Corporate Environmental Management 2:

Culture and Organizations

EARTHSCAN
Earthscan Publications Ltd, London

First published in the UK in 1997 by
Earthscan Publications Limited

Copyright © Richard Welford, 1997

A catalogue record for this book is available from the British Library

ISBN: 1 85383 412 2 (paperback), 1 85383 417 3 (hardback)

Typesetting and page design by Oxprint Design Ltd, Oxford

Printed and bound by Biddles Ltd, Guildford and Kings Lynn

Cover design by Andrew Corbett

For a full list of publications please contact:
Earthscan Publications Limited
120 Pentonville Road
London N1 9JN
Tel. (0171) 278 0433
Fax: (0171) 278 1142
email: earthinfo@earthscan.co.uk
http://www.earthscan.co.uk

Earthscan is an editorially independent subsidiary of Kogan Page Limited
and publishes in association with WWF-UK and the International Institute
for Environment and Development.

Contents

List of Acronyms and Abbreviations

ADL	Arthur D Little
BATNEEC	Best Available Technology (or Techniques) Not Entailing Excessive Cost
BFI	Browning Ferris Industries
BSI	British Standards Institute
CEO	Chief Executive Officer
CFC	Chlorofluorocarbon
DFE	Design For Environment
EHS	Environment, Health and Safety
EIBTM	European Incentive and Business Travel Meeting
EMAS	Eco-Management and Audit Scheme
EMS	Environmental Management System
EPA	Environmental Protection Agency
GCC	Global Climate Change
HRM	Human Resource Management
ICC	International Chamber of Commerce
ISO	International Standards Organization
LCA	Life Cycle Analysis/Assessment
NBER	National Bureau of Economic Research
NGO	Non-Governmental Organization
OB	Organizational Behaviour
OT	Organization Theory
R&D	Research and Development
TQM	Total Quality Management
TRI	Toxics Release Inventory

List of Figures, Tables and Boxes

Preface

There has been a great interest in the last ten years in developing tools and techniques to improve corporate environmental performance. We have seen environmental management systems become standardized, environmental audits more and more the norm, increasing numbers of environmental reports being published and interesting and innovative work on life cycle assessment, environmental performance measurement and even some attempts at developing sustainability indicators. To date, however, the literature on organizations and corporate culture has not embraced the notion of environmental responsibility. This partly reflects the fact that these 'softer' issues are less well suited to the imposition of generic tools and techniques. Every business will have its own organizational structure and will have a culture unique to itself. It is difficult therefore to be prescriptive in terms of what ought to be done. Nevertheless this book raises a number of issues which do need to be tackled if we are to improve the environmental profile of businesses. And there are themes which we constantly return to in this text: the need for more participative structures, the role of organizational learning, the need for explicit values statements, the importance of human capital, the need for appropriate training, reward systems linked to environmental performance, leadership and industrial democracy. Most of this is in the sphere of human resource management. We identify organizational and cultural issues which every business needs to grapple with. There are no easy solutions but here we present some ideas for action.

This book is a companion volume to the text *Corporate Environmental Management: Systems and Strategies* published by Earthscan in 1996. The focus of that previous text was on management techniques which could be implemented by business in order to improve its environmental performance. It identified best practice and examined the key tools within the framework of corporate environmental management. However, in recognizing that no technique or technology can be successful without the human element – the co-operation of everyone involved in the organization – I put together this book. In it we explore various organizational and cultural concepts which firmly place the corporate environmental management agenda within the human dimension.

Like the first text, this book provides only a start: early days in the move towards creating a more sustainable and equitable future. Sustainable development has to be our ultimate aim and corporate environmental management techniques are necessary but not sufficient to attain sustainable development. This book, like its companion, nevertheless ends by addressing the issue of sustainable development, pointing towards some of the practices which can be developed which (in a business context) are compatible with that concept. It is not an easy issue to tackle because it is surrounded by great uncertainty; nevertheless these two books are (we hope) able to provide managers, human resource practitioners and students of the subject with a road down which to travel. After the introductory chapter the book is divided into two parts. In Part 2 (Chapters 2 to 4) we construct a picture of the linkage between environmental problems and organizational issues. This raises the problems, challenges, contradictions and complexities which we then try to deal with in the third part. Part 3 therefore shifts to more practical and pragmatic approaches. Chapters 5 to 8 examine ways in which proactive cultures can be introduced into business, the role of values and leadership and an overarching agenda for human resource management.

Although this book and its companion volume provide only a start, it is vital to recognize that we must move swiftly and effectively. The environmental crisis has started – it is not a vague future threat. And it is starting in precisely those places where economic growth is the fastest and industrial development most intense. There are water shortages in China, deforestation is causing the collapse of agriculture because of topsoil erosion in other parts of South East Asia, and particulates in the air are responsible for a significant increase in respiratory diseases in Brazil. Change must be swift, effective and significant. But corporate environmental management tools alone will not be enough. The industrial change process will have to take human beings with it. This is what we tackle in this book.

This book would not have been possible without the help and support of a number of people. As well as the contributors to the text I would like to thank a number of people who have all helped in their different ways. These include: Chris Maddison, Elaine White, Tina Newstead, Richard Starkey, William Young, Walter Wehrmeyer, Michael Brophy, Linda Orwin and all the staff at Earthscan. I would particularly like to recognize the contributions of Ralph Meima who helped me with the introductory and concluding chapters and whose experience in the field helped me to structure the text.

Richard Welford

About the Contributors

Richard Welford is professor of Business Economics at the University of Huddersfield and Director of the Centre for Corporate Environmental Management. He is also visiting professor of Sustainable Management at the Norwegian School of Management in Oslo. He has written widely on the subject of corporate environmental management, undertakes consultancy work and training for selected companies and organizations and is a director of two companies. He is also editor for the leading academic journal, *Business Strategy and the Environment* and the practitioner based journal, *Eco-Management and Auditing*. Richard is a Director of ERP Environment, a member of the Advisory Board of the Greening of Industry Network and member of the ESRC Global Environmental Change Programme Committee. He has undertaken consultancy work for the European Environment Agency and a number of companies. His mix of academic and practitioner experience make him one of the leading authorities on corporate environmental management.

John Dodge is a professor in the School of Commerce and Administration at Laurentian University, Sudbury, Canada. He has undertaken research into organizational perspectives on strategic environmental management and performance. Before entering academia John held a number of senior management positions and was a consultant to a number of firms.

Tony Emerson is researching the implications of sustainability for personnel and training professionals at the Centre for Corporate Environmental Management, University of Huddersfield. He also lectures on human resource management at London Guildhall University. He is an active member of the Sustainable Development Network of the Association for Management Education and Development. He was formerly a lecturer at South Bank University.

Minna Halma is a research fellow in the School of Business Administration, University of Tampere, Finland. She conducts research into corporate environmental management, environmental reporting and corporate culture. She has been visiting research fellow at Georgetown University, Washington DC and at the International Institute for Industrial Environmental Economics, Lund University, Sweden.

David Jones was, at the time of writing, a researcher with the Centre for Corporate Environmental Management at the University of Huddersfield where he completed a PhD examining corporate culture change strategies for sustainable development. He has previously worked in industry.

Ralph Meima has an engineering degree and an MBA, and has worked in industry in Europe and the United States. Since 1992, he has focused on corporate environmental management and sustainable development, and has researched, published, taught and consulted in this area. He is currently a researcher at the International Institute for Industrial Environmental Economics at Lund University, Sweden, and is a US citizen.

Romney Tansley is an independent human resource and development consultant. He worked previously as an Anglican priest, as a social worker and as a local authority training officer and manager. He is a director of the London Cycling Campaign and a keen cyclist.

Part 1

Introduction

Chapter 1

The Ecological Challenge in Organization Theory and Organizational Behaviour

Ralph Meima and Richard Welford

If resolving the global environmental crisis were simply a matter of 'techniques', in other words installing new production technologies, converting to zero-emissions vehicles, using less packaging, changing to 'green' fiscal policies and strengthening emissions laws, then why haven't we already implemented them? The technical principles of a shift to a sustainable society are simple and straightforward, and have been discussed in great detail for at least 20 years: rooftop gardens; electric cars; windmills; solar architecture; triple-glazing; vegetarian diets; composting; recycling; pollution prevention; waste minimization. The list goes on, and makes up the utopian vision characteristic of the late '70s which in those days was often labelled 'appropriate technology'. We are now less driven by technical fix solutions and more enticed by the espoused beauty of management systems techniques enshrined in standards such as ISO 14001 and the EU Eco-Management and Audit Scheme (EMAS). Industry calls for voluntarism and a drive towards less resource depletion through eco-efficiency and it has successfully become the arbiter of ecological action through its powerful lobby groups and business clubs.

In fact both the technical fix approach and the techniques-oriented systems approaches have the same roots in that they provide apparently easy solutions to very complex issues. However, this technique-oriented, 'hardware' approach to building a sustainable society has its 'softer' aspects as well. As the alternative technology movement of the 1970s metamorphosed into the Green political movement of the 1980s, social aspects of sustainable development came to play a greater and greater role in the debate. The 'Four Pillars' of the West German Green Party (first elected to legislative positions in 1983) were ecology, social responsibility, democracy and non-violence. Industry and policy-makers nevertheless too often remain wedded to a technocratic approach which has denied the legitimacy of environmental themes outside of such narrow areas as environmental impact assessment techniques, pollution control equipment, the actuarial aspects of endangered species protection, and the local impacts of point source emissions on ambient environmental quality. Too often the implementation of corporate environmental management reflects this history. In the past it was an engineer's and lawyer's world. And so it remains, to a great extent, even today. The thrust of eco-efficiency, for example, is still a results-based technique, more driven by the size of its solution than the effectiveness of its action.

The Brundtland Report of 1987 and Agenda 21 of 1992 (cited only because they represent a kind of global apex of the environmental debate as we entered the 1990s) made it clear that a consensus was arising that social organization was in just as urgent need of consideration as its physical twin, technology. The hardware fixation of an earlier generation of ecological revolutionaries is slowly maturing into a more complex, nuanced, and balanced understanding of our predicament. Issues of intra- and international social justice, economic equity, gender and sexual equity, intra- and inter-generational equity, futurity, the rights of minorities and indigenous peoples, the rights and intrinsic value of nature, self-esteem and spiritual well-being, the meaning of work, quality of work life, lifestyles and consumption patterns, education, creativity and innovation, and many other social issues are increasingly found to be inextricably entwined with the more 'objective' aspects of sustainable development. Along with all this has come the realization that social science must play a part in the discovery of a sustainable path for human civilization, and that this part must consist of far more than partial analyses, superficial prescriptions, or mere extrapolations of social–scientific constructs developed before ecology had ascended to the level of concern it occupies today. Another realization to emerge is that the social science of people in organized groups – companies, research teams, corporate staffs, government agencies, non-governmental organizations (NGOs), universities, and so on, must figure prominently in this effort. The consideration of, on the one hand, individuals' systems of meaning and patterns of action, and, on the other, broad inquiries into the paradigms and ideologies of whole societies may also be important, but they leave out a tremendous middle segment: the world of organizations.

Begun only recently (although building on a long scholarly tradition) the effort of describing, explaining, and prescribing action for organizations in the context of the natural environment is gathering momentum, and occupying the energies of a growing number of management researchers, sociologists, social psychologists, anthropologists, political scientists, and other social scientists. Organization theory (OT) and theories of organizational behaviour (OB), which cut across these disciplines and unite students of organizations, comprise a large and unruly jumble of competing theories, so it is not surprising that the diversity and incoherence of OT and OB which charac-terize conventional areas of inquiry are being reproduced in the organizational investigation of sustainability. Looking around at what is now beginning to appear in books and journals and be heard at conferences, we recognize applications of rational choice theory, organizational economics, social systems science, contingency theory, adaptive theories, complexity theory, population ecology, psychodynamics, institutional theory, the resource-based perspective, interpretive and sense-making approaches (including quite a bit about cultures and paradigms), postmodern deconstruction, and much more. The core elements of OT and OB – meaning, values, attitudes, beliefs, habits, power, authority, responsibility, decisions, goals, interests, perceptions, incentives, communication and action – are being sculpted into an infinite variety of academic and practice-oriented forms in attempts to tackle the questions surrounding the ways in which organizations, especially companies, either influence or are influenced by ecological reality. Much of this work is repetitive and inward looking, using a language more designed to boost the egos of its proponents rather than engage people. Its techniques are often of the 'Absolutely Fabulous' school – names with little meaning, used to impress with very little consideration for practical usefulness. But some of the more important and understandable issues are contained in this book.

Thankfully while much of the academic side of this discourse is still rudimentary, closeted and pretentious, practitioners are putting considerable energy into organizational formulations and prescriptions. A typical 'practical' area where we see this arising is in connection with the new and popular environmental management systems (EMS) standards, primarily represented by EMAS and ISO 14001. Reflecting their recognition of the significance of the organization for environmental management (as opposed to the rational analysis and guidance of managers and the objective configurations of technology alone) the civil servants and industry representatives who have crafted these standards have made sure to prominently include such elements as organizational structure, responsibility, training, awareness, competence, employee participation, attention to good management practices, the philosophy of continual improvement, and relations with stakeholders. Similar checklists of the 'softer' side of companies appear in association with other corporate environmental management practices, such as design-for-environment, cleaner production, extended producer responsibility, and the social auditing movement. We can therefore assume that organizational treatments of environmental management are here to stay. But the journey has just begun, and we have hardly left the starting point. What today occupies centre stage must be seen as a transitional, ad hoc response – an improvisation using available knowledge and odd bits of scrap – but not anything even resembling what we ultimately need to achieve.

Along with this, it can be argued that the engineers and lawyers of yesteryear have changed their spots – no longer dominating the debate through an emphasis on technology and regulations, but instead reappearing in the context of corporate environmental management systems, standards, procedures, routines, indicators, and so forth, and retaining an approach which remains fundamentally the same. Aspects of organization have now come to be included in their diagnoses and prescriptions. They tell us to 're-engineer the culture', 'modify the paradigm' and 'integrate environmental values into decisions'. But the mindset of many in the developing field of corporate environmental management is still very technocratic, instrumental, results-driven and solution-oriented, rather than theory-based, dialectic or problem-driven.

What is now of concern to more thoughtful social scientists is that, by including, but at the same time trivializing, organization, the new wave of architects of the sustainable society will erect an edifice of complex procedures and routines in industry without the benefit of much insight into how organizations actually work in the ecological context. It will be a triumph of unexamined, taken-for-granted 'common sense' which, upon closer examination, will reveal such typical and simplistic (although not mutually consistent) assumptions as:

- decision-making processes are for the most part rational;
- an organization is a hierarchy of authority in which formal relationships dominate;
- the goals of organizations and their individual members are largely the same, and only deviate in dysfunctional circumstances;
- what gets measured gets managed;
- happy people are more productive, or, alternatively, the stronger the monetary incentive, the more efficiently people work;
- organizational culture can be instrumentally manipulated by managers to fit organizational goals;
- managers are becoming 'greener';
- increased employee participation is always a good thing;
- values can be transmitted down through organizations from the top levels; and
- equal opportunities policies make us socially responsible.

What such assumptions reflect is the evolution of organization theory of decades ago (eg scientific management, the administrative school, behaviourism, and other lingering types of positivism) into the accumulated conceptual sediment of the modern manager, organizational consultant, and not-very-critical academic researcher. While sometimes accurate, given the right qualifiers, they have been for the most part uncritically made a part of the apparatus of theories-in-use which we see manifested in the technocratic approach presently being redeployed as 'the corporate environmental management toolbox'. Such a toolbox may have some useful equipment but in the wrong hands it will be useless. Given the massive complexity, paradox, uncertainty, and ambiguity inherent in the ecological challenge, we must be very wary of this kind of facile, hey-ho-and-away-we-go approach. A great deal of more critical post-positivist organization theory has been worked out and empirically reinforced in recent decades, and this must be given careful consideration as well. Despite periodic ideological excesses, we still must keep our faith that knowledge – even in the social sciences – is gradually improving.

This book represents an attempt to collect some of this recent work in an accessible way. The chapters reflect a variety of theoretical foundations, and no attempt should be made to see the chapters as part of some coherent whole. In any case, coherence, like beauty, is in the eye of the beholder. Rather, the chapters explore a number of ideas and experiences from corporate environmental management using prominent theories in OT and OB in such areas as organizational culture, group dynamics, and sensemaking – areas in which very little work has been done to date. While all attempt to relate their theoretical formulations and assessments to practice, most do so in an appropriately tentative fashion, and establish more of a colourful collage than a set of principles for practitioners. Both the researcher and the critically disposed manager will find many useful ideas in the chapters ahead. Overly simplistic assumptions are questioned. Roadmaps for research and managerial and organizational action are charted. A number of techniques for making sense of things are proposed which could, given adequate insight and background, be useful in specific circumstances.

In Part 2 of the book (Framing the Organizational Dimensions of the Natural Environment), several schools within OT are employed in efforts to develop ecological critiques of organizations: to formulate and elaborate environmental problems in an organizational sense. Chapter 2 asks how we might define the problem of unsustainable practices in organizational terms and, using a mainly psychodynamic approach, presents a diagnostic method of examining environmental management in broader, multimodal, more holistic terms. The authors arrive at a generally actor-based, interpretive, clinical, and language-based means to perform such a diagnosis. Chapter 3 looks at several salient organizational anomalies or binds which corporate environmental management appears to often become ensnared in, and, following a review of the OT which one could imaginably apply to understanding them, develops an understanding using notions of sensemaking, complexity theory, and the idea of organizational epistemology. Chapter 4 returns to a more conventional socio–psychological tradition, and assembles ideas of power, organizational culture, organizational learning, and the nature of employee contracts to develop an analogy between the abuse of power in organizations with respect to human victims, and the abuse of power with respect to the natural environment. This is used to explain why organizations may systematically ignore environmental quality, and engage in pathologies of carelessness and abuse. From this quite academic analysis are derived recommendations for managers.

Part 3 (Developing Strategies for Managerial Action) shifts into a more pragmatic and practical mode, although theory stills plays an important role. These chapters rely more heavily upon cases from industry. Chapter 5 looks into ways in which an environmentally proactive culture might be created and cultivated in a company, with a line of reasoning which relies on the culture-change literature in management and such ideas as organizational triggers of change, top-down versus bottom-up processes, characteristic phases of organizational change, and facilitators and barriers to change. A set of managerial practices and environmental management tools are proposed which might contribute positively to a change in the organization's culture toward a more sustainable basis. Chapter 6 examines the culture concept in more depth, and explores the links between culture (in particular, shared values) and corporate performance. A central theme is a presentation of the culture concept as a way to explain quite divergent behaviour by firms in the same industry which are for the most part exposed to the same environmental and other pressures. A survey-based tool for assessing the environmental culture of the firm is proposed, and developed through a number of industry cases. The roles of leadership and administrative control systems are also examined.

Chapter 7 takes another approach to organizational culture, this time from a more emancipatory standpoint, emphasizing the kinds of ideas, values, and behaviour which a sustainable future might require of cultures. Making the assumption that strategic management must anticipate such a future, the authors take up cultural change and change programmes in companies, and develop an agenda for cultural change based on sustainable development. The significance of an organization's cultural paradigm for the way in which decisions are made is examined. The authors conclude that organizations must take a pluralistic approach to culture change, and tie this discussion into principles of learning organizations. Finally, Chapter 8 explores human resource management issues and, importantly, the role of the human resource manager. This person is identified as someone who is potentially able to drive the sort of changes identified in the book. The chapter argues that the human resource function should be integrated into environmental management strategies by being part of the vision for the environmental dimensions of the company. Through training, performance appraisal and reward setting employees can be an important part of the change process. Ultimately the human resource manager should raise the broader issues of sustainability in the company context, designing and implementing culture change programmes and tracking progress towards sustainability.

Although this book maps out many issues and provides the reader with ideas for action, we must not forget the aphorism that 'the map is not the territory' – a piece of wisdom frequently useful in both the academic and practical worlds of strategic management and organization. On the other hand, the difficult territory which this book deals with requires good maps, for what they're worth. A consultant who is only concerned with the formal, procedural aspects of an EMS is either a consultant with a pretty simplistic map of an organization or someone who has chosen, for whatever reasons, to only concentrate on one aspect of his or her map. Another person who is concerned with changing broad social institutions and personal values, but who ignores such things as organizational goals, formal procedures, and informal dynamics, is also either bereft of a good map or determined to only see part of one. The maps which emerge as one reads the following chapters are multi-faceted and strive to consider all of the relevant dimensions of organizational reality in their efforts to place environmental concerns in the context of the operations of a business organization. They are all of course limited by the assorted traditions on which they build, reflect research (and in some cases research careers as well), are young, and must stay within narrow confines due to the size and scope of this book. Nevertheless, together they present an organizational approach to corporate environmental management and sustainable industrial development which can be expected (and is urgently required) to bear fruit in the coming years.

Part 2

Framing the Organizational Dimensions of the Natural Environment

Chapter 2

Defining the Problem: Diagnostic Tools to Explore the Evolution of Unsustainable Practices in Organizations

Tony Emerson and Richard Welford

INTRODUCTION

Management theorists and consultants have developed a range of models or methods to enable the in-depth analysis of organizational problems and cultural issues. These approaches are rarely applied to corporate environmental management in the context of the individual firm. This chapter argues that an in-depth diagnosis of organizational culture is essential for the identification of underlying factors that give rise to unsustainable practices. Indeed, this diagnostic process is an important component of any change process.

The global environmental problem is highly complex. Various physical environmental issues interact with each other, with population and with international and inter-community political tensions. The identification of the causes of such problems is equally complex: macro-political and economic factors, technological change, business strategies adopted by companies, individual attitudes and behaviour – they all make a contribution. Faced with a problem of such magnitude, the danger is that we just feel overwhelmed and powerless. The answer however, lies in taking a broader systems approach to environmental problems rather than seeing each and every problem as requiring a specific solution.

This chapter concentrates on organizational culture, in other words on the norms, beliefs, customs and ways of thinking that people come to share with each other through being and working together. While other factors (impacting on sustainability) will be referred to, a clear focus is necessary if overload and confusion are to be avoided.

Cultural norms are manifested in decisions and activities. Cumulatively, these organizational decisions have contributed significantly to the development of environmentally unsustainable practices in the modern economy. How do we learn about this chain of causation and its evolution over time? This chapter suggests some diagnostic methods.

'A Problem Analysis Framework' (see below) develops a generalized problem analysis framework for viewing environmental issues at different levels. This framework can be applied to a wide range of problems and highlights the need to find explanations, or diagnoses, in terms of human and social systems, and to differentiate between types of environmental issues. 'Problem Analysis and Corporate Environmental Management' (see p17) is a critique of the approaches to environmental problem analysis which are explicit or implicit in many company environmental management systems and associated projects. We argue that there is little evidence of thorough diagnostic processes being undertaken within the traditional corporate environmental management framework and that the choice of environmental problems to be tackled is often arbitrary and questionable.

'The Importance of Diagnosis in the Management of Organizational Change' (see p19) looks towards more mainstream management literature to find diagnostic approaches or frameworks that might help us in the study of how unsustainable practices in organizations have evolved. A review of the methods of organizational diagnosis used in management consultancy suggests the need for a thorough, holistic and historical problem analysis, before attempting to design solutions, whilst recognizing that the diagnostic process in itself can lead to change.

'Organizational Culture and the Evolution of Unsustainability' (see p23) reviews some literature on organizational culture in particular, exploring some frameworks that might help explain the role of culture in the evolution of unsustainable practices in organizations. This section also discusses some methodologies for studying organizational culture.

The very nature of culture suggests the need for a historical analysis. As the 'Paradoxical Theory of Organizational Change' developed by Critchley (1994) states: One must fully experience what *is*, before all the alternatives of what maybe are revealed (p330). For Critchley, 'is' includes a recognition, and a valuing, of the past – the culture and the traditions of an organization and its members.

Another corollary of the Paradoxical Theory follows: a critique of problematic practices and consequences needs to be complemented by a study of positive achievements. Failure to acknowledge such achievements will inevitably provoke resistance from organization members.

A PROBLEM ANALYSIS FRAMEWORK

Global environmental problems can be viewed at a number of different levels. Figure 2.1 is a simple framework to help trace the chain of causation from overt symptoms to possible underlying causes. By following through this chain we will show that all environmental problems have their origin in human and social systems, and that different environmental issues may need very different analyses.

LEVEL 1: THE PHYSICAL SYMPTOMS

↓

LEVEL 2: BEHAVIOUR CAUSING THE SYMPTOMS

↓

LEVEL 3: EXPLANATION IN TERMS OF NATURAL SYSTEMS

↓

LEVEL 4: HUMAN AND SOCIAL SYSTEMS EXPLANATION

Figure 2.1 Environmental Problems at Different Levels of Analysis

As the study of human illness is more advanced than the study of ecological 'illness', a medical diagnosis analogy is useful to illustrate this multiple level analysis. At Level 1 (symptoms) we have, for example, the tired, overweight patient with digestive problems. At Level 2 (behaviour) the medical consultation reveals that the patient consumes six-plus units of alcohol per day. At Level 3, the diagnosis of physical illness might be sclerosis of the liver. This is a theoretical explanation: that the patient's liver is being damaged in a certain way because he has being drinking three times as much as his body can safely take in, for a substantial period of time. Such a diagnosis also leads to a prediction: continue in this way, any of a variety of bodily organs or functions may be damaged, but the exact form of malfunction, or the timespan of the ethology of the disease cannot be predicted with accuracy. Additionally, at some point in time, which cannot be predicted, the body systems will be so damaged that they will have gone beyond the point of no return.

This example was not chosen randomly. Firstly sclerosis of the liver is a good analogy of the overall global environmental problem, and of global climate change in particular. They both develop over a long period of time, the precise consequences of either, ie of the continued abuse of the human body or of the natural world, and the timing of those consequences, cannot be accurately predicted. But both are ultimately unsustainable.

The second reason for this analogy is because it illustrates the limitation of physical systems level diagnosis, and the need for the fourth level. Moreover, social and human factors (our Level 4) can get in the way of even the first level symptom recognition, as well as being barriers to treatment and cure. Thus an exploration of why the patient is drinking so much is required.

There is now a substantial body of literature questioning the adequacy of a purely physical level diagnosis in medicine. McKeown (1979) argues that health and illness need to be seen in their cultural, social and epidemiological context. Capra (1983) uses ideas from quantum mechanics and the 'new physics' to question a mechanistic, reductionist approach to illness and health and to argue for a holistic approach. Pietroni (1986) argues the need for psychological and social level exploration of the factors that give rise to an illness and challenges the simple notion that a disease has either a simple cause or that it can be cured by suppressing the symptoms or cutting out the diseased parts.

Applying the Framework to Major Ecological Issues

Three examples of major environmental problems are used to illustrate the use of this framework:

1) Major oil spillages;
2) pollution arising from synthetic chemicals; and
3) global climate change (GCC).

In a Symptoms Level analysis, the first example is the most straightforward. Oil slicks are all too visible, so the need for action is apparent. The second (chemical pollution) may not be so visible – indeed it is a characteristic of some synthetic chemicals that they cannot be detected by human senses. Physical symptoms, in the form of ecological damage, may take many years to detect. The third, global climate change (GCC), may be equally difficult to detect. It is the likely consequence of the accumulation of excess amounts of a number of gases in the atmosphere, accompanied by deforestation, is imperceptible in the short-term, with no perceived consequences for existing, live stakeholders.

At Level 2, it is the behaviour which (it is postulated) contributes to the causation of the symptoms. The cause of oil spillage and chemical pollution can usually be traced back to the decisions and activities of major industries. It is also relatively straightforward to predict the ecological consequences of such activities from scientific knowledge (Level 3) and to identify the political and economic forces that influence these decisions (Level 4). It may not be so easy to get the actors in this politico-economic system to accept responsibility for their decisions – but it is still easier than gaining acceptance of responsibility for GCC, the third environmental problem example, where the identification of the contributory behaviour becomes more difficult. GCC is the consequence of a myriad of decisions within producer organizations, as well as decisions by individual consumers and by governments and their agencies.

GCC is also a complex issue at Level 3 (an explanation in terms of natural ecology theory, ie a theory) where we seek a diagnosis that links behaviour to symptoms, and which predicts further ecological consequences. GCC links excess fossil fuel burning, deforestation, and other factors to disruption of the natural climate regulation process. It predicts that the disruption will be ultimately calamitous and irreversible. But, because of the complexity of the Earth's climate system, it is not possible to predict how or when this incremental and imperceptible accumulation of emissions will lead to any particular ecological events (Leggett, 1994).

At the fourth level (explanation of the behaviour in terms of human and social systems), fossil fuel use must be seen as being intrinsic to modern economic, human and social systems and to all sectors of it. It is not just a 'dirty industry' problem therefore, but at the core of the very system which we have developed in the West and continue to rely on. Let us examine a few elements or a sub-system of that system in more detail.

Here we take the example of transportation, as it vividly illustrates the need for analysis at the human and social systems level, as well as being a major cause of ecological problems. According to Whitelegg (1993), transport accounts directly for 22 per cent of UK CO_2 emissions, road transport accounting for 17 per cent of the total (or 77 per cent of transport emissions). Indirectly it leads to further emissions, in the making and servicing of vehicles. Whitelegg (1995) also estimates that air transport, in particular, now accounts for about 10 per cent of greenhouse gas emissions globally, although this may be conservative given the long-lived nature of some greenhouse gases in cold temperatures at this height. Other major contributors are industrial and domestic use, each accounting for 30 per cent or so of the total. The heating and lighting of commercial and public buildings account for 5.5 per cent of CO_2 emissions directly.

To help us to see the contribution of transport in its full perspective, Table 2.1 provides data on the degree to which the developed world now exceeds the planet's carrying capacity. Only a substantial reduction in the consumption of resources will enable us to avoid passing on the legacy of GCC and other major problems to future generations. As a start the data indicates the need for a 77 per cent reduction in CO_2 emissions.

Table 2.1 Current European Consumption and Sustainability Targets for 2050

Resource	Current consumption (per capita per year)	Sustainable consumption (per capita per year)	Percentage reduction required
Energy use	123 GJ	60 GJ	55
Fossil fuels	100 GJ	25 GJ	75
CO_2 emissions	7.3t	1.7t	77

Derived from Spangenberg, J et al and quoted in McLaren (1995)

If we are three to four times over the 'safe limit' for CO_2 emissions and if transport (including its indirect effects) accounts for something of the order of 30 per cent of total emissions, then transport could, ultimately, bring about GCC on its own! And, according to a UK Department of the Environment (1996) report, transport emissions are still increasing, while industrial emissions are declining.

We now move to an analysis of transport behaviour in terms of underlying social systems and psychological systems. Here we draw on a study by Marsh and Collett (1986) of the attitudes and behaviour in relation to the car, and of the role of the car in the culture of the firm. Marsh and Collett are apologists for the motor industry and dismiss the ecological argument irresponsibly in our view: '[Environmentalists] ... still continue to rehash the old warnings about dwindling oil supplies and the negative impact of the automobile on the ecology...' (p207)

However, their work illustrates the need to consider psychological and cultural factors if we are to bring about change in environmentally damaging behaviour. They discuss the car in terms of the status it brings in life. In particular, they argue that the company car expresses directly one's position in the business world and that for executives, even quite humble ones, the most important aspect of a job, after pay and working conditions, is the automobile that goes with it. Even after erosion of tax advantages of a company car, it is argued that the car a company supplies to you gives to you an immediate indication of how much your work is valued relative to your colleagues and communicates to others in the business world your standing: the visible reflection of the otherwise concealed pay cheque.

Upgrading company cars can provide people with an illusion of going up in the world, even though their status and salary remain the same. Marsh and Collett note in particular its role in maintaining within organizational status differentials:

> *It is essential ... to prevent the man at the top from downgrading his own car, even if it seems right and proper to do so in the interests of the economy or of a gloomy balance sheet. If your boss changes his Rolls for a Jaguar then you can be certain ... (that all the fleet) will be downgraded.* (p60)

They are quite explicit about the psychological roles played by this major consumer item:

> *The fundamental symbolism of the car is both complex and inescapable. It conjures up images of speed, excitement and vitality. At the same time it also communicates a sense of cosy seclusion – a womb-like refuge. Its potential deadliness give it an air of aggression while its power and shape endow it with a sense of sexual potency. It is precisely because the car can communicate such a variety of messages that it has captured our imagination ... and a second set of symbolic messages. These are to do with style and class, status, elegance and personal taste ... the combination of both types of symbols make the car the most psychologically expressive object that has so far been devised.* (p26)

and, in relation to other emotions:

> *... Studies of arousal demonstrate that people are able to use their cars as means of regulating their own internal states. In this way a car takes on the properties of alcohol or nicotine. Just as one smokes a cigarette to cool one's nerves or to increase one's arousal, so too one can use a car to regulate one's sense of excitement. The car puts us in charge of our own emotions. Acceleration, speed and emotional self-pacing, the three basic ingredients of the thrill of driving, coupled with all the other things that the auto. offers in the way of self-presentation and image enhancement, are at the root of the continuing success of fast cars.* (p185)

When the Director of Transport 2000 (Joseph, 1996) refers to the car as a 'drug on which we are dependent,' or Galbraith (1969) refers to 'consumer addiction' they may be quite accurate. The car, like the drug, is used to gain a sense of excitement or otherwise to regulate emotional states. The car, according to the above analysis, could also be seen to play a role in 'regulating the emotional state' of the organization.

This is obviously a partial study of the underlying human and social factors influencing transport behaviour. A similar analysis might be made about the role of business travel (especially overseas air travel) within organizational dynamics; or even of fashionable clothing, or other items of lesser ecological impact. But this example illustrates the power of the social and psychological factors, and the importance of analysis at this level if environmentally damaging behaviour is to be changed.

PROBLEM ANALYSIS AND CORPORATE ENVIRONMENTAL MANAGEMENT

If few medical scientists study the human and social factors underlying physical illness, we find virtually no indication that company environmental management studies and projects search for human and social level root causes. How well do they analyse issues at the physical environmental levels? A few examples follow to show the range of approaches.

Ballard (1994), in his work with Thorn EMI Rental (UK), an electrical goods firm, acknowledged the importance of human factors in a change process, without asking how such factors contributed to the problems in the first place. His work (like that of most practitioners in the study of corporate environmental management) aimed to identify the particular activities or functions which had the most significant ecological effects. Thus priority areas identified included energy used in heating and lighting and in in-bound logistics, and the impact of chlorofluorocarbons (CFCs) used in refrigeration. In this way it identified priorities in terms of the direct and indirect effects of its activities and, implicitly, non-priorities, for example paper recycling, which was judged to be of comparatively little environmental importance.

Such an attempt to identify and to prioritize the most significant causes of the most significant ecological effects (ie 'behaviour' and 'symptoms' at Levels 1 and 2) is about as far as traditional corporate environmental management tools take us. Any attempt to examine underlying systemic issues is extremely rare.

Rees (1994, p225) discusses an environmental management programme in John Laing, a large construction firm. 'Strategically, it was decided ... (to) establish a list of topic headings where real and practical initiatives could be introduced to improve environmental performance.' This led to attention being given to important issues such as the use of soft rather than hard wood, and to the protection of water courses. But a critical look at this report raised a number of questions about priority areas. The John Laing 16-point action list included both recycled paper and recycling paper but gave transport only one mention relating to the type of fuel to use in company cars (not their desirability or necessity per se).

Additionally, there was no reference to the location of their housing schemes or other construction projects. According to ECOTEC (1993), the location of housing in relation to various services and centres of employment is a crucial factor affecting transport demand. There may be a consumer demand for housing in dispersed locations, thus creating this extra demand. But if consumer demand is for unsustainable products or services, the firm needs to at least acknowledge this in its environmental strategy.

In summary, this 'real and practical' approach, so common in corporate environmental management, seems to be somewhat selective in its problem analysis. Issues of ecological significance are often ignored if there is no easy solution in sight, while issues related to organizational cultural issues are rarely on the agenda. Companies which are really serious about environmental issues need to relate their environmental strategy to an underlying ecological theory and an analysis of ecological, human and social systems. In so doing they are more likely to choose more ecologically significant issues to tackle.

Generally organizations seem to be defining, not necessarily consciously, as 'environmental' those issues which would not question the fundamental nature of their business. Fineman (1997) in his study of the UK automotive industry concluded that environmental issues were being incorporated into existing concerns (legal, technical, financial etc) and not leading to any fundamental review of the nature of their business. So often, business views its environmental problems as insurmountable and then chooses to do nothing or to make some piecemeal changes in order to look as if they are trying. One automotive firm which after thinking about its overall environmental impact and discussing a range of possibilities for action, all of which were too difficult to progress, adopted one proposal: to increase the reuse of the plastic cup holders in the staff coffee machines!

For firms which are really serious about tackling environmental issues a Level 3 physical environmental-level diagnosis involves asking questions about the total impact of their activities on life support systems. According to Fischer and Schot (1994), sustainable development needs to integrate this sort of 'limits thinking'. Its aim should not be to (just) make existing systems more efficient, but rather to set absolute limits. Moreover, Welford (1994) argues that sustainable development is about more than environmental protection. It is also about futurity which means taking a longer term look at the way we do business and it is also about equity and equality widely defined. By contrast, traditional corporate environmental management seems to be concerned with minimizing problems from existing activities (which are accepted as given) – particularly damage from more immediate and specific environmental hazards. A thorough Level 3 analysis would therefore suggest a fundamental review of business policy. This, in turn, requires an examination of the cultural norms and beliefs underpinning the policy-making process.

Some company environmental change agents do acknowledge the need for fundamental change in policy and/or culture. But where they do, they seem to advocate a top-down approach. It is commonly argued that environment policy change starts with a 'commitment from top management', which is 'enshrined in the mission statement', which includes 'total change in organizational culture and strategy' and then 'policy is defined' which is 'cascaded down the organization'. Rarely do we see the whole process being owned by those who will have to ensure that it is operable. Workers, it seems, cannot be trusted with such responsibility.

This reflects a fairly prevalent approach to the management of change generally. Fowler (1993) sees top management determining the objectives as the starting point, and then elaborates a step by step approach for managing the change programme down the organization. A study by Klinkers and

Nelissen (1995) illustrates this approach in the environmental field. They developed a model of a company campaign in their work with companies in the metal industry in the Netherlands, the first five principles of which were:

1) Announce your campaign ... in a simple and effective way;
2) address your personnel;
3) show a video about environmental care;
4) plant a tree;
5) publish an environmental newsletter.

The suggestion to 'organize a diagnostic workshop' was positioned nine on this list, and was confined to physical environmental issues. Not surprisingly, very little change in behaviour resulted from these campaigns (according to the report of the study). This study illustrates the limitation of a top-down approach. The more fundamental the change required, the more deep-rooted the problem, the more important the diagnostic phase – and a participative diagnostic process. While superficial and conveniently selective behavioural level activity is clearly inadequate, neither will a 'fundamental change' strategy be effective if it is not grounded in the experience and the perceptions of the organization and its members.

In summary, there is little evidence of environmental management work being based on a thorough diagnostic process. Much work is conveniently selective at the level of identification of organizational behaviours that lead to physical environmental consequences. When major change is considered, a top-down rational strategic approach is usually attempted. Analyses that attempt to explain ecologically damaging behaviour in terms of human and social systems are seldom, if ever, undertaken.

THE IMPORTANCE OF DIAGNOSIS IN THE MANAGEMENT OF ORGANIZATIONAL CHANGE

In contrast to the traditional literature on corporate environmental management, much more emphasis should be placed on diagnosis overall, and on human and social factors, in other management literature. Writers on management consultancy or on the management of change tend to emphasize the need for a thorough diagnosis or problem analysis before generating solutions (see for example Beckhard and Harris, 1987; Margerison, 1988). This section briefly examines four particular diagnostic approaches or frameworks that might help us study the evolution of unsustainable practices in organizations.

The Systems Model

This approach is developed from the work of Harrison (1987). The first stage of this model is a 'broad diagnosis' using an 'open systems' model of a firm in interaction with its environment. This should help us to see ecological problems in the context of traditional marketing and financial pressures, and also wider societal influences. The second stage of the model is a 'focused diagnosis' at (some combination) of the following levels as appropriate:

- the personal;
- the inter-personal;
- the divisional;
- the organizational.

Both stages are relevant to the study of the wide range of decisions that effect environmental impact. The first stage helps us to see ecological problems in the context of the firm's total interactions with its environment. At the physical level, this can be an analysis of the inputs and resources a firm uses (what, how much, how produced, where from), of how they are processed into outputs, and of how those outputs are distributed and finally disposed of. In other words, this systems model can incorporate the cradle to the grave analysis or life cycle assessment called for by many environmentalists.

But this diagnostic model also incorporates the societal, economic and financial factors that impact on the firm. An example may illustrate this point. Most supermarket chains are concentrating their services into a lesser number of larger, often out of town, outlets, thereby generating significantly more transportation. Such a strategy relates to the wish on the part of the firms to avail themselves of the economies of scale needed in a highly competitive retail business. Customers expect to see a large variety of products on the shelves, as well as wanting good quality at low prices. The advertising industry has helped to create such expectations. Most customers with spending power have cars and are willing to travel a few miles for shopping. There is, of course, pressure on the chains from shareholders to show high returns on investments. And so pressure from a range of stakeholders determines the overall strategy.

However, there is a danger in only examining the range of pressures which lead a firm to take a particular set of actions. The activities of a firm are never totally determined by external forces. Firms can be proactive in developing ethical and/or green markets for themselves (as have organizations such as The Body Shop and the Cooperative Bank). Moreover, some of the environmentally damaging activities of a company are not driven externally at all but are related to internal decisions about resource use, waste management and energy consumption. This leads us to the second stage of the Harrison systems model; to an analysis as to which level within an organization problems are occurring and to an exploration of factors influencing the decisions. Here, however, we will move on to other frameworks that place more emphasis on the cultural dimension in the diagnosis of intra-organizational factors.

Viewing Organizational Issues from Different Frameworks

Bolman and Deal (1991) suggest that four different frameworks can be used for viewing organizational issues:

1) The structural frame – an analysis of the effect of how a firm is divided into smaller units, of the number of layers of management, or reporting relationships, etc;

2) the human resource frame – an analysis in terms of the skills and motivation of people, and of the interdependence of organizations and staff;
3) the political frame – an analysis in terms of the distribution of power among individuals and groups in the organization, and the exercise of that power in competition for resources;
4) the symbolic frame – an analysis of how humans create and use symbols to bring meaning out of relative chaos and clarity out of confusion.

An analysis of a complex and multi-faceted problem area, such as the range of decisions that impact on environmental problems, will be very limited if any of these dimensions or frameworks are ignored. Once again, let us illustrate this approach with an example: energy conservation. In a large public sector institution, the responsibility for energy conservation was allocated to a relatively junior specialist officer. She had no authority in relation to managers who made major energy use decisions. She had to report through two levels of the management hierarchy to influence a manager with sufficient authority to affect the agendas of decision-makers. So the problem might seem to be structural.

But this structural problem may have reflected a political problem. The dominant forces in the organization seemed to be the marketing and finance departments, and an overtly power-oriented chief executive. They were interested in creating a 'flashy, up-market' image for their service, with newly carpeted, air-conditioned offices, cars with current year registrations in the car park etc. Environmental issues were simply not on the agenda. Aligned to this culture, overseas business trips, large offices and expense accounts seemed to have become the symbols of how successful people were and how they were valued. Additionally from a human resource frame, few staff had any awareness of the energy use implications of their activities.

Note the different insights to be derived from seeing the problem in each of the four frameworks and note how all the four dimensions interact. From a human resource perspective, an energy awareness programme would seem to be needed. But will it be effective, or even get implemented, unless it is accompanied by action at the political and symbolic levels? Upgrading the status of the conservation officer might reinforce action, it is therefore unlikely to be successful as a single strategy. This discussion leads neatly on to a third diagnostic approach: the holistic.

The Holistic Approach

Consultants and researchers like Pettigrew et al (1992) and Gummesson (1991) argue that the study of complex processes of decision-making, implementation and change requires a holistic approach, and either a longitudinal study and/or a historical study, allowing such processes time to emerge, evolve and change. The relevant decisions and factors need to be looked at in interaction (rather than in isolation), implying the need to spend a significant time on the diagnostic process.

Using the historical method, the analyst traces the decisions and influences within an organization that lead to the evolution of practices over time, and is particularly appropriate to the study of organizational culture. But as Gore (1992) points out, many environmental changes have been too gradual for human and social systems to detect as they occur. This presents a challenge for researchers and diagnosticians. It is difficult to trace the myriad of corporate decisions that have contributed to environmental damage over the years. So many decisions, spread over many decades, may have had an impact. The decision-makers are unlikely to have had much feedback about the environmental consequences of their decisions at the time. Even if you can trace who made a decision, and when, it may be very difficult to identify the subjective and other contextual factors that influenced the decision. Tracing decisions about the use of a particular industrial process, or the development of a major product, may be relatively easy. But it would be a difficult, if fascinating, challenge to trace the decisions about, say, the issuing of company cars to different groups of staff over the years, and the context in which those decisions were made (and remade).

An alternative method for the holistic (diagnostic) study of such an organizational sub-system is the action research model. This is based on Lewin's (1951) dictum that you only learn about systems when you attempt to change them – the threat mobilizes forces that would otherwise lay dormant or covert in their influence. What would actually happen if a firm withdrew company car provision from a group of staff, for example? Applying the Bolman and Deal (1991) analysis, and following from Marsh and Collett's argument that the car is a visible measure of the employee's value, we would predict that it would need to be replaced by some means of overtly and publicly valuing people. Whatever was tried, a significant amount of time is required to study how a system and its members adapted to change.

Change Intervention

Schein (1987) advocates two principles of organizational consultancy that might be of relevance to this discussion. Firstly, that where possible, members of the organization should participate in the diagnosis, and secondly, that the process of diagnosis is implicitly a change intervention (ie that once people start asking questions about an issue, changes are likely to occur).

To emphasize the latter principle in this context: no doubt many practical environmental projects are initiated by a genuine concern about the pace of environmental degradation – hence tree planting, paper recycling etc. But more action may actually occur sooner if the change initiators simply start asking questions about the more (ecologically) significant issues, and of relevant people, in a sensitive way. This can be desired action, as staff recognize that the firm is giving serious attention to environmental issues and start to consider how they can contribute in their job roles. But the questioning process can also lead to resistance and opposition, as people react to rumours and interpretations of environmental action in a more defensive way.

In summary, we can draw together a number of important principles forming a diagnosis of the organizational factors which will contribute to defining and investigating problems associated with ecological sustainability:

- view the organization in its wider social context;
- consider issues at the personal, interpersonal, divisional and whole organizational level;
- examine issues from a range of different analytical frameworks (structural, political, people management, symbolic/cultural);
- take a holistic and longitudinal perspective;
- attempt to trace the evolution of relevant decisions over time;
- attempt to involve a number of people in the diagnosis;
- recognize that the diagnostic process in itself can lead to change.

These diagnostic approaches can be used in the identification of all the internal factors that contribute to problems – from the 'hard' issues such as structure, strategy and information systems, to the 'softer' issues such as management style and culture (which we now turn to).

ORGANIZATIONAL CULTURE AND THE EVOLUTION OF UNSUSTAINABILITY

Stacey (1993) defines organizational culture as that set of beliefs, customs, practices and ways of thinking that (people in the organization) come to share with each other through being and working together; a set of assumptions people simply accept without question as they interact with each other. At the visible level the culture of a group of people takes the form of ritual behaviour, symbols, myths, sounds and artifacts. Stacey notes that culture is usually implicit (rather than explicit). Argyris and Schon (1978) argue that these implicit beliefs are often 'undiscussable' in organizations – and that such undiscussability militates against the questioning of fundamental aims and norms. Hawkins and Miller (1993) see culture as 'a rich multi-level perspective for viewing and influencing organizations.' They suggest an integrative model that views organizational culture as residing at four distinct but linked levels (see Figure 2.2) and argue that

> *it is important to recognise that only the top level of the culture is fully visible and conscious. The behavioral norms may operate without people being aware of the conventions they are acting within. The mind sets may be sub-conscious, for we see not the spectacles that we see through. The emotional ground may be fully unconscious* (p7).

These definitions suggest that norms, ways of thinking, etc, shape behaviour within organizations. They can be applied to the search for cultural issues underlying environmental problems. This approach recognizes the fact that behavioural change without tackling underlying issues will be short-lived. But they also acknowledge that behaviour is a part of culture, and imply that genuine cultural change will manifest itself in behavioural change.

However if culture or cultural norms are often invisible, undiscussable (Argyris and Schon, 1978), or unconscious (Miller and Hawkins, 1993), and if it/they have evolved over time, then we must address the issue of how we study them. As a starting point skilled, inter-personal intervention seems to

ARTEFACT – the rituals symbols/logos, mission statements, building, organizational structure.
BEHAVIOUR – the unwritten rules which constrain how people behave, what is and what is not talked about and how people relate to each other.
MIND SETS – the spectacles through which members of the organizational culture view themselves, the environment with which they interact and problems that arise.
EMOTIONAL GROUND – the collective feelings that underlie and influence the other three levels of culture; the emotional mood and feeling within the business.

Figure 2.2 Levels of Culture

be required in order to draw out those psychological and cultural issues surrounding any problem. Many writers argue the importance of first creating a climate of trust and respect, before asking perceptive and challenging questions.

Hawkins (1995) suggests the study of stories that circulate in an organization, and the unwritten rules highlighted by the behaviour of the people in the stories. Argyris and Schon (1978) suggested a technique whereby different people who experienced the same events are encouraged to share and contrast their stories. Hawkins (1995) also suggests the use of role play and visual representation to unblock barriers to awareness or discussability.

Relatedly, Bate (1990) argues that language is the primary cultural form of any society or organization. Therefore if we wish to study culture we must find ways of studying organizational language, recognizing that language is the property of a community, not of any single individual. Bate's research strategy is to use language to capture the 'living culture' of the organization in a (longitudinal) organizational development project. He argues that culture change must focus primarily on changing the network of relationships, commitments and scripts that bind people together in organizational settings.

A common feature of many writers is an emphasis on learning about the history of the organization and its members. This theme is also strongly emphasized by Critchley (1994) who argues against any change process initiated solely by top-level-inspired vision. Such vision is usually based on idealized states which are unattainable and therefore result in disillusion. Moreover impositions from the top tend to be resented and they implicitly denigrate the staff who have built their career with the organization, and who derive part of their self-worth from their achievements and their identity within it.

In summary, this section emphasizes the multi-level and only partly conscious nature of culture in an organization, and the importance of those deeper manifestations of culture that shape an organization's total performance – including its contribution to ecological problems. It suggests the use of such qualitative approaches as language, history and story analyses in learning about culture. Skilful cultural enquiry will not only enable the shared learning about what has gone wrong (in relation to sustainability or any other issue), it will also, if honestly applied, give the message that the feelings, views and information possessed by organizational members are valued. That such a message is an essential prerequisite for change is brought out in other chapters of this book.

CONCLUSIONS

A transition to a more sustainable world requires changes at all societal levels, including changes in the business practices of firms. We cannot expect to change behaviour unless we understand the processes that gave rise to it initially – including those cultural factors within organizations that contributed to the evolution of unsustainable practices. These processes or factors that gave rise to environmentally abusive behaviour may be complex and may be buried in time or in the subconscious of organization members. Management consultancy and theory have developed a variety of insightful approaches to the study of organizational culture, but these do not seem to have been applied to company environmental work. Two of the key features of these consultancy approaches are, quite simply, asking good questions and actively (but critically) listening to people.

Chapter 3

The Challenge of Ecological Logic
Explaining Distinctive Organizational Phenomena in Corporate Environmental Management

Ralph Meima

INTRODUCTION

The purpose of this chapter is twofold. First, it aims to provide managers and researchers with a number of concepts and perspectives which are relevant to understanding the evolution of environmental management as a corporate function. Second, in adopting and developing a critical position toward a number of current conventions or common assumptions, it aspires to add something of value to the emerging debate about ecologically sustainable organizations.

In the first section, a number of practical and theoretical problems which have given the environmental management debate much of its character are discussed. In the second, a variety of rival theories which seek to explain these phenomena are reviewed. Finally, in the third section, I propose a critical approach to thinking about organizations in the ecological context based on the concepts of organizational epistemology, sensemaking, emergence, and logics of action, and explore the implications of this approach for practice.

The reader is urged to consider the proposition that, although an academic and at times rather abstract tone is maintained in this chapter, its implications have a direct bearing on the practical conduct of corporate environmental management. The thing is, management practice and the political concerns of society have as usual outrun the development of theory, meaning that academic environmental management is now struggling to catch up with experience from the field and organize it in ways that add value and insight.

Gabel and Sinclair-Desgagne (1993), for example, make the comment that 'virtually no attention has been paid in the environmental economics literature to problems of organizational failure within firms.' (p1) At the 4th International Conference of the Greening of Industry Network in Toronto in November

1995, a number of poignant reflections were made which to me signified the increasing need for research into 'greening' as an organizational area. Kurt Fischer, one of the network's founders, had recently returned from a research tour of Europe and North America. On this trip, he had solicited opinions from academics, businesspersons, and policy-makers regarding research needs in the intersection of sustainable development and enterprise management or business administration. A common reaction was:

> We don't need more research! We have plenty of research already. What we need to find out is why people aren't using the environmental management tools that have been developed!

At the same conference, Dr. Philip Vergragt of the Netherlands expressed a similar perception to the effect that a great deal of conceptual research and model-building has already been accomplished, but that it remains to be implemented, and that this is proving to be a much harder project. What these comments point to is a tantalizing abundance of constructs, but a frustrating lack of practical guidelines or skills with which to make sense of and apply them.

To me, such statements and complaints underline the need to increase our understanding of the relationship between environmental issues and the collective action of humans in organizations. In other words, more research is on the contrary very much needed, but of the type which frames, problematizes, and seeks to understand organizations, as opposed to that which seeks to identify and solve essentially technical problems. This perception is incidentally not new. At the first Greening of Industry Conference in 1991, Thomas Gladwin laid out just such a research agenda, which later became published as *The Meaning of Greening: A Plea for Organization Theory* (Gladwin, 1993).

PROBLEMATIC OBSERVATIONS FROM ENVIRONMENTAL MANAGEMENT PRACTICE

The subjects of sustainable development and corporate environmental management are replete with paradoxes and anomalies – theoretical outcomes and practical experiences in which are manifested unacceptable trade-offs, uncomfortable contradictions, unintended consequences, stubborn impasses, and so forth. Paradox and anomaly seem indeed to be more the rule than the exception in questions relating to sustainable development and the management of corporate environmental performance.

There have been many assertions by organization theorists during the past several decades that research has been too concerned with the exceptional and deviant (cf Weick, 1969), and not sufficiently informed about what is routine, normal, and taken for granted in organizations. But, against the background of turbulence, ambiguity, and gravity which has defined the environmental crisis since the 1960s, we have to ask: What is normal? What is routine? Where can we find examples of corporate environmental management which has become routinized and pedestrian, and achieved stability which has lasted years or decades, and, moreover, is consistent with the requirements of sustainable development? Whereas organizations as whole entities appear to exhibit remarkable durability and stability, it is hard to find this bedrock in the corporate environmental management context. It will consequently be assumed here that most of what we have to work with is quite exceptional, anomalous, and problematic, and that it is with these fragments alone that we must go about developing theories of ecologically sustainable organizations and of corporate environmental management as praxis.

The Tragedy of the Commons

Garrett Hardin (1968) articulated what has now become recognized as one of the classic natural resource management paradoxes nearly 30 years ago under the label of *The Tragedy of the Commons*. The essence of this idea is that, when a natural resource is held in common by many actors (eg herdsmen, fishermen, air-breathers) for whom access is free and uncontrolled, each actor will attempt to maximize the benefit he or she derives from the use of the resource without paying for the harm inflicted on other actors because of its exploitation. For instance, this might involve fishermen who overfish an ocean without having to pay compensation to other would-be fishermen because stocks (and thus regenerative capacity of the fish species) have been depleted. The paradox is thus that owners of common property, in pursuing their individual welfare, together unconsciously conspire to undermine their collective welfare. This idea has obviously wide relevance in the environmental context, where free-riding firms, for example, can be substituted for individuals in the model. Solutions to the tragedy of the commons that have been proposed usually involve assigning property rights to the actors so that they can claim a rent or other form of compensation from anyone who exploits or damages their share of the natural resource. In this way, externalities become internalized into the price of using the natural resource, and the idea is that the resource will in turn be conserved and maintained rather than overexploited and exhausted.

We know, however, that many natural resources, including the atmosphere, the oceans, the genetic viability of species, and the ecological services provided by ecosystems or biomes, cannot readily be fenced off and parcelled out to private owners to be maintained in an enlightened spirit of market valuation and internalized externalities. So, although the paradox can be resolved in theory, it persists in practice. A very large proportion of current environmental regulation and international negotiation revolves around limiting and allocating access to various common natural resources. In many cases, important actors in these contexts are firms.

In the economic literature, most efforts have been focused on the environmentally related paradoxes and failures which occur at the levels of markets and public policy, of which Hardin's tragedy is one example. Others include the failure of command and control environmental policies, the capture of public institutions by private interests, and the general difficulty of what Daly and Cobb (1989) call 'pervasive externalities.' However, as Gabel and Sinclair-Desgagne (1993) noted, far less research effort has been devoted to what they call 'organizational failure' – ie mistakes committed within firms – in the environmental context.

In the remainder of this section, some of the key environmental organizational paradoxes, anomalies, and failures will be reviewed. Although some researchers have attempted to formulate and model them in theoretical terms, they will all be readily familiar to corporate environmental managers.

The Problem of the Low-Hanging Fruit

A common joke about economists in environmental management circles is that, if an economist saw heavily laden boughs of fresh apples hanging low within reach as he walked through an orchard, he would pass them by, muttering that, by definition, they should not exist, as somebody else would already have picked them. The implication is that opportunities to generate positive returns through investments in, for example, energy efficiency and pollution prevention should not exist in industry in much abundance, as firms rationally maximize value and are quick to identify and exploit cleaner production opportunities as they arise. However, considerable evidence has now accumulated that firms often commit what are called by economists 'type II errors' and systematically fail to pick the low-hanging fruit. The evidence builds mainly upon many accounts of pilot projects by environmental advocates and consultants which readily yielded a positive return through relatively simple, obvious investments that had previously been overlooked (Huisingh et al, 1986; Dorfman et al, 1992), although broader, more methodical evaluations of entire corporations or industries in search of an aggregate latent cleaner production dividend do not seem to be as yet available. Gabel and Sinclair-Desgagne (1993) indeed call into question the argument against further command and control regulation and in favour of self-regulation employed by many industry associations by pointing out that, if there is no need for regulation because corporations can profitably and continually improve their environmental performance without pressure from the state, then, given the persistence of environmental problems in many areas, why have they not already done so? Something other than ignorance, laziness, or sheer nastiness must be at work.

The Mystery of Persistent Overshoot

At the other end of the spectrum along the same dimension implied in the low-hanging fruit problem is the phenomenon of firms which not only zealously exploit profitable opportunities for energy conservation, cleaner production, cleaner products, extended producer responsibility, etc, but do it to and even beyond the break even point. In the language of economists, this means that, throughout the firm, the net marginal benefit of environmental investments has been whittled down to or past zero. In the neo-classical economist's world, all firms should be at this zero-margin when the system is in equilibrium (and no fruit should be left hanging in trees or 100-ecu bills lying unnoticed on sidewalks). They should not, however, have passed it.

Some firms purport to have nearly achieved such an ongoing state of fully realized returns to cleaner practices. The 3M Corporation is a good and oft cited example. Its Pollution Prevention Pays programme, in which employees are encouraged through an incentive scheme to find ways to reduce or eliminate a variety of chemicals from production processes, has reportedly yielded environmental performance gains and at the same time saved well over $500 million since its establishment in 1975 (Smart, 1992). Other programmes which have received favourable public attention – to take some examples from the United States – include those at Compaq, Kraft General Foods, Reynolds Metals, Polaroid, DuPont, and Monsanto (Denton, 1994), and at ARCO, AT&T, and Warner-Lambert (Piasecki, 1995).

We can only speculate as to whether such programmes are becoming the norm at such corporations. It is likely that many other positive return opportunities remain even there. It is also likely that pollution prevention programmes of this type are still very much the exception in industry as a whole. Nevertheless, their existence does not represent a paradox or anomaly. On the contrary, they represent firms behaving in a most neo-classical manner. What are anomalous, on the other hand, are firms which appear to overshoot the margin – to engage in investment projects which appear to yield no positive return at all, or which are justified as indirectly contributing to the overall success of the company over the long run in at best intangible, fuzzy ways. Whether large or small, such projects appear to make little sense in traditional business terms, and would generally not be selected according to conventional capital budgeting methods.

Again, there is a lack of a firm empirical base for evaluating such phenomena or claims to the contrary. Some companies have become famous for having developed environmental practices and positions in all aspects of their operations, with The Body Shop, Ecover, the Kalundborg (Denmark) industrial symbiosis coalition (Novo Nordisk, Gyproc, Statoil, the Asnaes electric power generating facility, and the municipality of Kalundborg), and Southern California Edison as conspicuous examples. They appear to be doing far more than their competitiors. Have they gone much farther than they had to, and if so, why? Conventional economists would argue that there is nothing irrational or mysterious about their actions; their indifference curves, discount rates, marginal propensities to invest, etc are simply based on distinct preferences or possession of unique information. This fits into the 'beyond compliance' argument (Smart, 1992) that wise, far-sighted companies prefer to stay a step ahead of the demands of regulators and other constituencies because they have determined that it is likely to pay off. So, put in these terms, it does not sound anomalous at all, and just involves staying a step ahead of the pack. The problem is that this line of argumentation is circular, and amounts to saying that whatever firms do makes sense to them, and whatever makes sense to them, they do, and nothing they do does not make sense. This still does not explain why a particular company embarks upon environmental projects which make sense only to them, and not to anyone else. Or, to phrase this problem as the converse of the low-hanging fruit question, why do some firms expend the effort to climb up to harvest even the high fruit (where there may, by the way, not even be much fruit), when sticking to low-hanging fruit is a seemingly more profitable strategy at the time?

Violations

A third problematic category of organizational phenomena is what economists call the 'type I error.' In contrast to the low-hanging fruit problem (type II error), which involves failing to do what is good for one, the type I error involves doing what is bad in full possession of the knowledge of how to avoid it and information about the potential consequences (eg fines, lawsuits, bad publicity). In the environmental context, this refers to conscious violations of regulations and permits, accidents due to human errors in judgement which could have conceivably been prevented, and cases in which corporations were aware of risks inherent in, for example, products or facilities, yet neither informed customers nor employees about these risks, nor took the necessary steps to mitigate them.

It could be argued that, in some cases, executives had full access to relevant information and yet calculated that the gamble was worth the risk (ie that the net expected value was positive). This seems heartless yet plausible. In other cases, it could be argued that accurate information and/or cognitive capacity to assimilate the information was lacking (ie rationality was bounded), leading to errors and misjudgements and a regrettable outcome. However (and the purpose here is only to describe a certain category of phenomena, not to dredge up some of the many regrettable examples which are documented in the literature), it also appears plausible that organizations in many instances have had access to relevant information, have possessed adequate cognitive capacity, have not deliberately calculated that getting into trouble was worth it, and yet have consciously created the conditions in which type I errors can and do occur – with a sometimes catastrophic effect on the firm.

If neither evil, ignorance, nor sloth is to blame, then what might be?

More Complex Images of Environmental Organizational Phenomena

Up until this point in the discussion, environmental organizational failure has utilized the image of the firm as a unitary actor making rational choices – and missing obvious opportunities, seeing opportunities where others see none, or deliberately getting into trouble. The discussions about these kinds of anomalies extend back into economic debates which took place long before organization theory of a more psychological or sociological flavour took up the environmental theme, and are, due to their empirical elusiveness, based more on logico-deductive reasoning than on observation in the field. However, there is another group of anomalies which I will now turn to: organizational failures – or at least puzzles – which have been noted by practitioners specifically in the environmental management context and which require a more subtle image of the firm as a coalition of diverse actors, systems of meaning, interests, and other things.

A limited selection of recent qualitative, idiographic organizational research – particularly of the action-research and ethnographic variety – has pointed to the importance of such phenomena as bottom-up initiatives, the role of champions or vanguards, the resistance of groups to the initiatives of other groups, and the general role played by employees in the corporate environmental management function. This research, begun for most part in the early 1990s, has studied environmental management change processes, managerial innovation, and related subjects in much greater depth than was formerly the case. In a sense, it could not really have started much earlier, as elaborate corporate environmental management (as exemplified by such things as environmental auditing programmes, extended producer responsibility schemes, environmental reporting, and environmental management systems) is a new area of practice.

Researchers have brought with them to the study of corporate greening a great variety of different theoretical backgrounds and research traditions. In addition, students of greening have now had the possibility of conducting longitudinal and comparative studies in ways that were impossible before. This has led to an accumulation of empirical material on diverse aspects of organizations, and paved the way for the characterization of organizational mistakes, anomalies, and paradoxes of a more complex, process-based character than was the case with those discussed above.

Taken together, regardless of which type of theory one might use for analysis, this field material presents a more subtle picture of the firm than that of a unitary decision-maker. Power struggles, personal and conflicting interests, ambiguity and uncertainty, traditions, rules-of-thumb, group identities, and values, attitudes, and beliefs emerge as important features of this picture.

One broad conclusion at which a number of studies have arrived is that groups outside the top management of the corporation, including corporate staffs, middle managers, and operational-level employees, often define, initiate, drive, or oppose many of the developments which later become established as corporate practices.

A New Case of the Hawthorne Effect?

Studies carried out during the 1920s at the Hawthorne plant of the Western Electric Company (an AT&T subsidiary) in Cicero, Illinois produced the surprising result that workers' productivity can improve merely when they are given special attention and treatment, regardless of concrete variations in their working conditions. Experiments in which parameters such as lighting and rest periods were varied consistently yielded productivity improvements, even when conditions were deliberately worsened. This effect, documented in the writings of Mayo (1946) and Roethlisberger and Dickson (1947), became widely known as the 'Hawthorne Effect,' and lent impetus to a branch of organization theory called the Human Relations school.

Something similar may be occurring in the environmental context. There are indications that deliberate involvement of employees in environmental management efforts, such as source reduction programmes, yields far greater increases in environmental performance than do top-down programmes of a more technocratic nature. In other words, some kind of performance gain appears to be being achieved through participation. Bunge et al (1995), for example, have studied the effects of employee participation in source reduction programmes related to substances listed in the United States Environmental Protection Agency's (EPA) Toxics Release Inventory (TRI); they found that manufacturers using a certain combination of three formal employee participation approaches (internal pollution prevention opportunity audits, participative team management, and formal solicitation of employee recommendations) attained triple the reductions in emissions attained by manufacturers using none of these practices.

Other research supports the converse as well – that lack of adequate employee participation impedes attempts to improve environmental performance. Nielsen and Remmen (1994), in studies of two Danish food processing companies, found that excessively rule-oriented, top-down attempts to implement an environmental management system according to British Standard 7750 were less successful when employees were not involved or consulted, and more successful when they were given a meaningful role in the implementation process.

Continuous improvement is a central concept in new environmental management standards such as the European Union's eco-management and audit scheme (EMAS) and ISO 14001. In the interest of achieving this, Annex I of the EMAS regulation text (Council Regulation No 1836/93) emphasizes the importance of employee awareness, involvement, training etc, and the ISO 14001 standard uses similar language. One could always interpret this as simply meaning a way to better utilize the cognitive capacity of the organization as a whole, and to move information around more efficiently, but what about the positive effects that employee participation produces which may be more related to the kinds of social needs represented by the Hawthorne Effect than they are to information processing efficiency?

Lean and Clean Management

The preceding thesis suggests that employee participation can raise corporate environmental performance. Romm (1994) goes a step further and argues, based on an abundance of examples and statistics, that 'lean and clean management' which involves all employees of a firm in programmes to eliminate waste and other environmental risks and liabilities leads almost inevitably not only to better environmental performance but to significantly better business performance as well. Romm's orientation is more toward ways in which US industry can preserve international competitiveness and jobs (especially with respect to Japan), than it is toward an in-depth investigation of the organizational phenomena of pollution prevention and cleaner production. However, in developing his argument, he goes beyond the simpler cost-based wisdom of pollution prevention pays to suggest that broadly based lean and clean programmes in companies can yield many positive intangible results related to improvements in the intelligence, learning capacity, and flexibility of the organization as a whole. The result can be summarized thus: progressive, vigilant investments in environmental performance almost always carry with them improvements in business performance and competitive position. This begs a closer look from an organization-theoretical point of view. Can it really be this simple?

Signs of Strong Latent Potential

A general characteristic of organizations in the process of implementing more elaborate forms of environmental management appears to be a strong latent potential for employee interest, commitment, motivation, and staying power in this specific context. One could even argue that environmental programmes and projects tend to enjoy a significantly higher level of interest, motivation, etc than those in other areas such as quality management, technological innovation, and brand management. Aldrich and Lorentzen (1994) discovered this in a study of Danish companies in five different industries. I have also encountered this in a study of a global information technology company (Meima, 1996). An important hunch which can be drawn from such studies is that the members of organizations outside of the top management group should not be seen as passive – albeit possibly 'Hawthorne-affected' – recipients of top-down initiatives to prevent pollution or otherwise raise environmental performance, but instead as potentially very active, driving agents in the change process.

Bottom-Up Processes, Self-Organization, and Vanguards

Corporate staffs, middle managers, and lower level employees are naturally not normally free to start spending company time and money on anything which catches their fancy. Corporations are characterized by strong formal and informal (or institutional) control processes. However, when a strong latent interest receives some kind of activation or starting signal (Aldrich and Lorentzen, 1994) from the corporate leadership in the form of a meeting, memorandum, project initiation, or appointment of a new upper level executive, then bottom-up or middle-top-down processes of change or sub-group self-organization can be triggered. This seems to be a fairly common phenomenon in the corporate environmental management context. On the one hand, active steering by top managment may prevent the occurrence of such processes, since employees, despite their interest and potential commitment, are kept in a more passive, receiving role. This may likely be the case in corporations which have experienced an accident, change in customer preferences, or sudden imposition of a regulation, and must act expediently. It may also be the case in situations where the arrival of a new Chief Executive Officer (CEO) or owner with strong environmental ambitions sets a new corporate course. On the other hand, an insufficient level of interest, motivation, or sense of empowerment among lower level employees – a kind of apathy – might also hinder the emergence of a self-organizing change process, despite legitimizing signals from management.

However, in the middle ground between active top management control and organizational apathy, there is considerable room for self-driving, self-organizing employee initiatives to blossom, including those in which labour unions or local works councils play a role. Two variants are:

1) Shopfloor initiatives: Aldrich and Lorentzen (1994) found that awareness of environmental problems was fairly high at the factory floor level, that employees were ready to actively contribute, and that their interest was

closely associated with concern for their own working conditions. In some instances of poorer working conditions and repetitive, boring work, the employees in fact made improvement of working conditions a requirement in exchange for their participation in environmental programmes. When given a starting signal in the form of a general meeting and the creation of smaller quality-circle-like discussion groups, employees were able to develop considerable momentum on their own initiative, and work quite independently from management. The initial scepticism of employees towards putting unpaid time and effort into what might prove to be another spurious management fad was overcome through use of a course which demonstrated that management was serious about environmental performance. Aldrich and Lorentzen also found that employee interest was stronger for concrete measures than for the establishment of systems and procedures of a more abstract nature. Finally, the perception of environmental management as a new policy area or corporate function appears to have emerged as management and workers negotiated and interacted, but was not fully appreciated in advance.

2) Corporate staff initiatives (Vanguards): In many corporations, the creation of a corporate environmental staff and/or environmental vice-presidential or board position is preceded by a preliminary period of a number of years of ad hoc corporate environmental management. This may involve working groups which are set up from time to time to handle pressing issues (eg elimination of CFCs). It can also involve someone at a high level who is given a part-time responsibility for managing environmental affairs (eg a corporate spokesperson, quality manager, or personnel director). Another kind of ad hoc corporate form arises when other corporate staffs, such as a legal department, government relations staff, health and safety department, or public relations unit, must from time to time address environmental issues along with their other more routine areas.

In research I have been conducting of large international corporations in the information technology industry, I have found that, during such ad hoc periods, close relationships and new, shared knowledge develop among the protocorporate environmental staff. When a formal move is made by top management to establish a permanent corporate environmental function which has some budget discretion and which takes over the reins of prior environmental programmes (such as internal environmental auditing or pollution prevention) and begins to create its own, the newly empowered and invigorated proto-staff emerges into a vanguard of more ambitious, elaborate environmental management practices in the company. My research suggests that the language, identity, priorities, and direction of this vanguard rapidly differentiate themselves from other areas of the business, and the vanguard constructs a distinct area of management practice, bringing in many concepts and terms from networks external to the company with which it intensely interacts (eg the ISO 14000 committees, the World Business Council for Sustainable Development, associations of environmental managers or auditors, environmentalist membership organizations, etc). This process can occur in the absence of top management leadership or control. In short, establishment of a corporate staff responsible for environmental management in its increasingly more elaborate forms seems to set in motion a distinct process of self-organization which puts corporate environmental management into an entirely different category of organizational phenomena.

Intrapreneurs and Corporate Guerrillas

However, what can occur in the absence of a legitimizing, catalysing starting signal from above? One answer might be nothing. However, a variant of the self-organizing processes described above, currently available to me at least in the form of anecdotes unsystematically chanced upon, involves the spontaneous efforts of individual 'intrapreneurs' (Pinchot, 1985) or small groups of 'organizational guerrillas' to pursue environmental management discussions or projects that go beyond what management has initiated or sanctioned.

One version of this story seems to arise with regularity in Sweden in connection with the activist organization *Det Naturliga Steget* (The Natural Step), founded by Dr. Karl-Henrik Robèrt. The Natural Step is dedicated to educating the public at all levels about ecological principles (the 'four systemic conditions for nature's cycles') on which a sustainable future is supposedly to be built. These principles are essentially thermodynamic/systems-theoretical in nature, and confront current day business-as-usual with a message of priorities based on a scientific view of the environmental crisis. They can be expressed as follows (Robèrt, 1994):

1) Substances from the Earth's crust must not systematically accumulate in nature;
2) substances from society's production must not systematically accumulate in nature;
3) the physical basis of nature's cycles and diversity must not be systematically impoverished;
4) efficient and equitable turnover of resources is necessary.

A part of The Natural Step's activities has involved creating a network of local professional clubs, such as 'Economists for the Environment' and 'Technologists for the Environment.' Many members of these clubs work in industry, possess a high level of environmental awareness and concern, and seek to implement the principles of The Natural Step in their working lives, even when there is no formal, legitimate outlet for such initiatives in the organization to which they belong. Their spontaneous activism may involve starting networks and discussion groups, or petitioning management for new projects and programmes. This may in a sense today be no longer applicable in many companies, as environmental managers, policies, training courses, etc are popping up all over, creating an organizational space in which such things may be discussed. However, in past years, and probably also in companies today where change is very halting and irregular, this kind of intrapreneur or lone guerrilla appears to have been or be endemic. Examples have come to me from a number of Swedish companies, including an insurance company, an electronics firm, and an auto manufacturer. These agents generally achieved no lasting impact on formalized systems and procedures, but played a key role in starting environmental discussions that later became legitimate, and now personify the start of corporate environmental management in the accounts that other organization members recite. Many of them appear to have subsequently left the company, due either to retirement or to dissatisfaction with their possibilities for advancement, and thus not become a part of later, more systematic steps in the development of the environmental function.

An alternative to the image of the lone environmental campaigner who finally drifts away to other pursuits is the persistent technical specialist who turns out, when environmental practices eventually attain a high level of corporate priority, to have been quietly working away at a significant project under everyone's noses that proves to have been years ahead of its time. An example of this arose in a Scandinavian electronic equipment manufacturer, where it emerged, when the corporate environmental staff began to evaluate life-cycle assessment as a possible product design tool, that an engineer in one of the business areas had, on his own initiative and in collaboration with other engineers he personally knew at other industrial companies, already made considerable progress in several pilot life cycle analyses of selected products. This resembles the 'skunkworks' phenomenon (Peters and Waterman, 1982) noted by many management researchers, in which engineers who believe in the soundness and common sense of a technology overlooked or cancelled by higher level executives manage to somehow continue with its development, even if it requires working extra hours or 'borrowing' corporate research and development (R&D) resources.

One could argue that the strong personal interest and commitment which some individuals feel towards environmental work sometimes, even in the absence of formal signals and support from top management, leads to organizational events which contribute to the development of corporate environmental management. While this has been noted in other contexts as well, particularly those associated with new product innovations, it seems to form a distinct and not entirely insignificant category of organizational environmental management phenomena.

The Green Wall

It is safe to say that few corporations had well developed corporate environmental management programmes and organizations before the late-1980s. Those that did exist were, as many have already noted and discussed, primarily concerned with legal compliance and with the technical measures needed to achieve it. This state of affairs began to change, and corporate environmental management now often involves a much wider range of activities. Many corporations have by now launched new programmes, created new positions, established new or very much modified corporate staffs, experimented with new technologies, explored green market strategies and corporate images, and generally plunged into new terrain. And, what is now becoming apparent in recent studies is that much of this has not lived up to initial hopes and expectations – in both business and environmental performance terms – and has encountered what consultants at Arthur D. Little (ADL) have named 'The Green Wall' (Arthur D. Little, 1995a).

ADL conducted a survey in 1995 of 185 North American executives responsible for environment, health, and safety (EHS, a common American term for the corporate function which usually subsumes corporate environmental management). They discovered that there were widespread sentiments that EHS faces barriers to integration into corporations' business as a whole. Respondents cited 'lack of acceptance of EHS by business staff' (39 per cent) and 'EHS culture and separatism' (34 per cent) as the two by far most important impediments to integration. In a similarly formulated question, they replied that the 'single largest internal roadblock to managing environmental issues successfully in most organizations' was, first, 'failure to convince management that this is a business issue' (30 per cent), second, 'lack of integration between environment and business' (25 per cent), and third, 'insufficient or lack of resources' (22 per cent). Respondents noted with roughly even frequency that, in their companies, environmental issues were managed as either part of an integrated ('combined') EHS function, (or) 'increasingly, a part of the business management and decision-making process' or as a separate environmental function. Only a small minority of respondents said that their EHS was managed as a part of line responsibility or 'as a full-fledged partner on the business team' (Arthur D. Little, 1995b).

The results of this survey are consistent with observations of a more qualitative nature which ADL and others have made: many corporate environmental management initiatives, however well-conceived and sincerely supported by members of organizations, frequently run into trouble. ADL's promotion of the Green Wall metaphor for the organizational challenges which corporate environmental management faces has stimulated discussion and debate about various aspects of the phenomenon. The basic idea seems to be that many companies are backing away from earlier ambitions and commitments, with corporate environmental management retreating to a more traditional compliance-oriented role as compared to its recent promises of new ways of creating business value. Hitting the Green Wall is defined as reaching 'that point at which management refuses to move forward with its strategic environmental programme and the initiatives stop dead in their tracks' (Arthur D. Little, 1995). ADL names such symptoms as 'an increasingly fuzzy focus for environmental, health, and safety programmes, deferred decisions because of reduced management support, and an inability to demonstrate return on investment in the environmental programmes.' Outcomes may include an inability to move projects beyond a pilot or demonstration phase, budget cutbacks, organizational turbulence (eg a reorganization or re-engineering) which lowers earlier priorities, and burnout and attrition among the environmental staff.

Inertia is one adjective used to imply why environmental initiatives encounter the Green Wall. It bears connotations of active agents, ideas, and other resources somehow losing their vitality when they must interact with agents, ideas, and other resources which are more tradition-bound, conservative, reluctant, or striving in opposite directions. However, it is always dangerous to borrow notions such as inertia, force, and mass from physics when explaining social situations, as physical systems and society are in many ways fundamentally different. It is usually possible instead to bring in more concrete events when looking at specific companies in order to shed light on such inertia. One such event which seems to play a recurrent role in the exhaustion of corporate environmental initiatives is the resignation or firing of a key personality – a champion – who has driven and symbolized the initiative, and perhaps also a simultaneous reorganization or even disbanding of the environmental unit. Aldrich and Lorentzen (1994) recount examples of this. I encountered this in a company I studied (Meima, 1996). There have been accounts of this type in recent years at Asea Brown Boveri (ABB), AT&T, Volvo, and Ontario Hydro. We can draw the conclusion that, despite the frequent usefulness of seeing the development of corporate environmental management in impersonal, self-organizing terms, key individuals – with charisma, strong personalities, perseverance, and a symbolic, identity-giving function – can be very important. The coming and going of such individuals can also define the beginnings and ends of particular cycles or epochs of corporate environmental management, and either signify the dissolution of structures and practices which had been painstakingly built up in an otherwise hostile or indifferent organization, or signify new beginnings and a new wave of innovation based on lessons learned in the earlier cycle (as appears to be the case at, for example, ABB).

Another concrete manifestation of such inertia occurs when top management simply cancels employee or staff initiatives which have 'gone too far.' Aldrich and Lorentzen (1994) found examples of this in both a paper mill and a fish filleting plant. In both cases, a demotivation and disenchantment among employees resulted, and environmental management efforts faltered.

ADL suggests two generic sources of Green Wall episodes – one more cognitive, and more cultural. The congnitive explanation is that strategic environmental management simply does not fit in conceptual, analytic terms with the other functions of the business. The cultural explanation is that organizations are composed of believers and non-believers who fail to communicate. In more concrete terms, they mention the following major factors which can threaten corporate environmental management:

1) The destabilizing influence of corporate downsizing;
2) excessive financial scrutiny and bottom-line orientation;
3) new, distracting management paradigms;
4) the common tendency to try to do everything at once with environmental strategies;
5) overselling of the benefits of strategic environmental management, thus raising false expectations;
6) creation of an environmental culture incongruent with the business culture of the company; and finally,
7) poor communications between the corporate environmental function and the company's business units about potential competitive advantage. (Arthur D. Little, 1995a)

A theme common to a number of these factors is the fact that many corporate environmental personnel have no business training, and thus fail to understand how their activities relate to the business goals of the corporation (Shelton, 1996).

The solution ADL offers basically requires that top management begin to take a more active role in the integration of strategic environmental management into the business-driven parts of the organization. This is to be achieved by putting the competitive benefits which environmental management can bring into terms which business understands and can act upon (eg return on investment, payback period, present value, value-added, etc). By doing so, the tension and mutual incomprehension between the business and EHS organizations, as symbolized by the Green Wall, can be dissipated. ADL claims to have identified companies which have achieved this strategic linkage between the business and environmental sides, including Sun Microsystems, where a programme focused on cost effectiveness, and AT&T, Hewlett-Packard, and Xerox, which have been successful in implementing Design-for-Environment (DFE) programmes. A key aspect of Xerox's success has arisen in connection with German movement toward legislated eco-cycle (or 'take-back') schemes for electronic products. By studying how business and environmental activities could be better co-ordinated in anticipation of this shift, Xerox reportedly saved over $200 million (Arthur D. Little, 1995a).

Other Phenomena

The objective here has not been to exhaustively identify all the ways in which corporate environmental management can fail or otherwise produce surprises and unintended consequences. There are other conceivable anomalies to which researchers might turn their attention as well. There is, for example, the question of why many environmental efforts which are successful as demonstration projects fail to be transferred into routine practice. Another question has been raised over whether the introduction of environmental management systems may improve short-term environmental performance but lock firms into longer-term courses which lead to sub-optimal or even mediocre performance results. Another subject which encompasses many interesting organizational phenomena is the stakeholder concept: its use in designing strategies, legitimating corporate claims, explaining events, reframing and channelling conflicts, etc.

My objective has been to assemble a number of observations from practice which can challenge and exercise theories about how things are and should be in firms – theories not only of an academic character but also the kind of theories-in-use or rules-of-thumb which managers carry around in the backs of their minds, like the theory that happier workers are more productive or that pollution prevention always pays. Put to use on a daily basis in the workplace, it is the latter type of theory which certainly carries more impact. In the next section, the question of how these observations relate to theory will be addressed.

ALTERNATIVE THEORIES OF THE ORGANIZATION OF ENVIRONMENTAL MANAGEMENT

Organization theory (OT) has perhaps always been one of the most diverse, conflict-ridden, and impractical areas within the field of management. The word impractical is not used to imply that organization theory lies far from the daily concerns of managers; on the contrary, OT deals with such pragmatic matters as the allocation of authority and delegation of responsibility in firms, the processes and outcomes of decision making, the loyalty, motivation, and productivity of employees, the management of conflict, and the processes of training, management development, and organizational learning. What is meant by the use of impractical is that the rich literature of organizational studies is not easily put into practice.

Strategic management, marketing, finance and accounting, research and development, and operations management – despite their own schisms and controversies, for better or worse – tend to be characterized by fairly well accepted paradigms replete with practice-oriented matrices, checklists, and prescriptive diagrams. OT in contrast seems to generally offer quite obvious banalities on one hand (we are reminded of the well worn slogan 'People are our most important resource'), and, on the other, dense, critical 500-page books which compare various schools, delve back into historical debates, and end up with the kind of elegant reflections that please academics but leave a managing director struggling with employee absenteeism totally nonplussed.

Perhaps this is more a reflection of the people who write about OT than of the topic itself. But perhaps not. Weick (1989) suggests that organizational theorists usually must work on problems that are wide in scope, limited in clear detail, inaccurate in their representation, and vague in terms of their assumptions. He compares the research problems of organizational theorists with those of natural scientists, for example, in the following manner:

> *Natural scientists pick problems they can solve, work for colleague approbation rather than lay approbation, collaborate with people who share their interests and values, and seldom worry about what others think. The world of the social scientist, poet, theologian, and engineer is dramatically different. These people choose problems because they urgently need solution, whether they have the tools to solve them or not.* (p521)

The organizational challenges of environmental management and sustainable development appear to certainly match this description. This may explain why 'ecological organization theory' is emerging as a timely and appropriate response to these challenges and yet, unfortunately, may probably have to go through a great deal of field research, theorization, and text before a consensus emerges around how it can be of practical use.

A Choice of Theoretical Paradigm

How might the collection of organizational phenomena that have been reviewed above be placed together in some kind of coherent, unifying theoretical framework? Or should we even try to fit a unified theory of organizational greening to what we can observe in practice? There are certainly a great variety of substantially different – even contradictory – organization theories to choose from. Perhaps we should mix and match, borrowing from a different theory to explain, predict, or prescribe a solution to each unique situation as it comes up. This would require a broad knowledge of the theories among which one could choose. As such, it would also be very time-consuming and inefficient, and moreover manifest the assumption that all plausible theories are equal, few situations are comparable, and each case essentially requires its own custom tailored amalgam of theory in order to be made sense of.

In this world of equi-plausible organization theory, there is another position which one could adopt as an alternative: the assumption that, since it does not really matter in scientific terms which theoretical paradigm one chooses, and since data and arguments can be found to defend any theoretical position, one is free to choose a paradigm on the basis of personal taste, ideology, fashion, or some other dubious criterion.

While it could be argued that many management researchers choose to go one of these two routes, this state of affairs is not without its critics. Donaldson (1995), for example, decries the fragmentation, lack of cumulation, fascination with novelty, and overall absence of a unified, coherent view of organizations in the organization theoretical literature. Even within the relatively narrow sub-range of theories based on the notion of organizational culture, concern has been expressed over the proliferation of different approaches (Martin, 1992).

In the remaining pages of this chapter is available only a tiny fraction of the space one would need to examine the broader typologies of organization theories and to argue the pros and cons of applying them to our experience in the areas of corporate greening and ecological sustainability. This is a massive project. To suggest the size of such an endeavour, a few examples of such typologies are provided below. They represent scholars' attempts to grasp and summarize the main features of the OT landscape, and condense the work of many other researchers. This chapter will proceed to focus on one particular approach, leaving untried the many other approaches listed below. However, before we go on, a critical question must be asked: what theories can help us find the way to the most realistic and useful formulation of the ecological crisis in organizational terms? Many voices thick with ideological accents clamour to be heard, but the real research has only just begun.

Four Typologies of Organization Theory

Approaches before and after 'the crisis'

Gherardi and Turner (1987) attempt to classify studies of organization into two major and 13 minor categories. For the major categories, they distinguish between earlier, 'pre-crisis' approaches tinged with natural scientific optimism, and emerging 'post-crisis' aproaches which have taken a more critical stance. Their system of classification is as follows:

Pre-Crisis Approaches

1) Structural-Functional Analysis: the main concern is with efficiency and organizations as kinds of machines.
2) Systems Analysis: very concerned with building models, and is based on General Systems Theory and cybernetics.
3) Socio-Technical Analysis: interested in laws of equilibrium, control, and self-regulation in organizations.
4) Action Research: uses ideas borrowed from psychology such as psychodynamics and psychoanalysis.

5) Social Analysis: also based on psychology, and especially concerned with unconscious reality.
6) Institutional Analysis: focuses on the dynamic processes which establish social structures and norms.

Emerging Post-Crisis Approaches

7) Organizational Learning: emphasizes co-operation, theories-in-use, mental images, organizational norms; images of cybernetic single and double feedback loops have inspired its notions of perception, learning, and retention of what is learned.
8) Interpretative Interactionism: pursues an understanding of the interaction of phenomena rather than causal explanations; basically a sociological approach; everyday social interaction is reframed as problematic.
9) Longitudinal Analysis and Life Histories: this is essentially a historical, evolutionary approach, concerned with processes of growth and social-ization, critical events, the influence of individuals' life histories, and with language as a manifestation and transmitter of change.
10) Corporate Culture and Organizational Symbolism: here, organization can be seen as an interplay between symbols and action, or as a network of shared meaning, in which ethics and symbolic forms – eg language, ritual, ideology, and myth – are used as part of the collective construction of reality; this approach is closely allied with anthropology.
11) Cognitive Mapping: concerned with how organization members represent reality on a cognitive level with recurrent mental models and scripts, the storage of knowledge; concerned with how shared mental maps in organizations can be either harmonious or fragmented and dissonant.
12) Semiotic Approach: focuses on language; an organization is built upon discourse, and the objective of organization studies is to highlight narrative structure and read visible signs, and to reveal the hidden messages which convey the values of an organization.
13) Dramaturgical Approach: here, organizational action is seen as theatrical performance, to be interpreted according to the five elements of the classical pentad: act, scene, agent, motive, agency.

Four Competing Traditions

A second typology originates with James March (1994), who sees four primary perspectives (or 'traditions') of organizational research currently competing for 'airtime':

1) Seeing organizations as systems of coherent goal-oriented action: the emphasis here is on co-ordination and control, processing of information, making decisions, and rationally allocating resources.
2) Seeing organizations as social structures: this includes notions of organization as a system of internal order; a network of communication, authority, or other links; a system of interrelated rights and duties; a normative structure; a trust-based system of relationships; and a system of differentiation and stratification, possibly hierarchical and possibly with factions. Organization as such is not so much conflict-resolving

as it is a conflict-organizing system. This view sees individuals, organizations, society, and other levels/groupings as varieties of social structures, and is fond of organizational diagrams as a way of making sense.

3) Seeing organizations as adaptive (or learning) systems: in this view, organizations work to match their environments, not necessarily through rational action but instead through learning, diffusion of experience, and differential, adaptive birth and death of practices, functions, businesses, etc. The adaptation results through the interplay of processes of variation, selection, and retention of characteristics. Organizational learning is not a panacea for theoretical problems, and has highly political interpretations. The reason is that it is actually very hard to learn from experiences, such as accidents; it is often unclear what really happened, and what the cause-effect relationships are. Systems may learn far more from near-accident experiences coupled with individuals' imagination than from actual negative lessons.

4) Seeing organizations as systems of meaning: this tradition centres around the idea of culture, with organizations as producers, organizers, and communicators of meaning.

Six Different Approaches to 'Greening'

Gladwin (1993) makes a plea for a very much expanded effort in the application of organization theory to environmental management and sustainability, and develops the following set of categories as part of the agenda he lays out. He considers 'greening' to mainly be a change process (one could thus replace 'greening' in much of the following with the more general 'organizational change').

- Greening as Institutionalization: this approach suggests that changes in the features of organizations are often introduced to bring organizations into line with the changing norms and expectations of the institutional environment – a process often called 'isomorphism.' Isomorphism can assist in the acquisition of such survival benefits as stability and predictability, legitimacy, status, and access to resources. Firms affected for the most part by the same isomorphic influences are said to occupy the same 'organizational field.' The emphasis in this approach is upon the normative role of the environment.

- Greening as Organizational Learning: such theories focus on how past experience is mapped into actions appropriate to the present. Learning occurs if, through information processing, an organization's range of possible behaviours is changed. Learning consists of four central constructs/processes: knowledge acquisition, information distribution, information interpretation, and organizational memory.

- Greening as Natural Selection: also known as population ecology, this approach suggests that organizational survival is the result of external pressures that discriminatingly select forms for retention or for extinction among an organizational population (eg industry, regional set of firms). The focus is not on the choices or change of individual firms, but rather on the content and variety of entire populations of firms over time. Individual firms have great inertia, and are mostly immune to managerial action, and environmental factors favouring greening will offer survival to those organizations which, primarily through random variation, are more 'fit,' and eventually destroy those which do not possess compatible characteristics.

- Greening as Strategic Choice: this view takes almost the opposite view – managers do matter, and organizations 'purposively enact, define, and affect their domains.' Strategic action is seen as 'rational, deliberate, premeditated, and orderly.' Accurate apprehension of the present and future environment, analysis, development of objectives, and allocation of resources are the keys to success. A modified variant of this approach assumes that strategy reflects some conscious intent, and is also intendedly rational, but that uncertainty and ambiguity, the incremental quality of time and change, and bounds upon rationality cause outcomes to often differ from original intentions.
- Greening as Transformational Leadership: here, the human factor – the leader – is the key to a description and explanation of organizational change. Such qualities as charisma, force of personality, vision, values, goals, etc which are adopted by the other members of an organization are what primarily determine outcomes. In a process of change as comprehensive as greening, transformational leadership becomes especially necessary.
- Greening as Organizational Evolution: evolutionary theories see the cumulative effect of history and the rate of change with respect to time as most important in understanding greening. During periods of stability, change is incremental and convergent, while during periods of sudden, dramatic change in markets, technology, regulation, etc organizational equilibrium is punctuated by rapid, divergent change which 'breaks frames.'

Eight Basic Metaphors for Organization

A rather unique typology of various ways of approaching organizations owes its existence to Morgan (1986), who examined eight basic metaphors for organization and then categorized a great many theories according to their central metaphor, whether explicit or implicit. In these metaphors, organizations are alternatively seen as:

1) Machines: this view underpins bureaucracies; it suggests that organizations are made of interlocking, deliberately fashioned parts that each play clearly defined roles in the functioning of the whole.
2) Organisms: the focus here is on an organization's 'needs' and relations between it and the environment. Different species of organizations are suited to different niches, and the organism metaphor can easily explain how organizations are born, grow, develop, adapt, decline, and die.
3) Brains: emphasis here is on information processing, intelligence, learning, and making decisions; the organization is a self-organizing computer.
4) Cultures: the essence of organization resides in shared ideas, values, norms, rituals, beliefs, etc that sustain organizations as socially constructed realities.

5) Political systems: dominant concepts are interests, conflicts, power, and legitimacy. Actors in organizations exercise power in pursuit of their many interests, experience conflict when interests diverge, and build alliances when it suits them.

6) Psychic prisons: people in groups become psychologically trapped by conscious or unconscious preoccupations, and the organization channels or amplifies them. A widespread anxiety, such as fear of unemployment or humiliation, can become part of a self-driving organizational neurosis. This view is relevant with respect to ideological and psychodynamic aspects of organizations.

7) Flux and transformation: organization is a manifestation of systemic logics which shape social life, such as autopoiesis, cybernetics, and paradoxical dialectic phenomena.

8) Instruments of domination: organization embodies the pursuit of the ends of the powerful: the imposition of the will of some individuals (the empowered) upon others (the exploited). This is possibly an extension of the political-system metaphor above.

From a Theory-Driven to a Problem-Driven Approach

There is practically no end to the organization theoretical typologies, comparative arguments, etc to which we have access. Donaldson (1995), for example, analyses five theoretical paradigms – contingency theory, population ecology, institutional theory, the resource-dependency view, and organizational economics – in developing his arguments for why a unified approach should build upon the first one. Räsänen (1994) examines corporate greening from five perspectives which characterize pioneering attempts to get a grip on the subject: greening as strategic choice, as a planned reform of strategic management, as a natural process of organizational change with an ethical shift as its basis, as ethical or cultural change, and as institutional change.

Where does this leave us? What was the point of this deluge of different alternative points of theoretical departure? One point is emphatically for those who are reading this without much of a prior background in organization theory: there are many competing approaches out there, but no management science that we can routinely rely upon to unambiguously solve our problems. A second point was to create a kind of creative tension between the environmental management phenomena with which this chapter started, on the one hand, and the theoretical universe which could potentially address them, on the other. A third was to set the stage for a discussion of how, using the phenomena collectively as a point of departure, a specific appropriate theoretical approach might nevertheless be developed. I note that this is seldom done; much management research moves directly from empirical material to theoretical analysis without attempting to justify why the particular theoretical path was chosen, and without discussing alternatives.

DEVELOPMENT OF A BASIS FOR A CRITICAL APPROACH TO CORPORATE ENVIRONMENTAL MANAGEMENT

A Matrix to Organize the Phenomena

Returning to the organizational problems in the beginning of this chapter, what common themes or handles might we be able to identify in order to force a unifying theoretical approach? Figure 3.1 illustrates an effort to put them into an ordered framework. The vertical dimension represents the organizational tendency which a phenomenon appears to display. This can either be expansive, stimulative, and creative, or restrictive, depressive, and dissipatory – in terms of performance, resources, formation of stable groups, and such things. The horizontal dimension represents the domain of action in which the phenomenon – at least in terms of how it has been formulated by researchers and consultants – appears to live. This can thus mean either the domain of rational, calculating decision-making, the domain of managerial action (in which employees are seen as primarily passive resources to be managed, and where managers manipulate conditions), or the domain of organizational processes in which neither rational decisions nor the goal-oriented management of human resources can explain what seems to be going on.

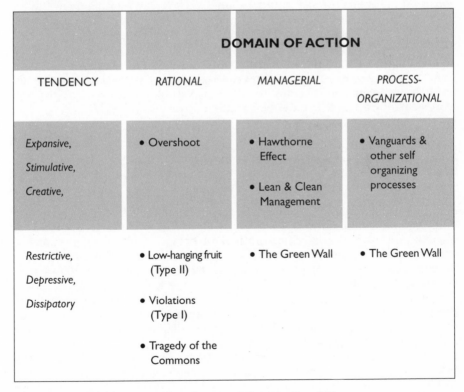

	DOMAIN OF ACTION		
TENDENCY	*RATIONAL*	*MANAGERIAL*	*PROCESS-ORGANIZATIONAL*
Expansive, Stimulative, Creative,	• Overshoot	• Hawthorne Effect • Lean & Clean Management	• Vanguards & other self organizing processes
Restrictive, Depressive, Dissipatory	• Low-hanging fruit (Type II) • Violations (Type I) • Tragedy of the Commons	• The Green Wall	• The Green Wall

Figure 3.1 A Classification of Organizational Phenomena

The selected phenomena can be distributed among the categories created by this matrix. For example, the problem of the low-hanging fruit has to a great extent been described and discussed by organizational economists, and relates primarily to a rational decision-making context which produces unexpected outcomes, and therefore begs an explanation which might, for example, make use of such qualifying assumptions as bounded rationality and the opportunistic behaviour of agents. The low-hanging fruit problem also can be placed in the lower row of the matrix because it represents lost opportunities, inefficiency, unrealized value, and so forth.

A second example is the vanguard phenomenon. To explain it clearly requires more than rational decision-making and the deliberate actions of managers. It seems to involve complex group processes, and evolve over time in unpredictable ways. It can also make possible considerable learning and give rise to elaborate forms of management in a self-organizing, spontaneous way. However, it might also be a route to the impasse of the Green Wall, which can either manifest itself in a more tightly steered managerial form or arise through vanguard processes which run out of their acceptable bounds and into organizational resistance.

What theoretical constructs does this simple ordering of the phenomena suggest? In one way, by suggesting a spectrum from rational decision-making via managerial leadership to impersonal, complex group processes, it leaves the door open to the wide range of different theories listed in the typologies above. Many explanations could be applied. Yet, in another way, taken together, it suggests that most specific theories are themselves insufficient and must be thrown out as general approaches. For example, strategic choice overlooks the role of complex bottom-up group processes, population ecology ignores the potential for individual organizations to adapt to changing conditions in their environment, and the various structuralist approaches do not take into consideration unique roles played by individuals. Something more generally applicable must be found.

Two Theoretical Critiques

Two recent critiques of the proliferation of theory can help us to narrow down our options. Stacy (1995) reduces the range of dominant theories of strategic and organizational change to two perspectives – strategic choice and population ecology – and criticizes them for being based on assumptions of causality and a tendency for systems to return to stable equilibria which – despite their neat logic – are not borne out by observation of actual practice. He proposes an alternative complexity-based perspective which instead sees organizations as near chaotic, unstable, characterized by positive as well as negative feedback, and self-organizing – with order emerging as a systemic property rather than as the effect of discrete, identifiable causes. How this order emerges depends upon the rules or logics to which the individual actors in organizations make reference when they act. And what is important here is that such action is a part of interaction among individuals; organization members continually receive feedback from other members as a result of their own actions, provoked earlier by the actions of others. As such, the picture emerges of an organization as a complex, non-linear feedback system. The order which emerges is a result of the overall systemic interaction, and is routinely remarkably stable in a dynamic way. An example of how to apply this image is by seeing the activity of an industrial company not as the mechanical output of formal systems of authority and information flow, nor as the realized intentions of rational planners and executives at the top, but as the outcome of the ongoing, nearly chaotic interaction of many actors following shared rules or logics which they reproduce in each interaction, and which have proven themselves through experience to be capable of maintaining the existence of the organization as a whole.

Von Krogh and Roos (1995) provide another critical perspective on theories of strategic and organizational change. They distinguish between a 'cognitivist' epistemology underlying dominant theories like strategic choice, which focuses on cognitive representations of reality and linear, analytic processes in the brains of organization members, and an alternative 'connectionist' epistemology which focuses on networks of agents which interact and learn according to locally applied rules. Invoking Weick and Roberts (1993), they argue that the value of connectionism lies in its ability to depict organizations as complex patterns of interaction by simple agents which, if richly enough connected, collaborate to produce the emergence of mind on a collective level. The emergent organizational patterns must be encoded in the rules used by the agents in their interactions. This derives in part from our growing understanding of how neural networks function in the human brain, but also can be traced back to early attempts in social psychology to build a model of organization which consists at its most basic level of interacting pairs of individuals who form their responses to each other using 'assembly rules' and learn in an evolutionary fashion from one interaction to the next (Weick, 1969).

Emerging Components of a Theory

Where does this leave us? If we bear in mind the problematic greening phenomena reviewed above, Figure 2.1 and these two critical evaluations of organization theory can be combined to suggest several points:

- A necessary component of a unifying theory is the role played by individuals throughout the organization.
- Another necessary component is the nature of their interaction.
- Their interaction may to a great extent depend upon local, temporary or context-specific rules, logics, or rationalities which are deployed when an interaction takes place.
- The deployment of shared rules, logics, or rationalities common to groups of organization members is what gives the overall organization its emergent patterns.
- The emergent patterns can lead to expansive, stimulative, creative circumstances, or to restrictive, depressive, or dissipatory circumstances. The former can usually (although not necessarily) be interpreted as success, and the latter as a kind of dysfunctional situation.

- The peculiar nature of environmental or ecological issues compared to other issues which arise in companies plays an important role in how and why certain organization members interact. While interaction of an environmental nature does not have to differ in any fundamental way from other contexts of interaction, it may often involve a consistent, distinct set of rules or logics which differ substantially from those which have evolved over decades and centuries in the service of conventional commercial enterprises.

- This 'ecological logic' appears to have originated outside of the traditional managerial control of corporations, and probably has its roots in cultural traditions, participation in various institutional networks, and the formation of values, attitudes, and beliefs through exposure to the news media, modern forms of entertainment, and the diffusion of new scientific knowledge about the environment. Therefore, although business logic is embodied in the overall ideology and rhetoric of modern corporations, and is generally the only legitimate rationale which can be invoked in analysis and discussion, ecological logic makes itself felt in local, micro-level interactions all over and throughout the organization because, in the instant it is deployed, it makes sense to the people who deploy it. However, what leads to tremendous complexity, variety, and seeming paradox is that conventional business logic is also locally deployed in many situations.

- A way to understand the organizational phenomena of corporate environmental management is to distinguish between business and ecological logic in the local interaction of organization members, and to then attempt to see the links between this pattern and the higher level patterns of the organization.

Sensemaking as a Theoretical Perspective

Weick (1995) has united a diverse body of organizational research and theorizing since the beginning of this century under the label of the 'sensemaking' tradition. This fits well with the theoretical components listed above. Sensemaking is what people in organizations do, and can be used to explain organizational life in diverse and subtle ways. He ascribes sensemaking with seven properties:

1) Sensemaking is grounded in identity construction: as people try to make sense in organizations, they construct notions of their own identities, of those of their counterparts, and those of various things like products, processes, and the organization itself. In other words, these identities cannot be taken as given and stored somewhere outside of the local interactions in which they are used. For example, an environmental manager will likely construct a personal identity in interacting with top management which differs from that used in meeting other environmental professionals at a conference.

2) Sensemaking is retrospective: in making sense of a situation, history matters, and while what has happened in the past cannot be retrieved in any kind of unambiguous, objective data-like sense, an interpretation of what worked in the past is usually available in determining how to act in the present.

3) Sensemaking is enactive of sensible environments: a central idea in the sensemaking approach is that people's subjective reality cannot be the same as a neutral, objective reality, and that they enact or construct the physical and social environments around them. This is not generally done in arbitrary solipsistic or psychotic ways, but rather in a sensible way that allows them to function as organization members, citizens, etc. What might even be considered remarkable is that we nearly always manage to make sense of our worlds even when bombarded with information and other stimuli, and subjected to great novelty and ambiguity.

4) Sensemaking is social: as already explored in connection with the complexity-based and connectivist approaches discussed above, sensemaking requires interaction. We cannot make sense in isolation, but instead require a counterpart – whether a living individual, the embodiment of a person's thought in a book or product, or an imagined encounter with someone who is absent – in order to deploy the logics and rules of interaction.

5) Sensemaking is ongoing: it is never switched off. The sense made in one interaction is reflected upon as individuals go on to their next encounter; one interaction has never quite ended before another begins. Sensemaking can be seen as a continual, never ending process.

6) Sensemaking is focused on and by extracted cues: every time we are presented with a situation of which sense must be made, we extract cues or indications from the situation with which we can work, such as the symbolic interpretation of a word or image, the tone of a person's voice, or a piece of factual information like a number or colour.

7) Sensemaking is driven by plausibility rather than accuracy: as sensemaking is an ongoing process, and there is always a new opportunity to revise one's sense of a situation as circumstances change and new cues become available, a greater premium is placed on plausible, adequate, expedient treatments of interactions than on strict accuracy. The latter would demand rational, exhaustive calculation, which is usually impossible.

Corporate Environmental Management as Ecological Sensemaking

An explanatory framework has now been established which links organizational phenomena observed in the actual practice of corporate environmental management to the sensemaking approach. A key distinction which can help us to understand how these phenomena arise and unfold is the difference or tension between business logic and ecological logic. A great deal has been left unsaid or undeveloped in this chapter.

What has been presented here can be used as a point of departure for researchers and practitioners embarking on their own projects in this larger context. The sensemaking approach, along with complexity-based perspectives and organizational epistemology, offers great promise in helping us get beyond simplistic models and false polarities as we struggle to figure out how industrial enterprises can become integrated into the quest for sustainable development. I believe this is a necessary undertaking because, as described in the beginning of this chapter, environmental management and ecological sustainability are as much organizational problems as they are, for example, technical, economic, or ethical problems. Organizational problems can only be understood using organizational theories, and solved through organizational practices. What has been developed here may be a start.

A Sensemaking Vignette: 'AdVance Corporation'

There has been a lot of abstract discussion in this chapter. Some readers may be left wondering how it relates to practical issues. To illustrate the idea of sensemaking, and to put the theoretical components above to use, I will provide here an account from the world of corporate environmental management which I have assembled from several situations encountered in my research. I emphasize that this vignette is a composite of several related situations in several case studies; it does not describe events which actually transpired as depicted.

AdVance Corporation is a global manufacturer of electronic equipment. After several decades of successful traditional pollution control at the plant level, the management of AdVance began to take steps during the late-1980s to introduce new forms of environmental management co-ordinated at the corporate level. For example, in connection with the Montreal Protocol in 1987 and subsequent national CFC legislation, AdVance was quick to organize a working group to eliminate CFC use which involved representatives from all business areas. When the national government in its home country began to suggest that it might require mandatory, externally monitored environmental audits, AdVance worked actively with other corporations under the auspices of the confederation of industry to develop a voluntary internal auditing scheme. As these and other projects arose, the executive committee decided to appoint one of its staff managers as environmental spokesperson, a part-time position.

Within a few years, the complexity and workload of the environmental spokesperson had expanded to the point at which it became necessary to establish a corporate environmental staff, with three additional full-time positions. The staff worked intensely together as soon as the unit formally came into existence because they had a great deal to do. First, they had to assume responsibility for a variety of corporate environmental programmes which already existed, including the auditing programme, several working groups for specific pollution prevention issues (such as chlorinated organic solvents, brominated flame retardants, and heavy metals), and a network of factory level environmental co-ordinators. Second, they received a number of assignments from the executive committee in connection with the elevation of environmental management to corporate staff function, including a revision of the environmental policy, establishment of company-wide environmental performance indicators, and launching of an annual environmental report. Third, merely through working together in their new capacity and associating with colleagues around the world via conferences and other fora, many new issues quickly arose which attracted their attention, including ISO 14000, EMAS, and the use of life cycle assessments (LCAs).

And so it went. As in most new units, the staff members spent quite a bit of time explaining their purpose to others in the company, building their identity and justifications for existence, and trading stories and ideas back and forth with each other as they worked through the pursuit of these things. A number of stories circulated quite vigorously. One involved copper. It seemed that one of their plants was in violation of its permit because it was releasing twice as much copper in its waste water as the permit allowed: seven kilograms per year instead of four. The permitting authority was threatening them with a large fine if they did not invest in a relatively expensive addition to their water treatment plant. Then, it was discovered that the copper runoff from the rooftops of the public buildings in that province totalled over 1,000 kilos a year – all entirely uncontrolled. It would be much cheaper for AdVance to pay for the refitting of a few rooftops to achieve the same reduction in copper pollution, but that was entirely out of the question. People shook their heads. The lesson was that not only was it dangerous to fall out of compliance, but one had to assume that the authorities were so narrow-minded and inflexible that even getting close to the compliance limit was unwise. Better to stay at least a few steps ahead of compliance.

A similar story arose in connection with pine resin. At a plant in a northern location, the occupational health and safety authorities were reportedly imposing a fine because there was too high a level of resin dust and vapour along an assembly line where it was used as a flux in speciality circuit soldering. Then it was discovered that the level of resin dust and pollen containing the same irritants outside in the parking lot was at ten times that level because of the surrounding pine and spruce forest! Members of the corporate staff laughed in disbelief. You certainly could not reason with the authorities when they work in these ways, but you had to stay ahead of them and get good at it if you wanted to avoid unnecessary costs and inconvenience.

In other contexts, it became obvious to the staff that staying a few steps ahead of compliance was the right policy. They all knew that environmental problems were serious and getting worse, and that regulation could be expected to tighten for a long time before it became any more lenient. They would have to achieve continuous and significant gains in environmental performance. A way of thinking about and communicating the kinds of efficiency gains that industry would have to achieve in the coming decades which staff members often used was the 'Ehrlich equation,' which the unit manager had found in a book.[1] It led one to the conclusion that, if the world's

---

[1] See Ehrlich and Ehrlich (1991:7–10) for an explanation of this model, which often has the form $I = P \times A \times T$, where I is environmental impact, P is population size, A is per capita affluence, and T is the damage caused by technology employed in supplying each unit of that consumption.

population could be expected to double before it peaked, and the overall average material standard of living of humanity could be expected to quintuple as, for example, Chinese citizens all acquired refrigerators and air conditioners, then, to simply hold the current rate of environmental degradation steady, the resource efficiency of technology would have to improve by a multiple of ten. To the staff members, this meant requirements in the near future for cars which went more than ten times as far on a tank of gas, houses which could be heated with less than one-tenth as much heating fuel, and cellular phones whose batteries lasted over ten times as long. This transformation would place tremendous burdens on industry, but also offer many commercial opportunities for the quick and the innovative. Merely complying with regulations as they currently stood would probably mean missing the opportunities and being repeatedly caught off guard. Staying a step ahead was a better policy.

Over the first months and years of the unit, this conclusion was reached over and over again. All sorts of stories, examples, and conceptual models arose which pointed toward a one step ahead policy. It simply made sense. Then, one day, in a staff planning meeting, the idea arose that they should propose to the corporate leadership that AdVance become a signatory of the International Chamber of Commerce's (ICC) 'Business Charter for Sustainable Development.' They felt that this would help to further consolidate the corporate environmental management function at AdVance (which, despite its successes, still often found itself battling to be accepted out in the further reaches of the global organization), and also help AdVance to enhance its legitimately deserved environmental image among the public and other stakeholders. So, this proposal was added to the agenda of the upcoming semi-annual meeting with the executive committee.

The staff unit manager entitled his presentation 'A Step Ahead,' and used some of the short anecdotes presented above as well as others in his argument for why AdVance should sign the ICC's charter and commit to a path of proactive environmental management. He felt it would make sense to the executives. After all, the charter would not have to be accomplished all at once, and many of its provisions were quite broad and fuzzy anyway. The point was that it would be a good overall way to communicate the unit's work internally, and to cultivate a new corporate culture of anticipatory, integrated environmental management.

To his surprise, the proposal met with resistance. The executives even joked about it putting them 'A Step Too Far,' or 'One Foot in the Grave.' The CEO reminded the unit manager that the corporate policy, even after the latest revision, required compliance using best available technology not entailing excessive cost (BATNEEC), and compliance in less stringent nations with norms in the home country, but said nothing about going *beyond* compliance. He said he understood some of what the manager was getting at, but that 'a step ahead' was impossible to define as a corporate goal, and that he furthermore did not see how the ICC's charter could help to clarify the situation. On the contrary, the charter might get them into unforeseen difficulties with respect to their image or legal liability. Better to leave the environmental adventures to The Body Shop or Ecover, and stick to what they were good at – 'building boxes with buttons on them.'

The environmental staff unit manager was very disappointed. He had succeeded in achieving a variety of piecemeal, albeit important, steps in the construction of the corporate environmental management programme, but had never managed to get an integrated approach accepted, whether of the more innocuous ICC variety or of the more massive, committing type as exemplified by ISO 14001. For various reasons, his disappointment but one of them, he left AdVance a few months later and accepted a new position as Environmental Vice-President at another manufacturing company in a different industry. While on holiday that summer, he was surprised to read in an environmental management newsletter that AdVance had just signed the ICC's charter with great fanfare and media coverage. The CEO was quoted as saying that he was excited and looked forward to putting his business where his own personal values were. The former unit manager immediately picked up his cellular phone and called one of his old colleagues.

'What finally made them do it? Did they see the light?'

'They saw a different light, a warning light,' his old workmate replied. 'CenTransit, our biggest customer now with that UK project, said that if we didn't, they would possibly go with the competitor on a big order.'

They had never thought of that argument. Staying a step ahead had just made sense to them in its own right ...

CONCLUDING REMARKS

Perhaps a sign that environmental management and sustainable development possess many challenges for OT lies in the increasingly frequent observations that – in this unknown and novel territory – companies either do unexpected things or fail to do what would be reasonably expected of them. A common reaction is to anthropomorphize their behaviour, and to accuse them of evil, greed, laziness, ignorance, or stupidity, or, alternatively, benevolence, altruism, alacrity, insight, or wisdom. While these might be appropriate labels for the individual people who make up an organization, they fall short of adequate frameworks for analysing and explaining corporate behaviour. What clearly must be part of ecologically grounded OT as well are, on one hand, the unexamined, partially shared systems of meaning to which individuals refer when they act as members of society, and, on the other, the informal and formal collective patterns which emerge when people interact, such as group dynamics and institutions.

This chapter has attempted to take several steps toward such an exploration of OT: by classifying organization anomalies, by skimming through a number of typologies of organization theory, by using two critiques (one complexity-based, the other epistemology-based) to argue for a sensemaking approach incorporating 'ecological logic,' and by describing this approach in brief detail.

The objective here has been more a kind of reconnaissance of theoretical and empirical territory than permanent settlement – winning terrain as opposed to consolidation. However, settlement must follow. Agenda 21, for example, makes it clear that social organization is as relevant to sustainable development as is technology. The air is still thick with ideological characterizations of the organizational and managerial side of sustainable development. Some reflect technological optimism, others a loathing of capitalists and markets, others green fervour. While a moderate belief in the usefulness of tools, a healthy scepticism of businesspersons, and reverence for the natural world are all positive things, the tendency of many to go to extremes may be partly due to the immaturity and lack of widespread awareness of theoretical perspectives. As a colleague of mine recently said, the map may not be the territory, but most territories require good maps. Sensemaking may thus be a sensible way to proceed.

Chapter 4

Power, Organizational Culture and Ecological Abuse

Tony Emerson and Richard Welford

INTRODUCTION

Often pollution and other ecological damage are seen as something external to the firm: smoking chimney stacks, discharges to water and toxic waste dumped in remote landfill sites all conjure up images of something outside the working of the business. Yet, factors within the organization where decisions are made and practices established are also responsible for the ecological problems that have built up over the last 50 years. Central to this internal process is the issue of power relationships since it is normally the few who take decisions which affect the many. This chapter therefore constructs a theory that offers an explanation of the role of the firm, based on the literature on power (vis a vis organizational culture), on organizational dynamics, on organizational learning and on the nature of employee contracts. These ideas on management have been applied to many other types of organizational problems but they have rarely been considered in relation to ecological abuse.

'Power and Organizational Culture' (p58 of this chapter) explores the role of power in the evolution of organizational culture, and sets ecological abuse in the context of power abuse. 'Psychoanalytical and Psychodynamic Models of the Organization' (p64) looks at organizational dynamics and human emotions, and particularly at schools of thinking based on psychoanalysis and other forms of psychodynamics. It relates this literature both to ecological abuse, directly, and to power abuse more generally.

A transition to sustainability requires very significant learning and change by organizations and their members. 'Organizational Learning and Environmental Responsibility' (p69) examines the organizational learning process, and the barriers to it – especially, organizational defence mechanisms and extremes of power culture. 'The Flexible Firm Model' (p71) looks at recent developments in the nature of the contract between the firm and the employee. It argues that the 'flexible firm' (or interpretations of this concept in which employee contracts are insecure and short term) tends to increase anxiety and stress, increase power concentration, and to reduce the likelihood of organizational learning and change towards sustainability.

'Power, Organizational Dynamics and the Learning Organization' (p73) integrates these ideas into a theory on organizational culture and ecological abuse, and 'Recommendations' (p74) concludes by suggesting a range of actions or action strategies that might be considered by managers, consultants or action researchers.

POWER AND ORGANIZATIONAL CULTURE

The starting point for our exploration of the function of power in the evolution of organizational culture is the classification of cultures developed by Handy (1985), and Harrison (1987) in Table 4.1.

Table 4.1 Types of Organizational Culture

Culture Type	Description
Power	Head sits in centre, surrounded by intimates; head is dominant, subordinates dependent; a personal, informal management style; power is valued.
Role	Organization is a set of roles or 'job boxes' joined together in a logical fashion in order to discharge the work of the organization; formalized communication, standardized procedures; 'roles not people'.
Task	Team of talented people or resources focused on projects or task; flexible, competent people, emphasis on planning and development; friendly, enthusiastic, co-operative management style.
Person	Individual comes first; organization sees its role as resourcing talented individuals, who value working on their own and making decisions; management by persuasion and negotiation (not commanding).

Different cultures are functional at different stages in a firm's development. Handy (1985) and Harrison (1987) suggest that a developing organization tends towards the characteristics of a 'power culture' firm: it is able to exploit opportunities, able to move quickly and to react well to threat or danger. Firms tend to move to a role culture when they become established and need to consolidate, but if the external world becomes very changeable, they need to move to the more adaptive and responsive task culture.

The features of all culture types have potential relevance to environment related behaviour. Organizations where the power culture dominates might be flexible and open to development but the emphasis given to the environment will depend on the attitudes and values of those at the centre of the organization. It may or may not be an environmentally responsible company. In the role culture, power is exercised through rules, systems and procedures. Such a culture may be conducive to keeping within environmental constraints, but not for bringing about change when the violation of such constraints are already the norm. The task or 'achievement' culture is oriented outwards, onwards, upwards towards a goal or ideal, and assumes people are internally motivated. In many ways, this culture is the opposite to the role culture: it may not always be conducive to running a tight environmental management system but it can be good for bringing about change within the organization. The person or 'support' culture motivates and bonds people through close, warm, relationships. Here we might expect participative styles of management and a caring attitude to the environment as part of a wider social responsibility.

For our purposes, however, the association of the power culture concept with the developing and dynamic organization leads us to a more detailed analysis of this type of culture. Most large organizations display elements of the power culture. Even the bureaucratic type role culture organization often tends to be a covert, complex version of the power culture, with power sub-groups alternatively co-operating and competing. Within these firms we may also get sub-units which can be characterized as task or as person cultures. However, in so many organizations it is the power culture which emerges as the most dominant. When there is conflict or change the importance of power relationships is heightened. Those who can ultimately wield most power will determine the direction of the organization. It is therefore useful to explore some positive and negative aspects of the development of this economic power.

Positive Features of Power

Many commentators put forward a relatively simple justification for the necessity of a power culture in an organization. Simply, if a firm is to carve a niche in a market and deliver a high added-value product or service, it must be powerful. In particular, it must have a clear and sophisticated organizational structure, with power differentiation related to organization function, where individuals or teams are delegated adequate power to act swiftly in the event of threat or opportunity.

In a model of the firm provided by De Board (1978) the organization is seen as importing energy, materials and people from its environment, then converting or transforming these resources into products or services, with added value, which it then exports back into its environment. Over time through a process of internal elaboration, the organization evolves to a higher level of order, sophistication and organization. In this way, a successfully developing entrepreneurial organization builds up power. Power is essentially the potential or capacity to do work.

It is thus the combination of both technological and organizational sophistication which explains the enormous growth in production this century. Even a writer like Tannenbaum (summarized by Pugh and Hickson, 1989), who argues for reducing power differentials in organizations, recognizes the need for some degree of differential for organizational efficiency. In addition, studies of organizations endeavouring to promote alternative and more democratic values, by Freeman (1972) in the US, by Paton (1978), by Landry et al (1985) and by the Co-operative Advisory Group (1986) in the UK, all argue for the need for clear and explicit decision-making structures.

Thus it is argued that power is necessary for the development of an effective organization. Power is required in order to run an organization capable of delivering goods and services to customers which, in turn, leads to success. In turn, success reinforces power. Internal power and success then deliver power to the firm as a whole. The successful commercial firm, performing optimally, maximizing added value and delivering marketable output at minimum input costs, remains in business, grows and develops a corporate power of its own.

Negative Features of the Power Culture

Power certainly makes things happen but the ultimate question surrounds whose interests are being served in the type of successful firm described above. As they elaborate on the features of the power culture, the originators of this concept discuss some problematic features as the powerful organization evolves. Harrison (1987) notes that a power culture tends to be dominated by a strong leader or coalition, who often run the organization for their own benefit. Successful people within such a culture are often preoccupied with striving for status, personal power and influence, and with building up relationships with other powerful figures. Political skill is important in getting ahead. The leader, Harrison suggests, is required to be all-knowing as well as all-powerful, while subordinates are expected to be compliant and willing to please their bosses, and are usually motivated by fear and dependency. Handy (1985) observes that power culture decision-making tends to be based on the balance of influence rather than on procedural or purely logical grounds, and that individuals will prosper and be successful to the extent that they are power-orientated, politically minded and risk-taking.

Both writers note a tendency for a power culture organization to degenerate with size. Handy sees it as analogous to the spider's web: such a web can break if it seeks to link too many activities. Harrison sees a tendency for the firm to degenerate into 'rule by fear', with the leaders, their friends and proteges abusing power for personal advantage.

In the power culture, therefore, status is vital, little respect is shown for those with lesser status and fear and insecurity is experienced by those with little power. People seem either to have to accept a low status, dependent and compliant position, or to engage in political striving for power and status.

The Power Culture and Ecological Abuse

Power cultures tend to drive progress and development within the firm. The power elites, and the culture underpinning their decision-making, should therefore bear prime responsibility for the consequences of business decisions. Here we explore how organizational culture features relate to pollution, resource misuse and other environmental problems. Four problematic features or tendencies of the power culture are suggested.

Marketing Practices Lead to Non-Optimal Use of Global Resources

Marketing practices focus on convincing us that more is better then less, that we actually need certain products, that some products will necessarily convey status, happiness and well-being and that without more and more consumption life will have little quality. In the West we know that overconsumption is the norm, that we consume vastly more than the majority of people in the world and that our consumption and demand for low cost goods leads directly to poverty and suffering in the least developed countries. Such inequity is, however, compounded by the inequity even within the developed countries.

Harrison (1987) notes that the internal (power) orientation of firms seems to be associated with an external orientation towards power and status differentiation in the market it serves. Thus:

> *Power orientation in service ... emphasises status and prestige ... makes the customer feel like a King. The hierarchical emphasis of the power orientation leads naturally to status differentiation in service ... typical of restaurants, hotels, resorts ... a more aggressive and competitive variety of the power orientation can be found in the salesrooms of car dealers.* (p9)

Thus, increasingly, the use of resources for production is devoted first to the luxury needs of the few who can afford the high prices of goods and services which, in turn, provide larger profits for the suppliers. From this starting point, firms will pursue a marketing strategy of product differentiation and market segmentation. Essentially, this means that the firm will seek out ever larger markets, providing goods and services which one particular segment can just afford (egged on by tantalizing marketing campaigns). In a finite world, with finite capacity to absorb greenhouse gases and other consequences of production, this is hardly in accord with the principles of sustainable development.

The Propensity to Externalize Costs onto Third Parties

According to neo-classical economists the traditional firm, seeking to maximize profits, will seek to minimize its costs, partly by resisting the internalization of costs associated with free goods (eg clean air). Thus where a company is virtually free to pollute the air, it will actually prefer to do this than install costly clean-up technology. Two features of the power culture actually contribute to making the generalized picture even worse.

Firstly, the rapid, unimpeded, decision-making process requires short-term results and does not allow the organization the luxury of considering the wider impacts of its actions. Satisfying the narrow aims and objectives of the organization, usually based around maximizing output, sales and profits, means simply that there is not the time or resources to ensure that this is achieved in a socially responsible way. Indeed, time will more likely be spent on avoiding and evading environmental laws than putting systems in place to ensure compliance.

Secondly, the power culture leads to a general disregard for the powerless. In effect their wishes and aspirations (even in many cases their rights) are discounted. Thus there is a tendency to externalize costs through pollution affecting, disproportionately, the powerless third parties whilst the organization pursues its own narrower goals. Those companies who act in accordance with blatant cost cutting strategies can often gain unfair competitive advantage, and, in doing so, also violate rights of more ethical competitors (Commoner, 1974).

Unilateral action which violates rights of others (Argyris, 1982) might be an apt definition of 'power abuse' in this context. The action may simply arise from carelessness, ie from a lack of consideration of the interests of parties who are not perceived as stakeholders with power, rather than from malicious intent. But this phrase may be a particularly apt description of a range of decisions and actions, in themselves often apparently innocuous, but which cumulatively lead to severe ecological problems where the ultimate bearers of the costs are not yet even born and are powerless in the extreme.

Beyond Control Mechanisms

Galbraith (1969) argued that all successful firms try to control the market, rather than to be subject to the disciplines of the market place. While such market disciplines are no guarantee against ecological abuse (which tends to effect third parties as much as immediate consumers), a more sophisticated market and increased consumer awareness and information provision can help ensure that organizations that degenerate into unethical and ecologically damaging behaviour will not survive. However, as companies become more powerful they are more able to manipulate the market and hide those aspects of their practices which might be seen as unacceptable. Moreover as companies become increasingly internationally oriented they can hide their more ecologically damaging activities from consumers in the final market. Thus the consumer who buys the high quality, high priced heavily advertised training shoes in America may be blissfully unaware that they were made with sweatshop, under age labour in Indonesia.

As many firms become increasingly transnational in their behaviour and outlooks so they begin to have the power to manipulate not only markets but countries and national cultures. Many transnational firms become more powerful than the nation states in which they operate, and are, to a great extent, beyond the influence of state regulatory bodies, such as environmental or pollution control agencies. Here they wield huge amounts of political power, playing government against government in the important function of attracting new inward investment. Deregulation becomes the norm and the large corporation does favourable deals with national authorities which allows it to increase its power base.

Together, these first three issues show that an optimal economic model in traditional neo-classical terms is unlikely to be optimal in ecological terms. The combination of a movement towards luxury production, market segmentation, the externalization of costs, traditional strategies for competitive advantage and egotistical power structures result in an increase in society's environmental costs. This traditional pattern is illustrated in Figure 4.1. The powerful organization uses technological and organizational skills (1) to build up power (2) and develop high productive capacity (3). In delivering a high volume of production (4) it produces pollution and other externalities (5) and

Figure 4.1 Organizational Psychodynamics and Ecological Abuse:
Power, Production and Pollution

makes excessive use of natural resources (6). This is the common tension which exists between business activity and care for the environment. However, a fourth issue compounds this problem still further.

Problems Arising from the Internal Dynamics of the Power Culture

March (1984) argues that organizational decision-making often serves the function of a power celebration ritual, rather than being a rational economic interest maximizing process. This view helps explain the frustration of environmentalists who would like to see business take their environmental responsibilities seriously. But in so many cases environmental issues are seen as secondary considerations and are easily dismissed as organizational trivia; not the stuff of power celebration. Even where environmental strategies are introduced into the organization, they are often managed by relatively junior staff or subsumed within other functions (such as health and safety) and given lower priority.

To appear to care about the environmental and other issues seen as external to the firm is often seen by the managerial elite as a sign of weakness. This is not the cut and thrust of business, where hard men are required to take tough decisions based on financial considerations alone and where one's self importance is measured by the fear which can be instilled into workers, suppliers and even vendors. Thus environmental issues are overlooked or even deliberately ignored.

Thus virtually all large and (economically) successful organizations will display at least some of the four ecologically damaging characteristics outlined here. One particular aspect of the power culture which arises again and again is the devaluation of lower status members of the organization and of weaker external stakeholders. As this process is, we believe, at the root of ecological abuse, it is important to consider it in more detail. In order to gain more detailed insight into such manifestations of the use of power in organizations, we turn to two other schools of management thinking: the 'Psychodynamics of the Organization', and the 'Organizational Learning' schools.

PSYCHOANALYTICAL AND PSYCHODYNAMIC MODELS OF THE ORGANIZATION

Originally developed by Freud from his therapeutic work with individuals, psychoanalytic theory is based on concepts such as the unconscious, anxiety, defence mechanisms and identification. De Board (1978) explains its application to group and organizational life:

> ... psychoanalysis helps to reveal those processes which occur within every individual and determine how each person will act. It shows how psychological pressures, especially anxiety, can neutralise productive effort and drain away human energy. It shows the ways in which people affect and relate to each other in groups, and the ways in which leaders are created. Above all ... it shows some of the basic causes of problems which are likely to occur in any organization, but which are rarely understood, and therefore rarely solved, by managers. (pviii)

Hirschhorn (1990) put forward a number of key propositions for the understanding of organizations from the psychoanalytic viewpoint. Three of these propositions are:

1) Feelings of anxiety are the fundamental roots of distorted or alienated relationships at work;
2) a work group manages its anxiety by developing and deploying a set of social defences through which people retreat from organizational boundaries;
3) the social defences at work frequently create a distorted relationship between the group and its wider environment, including its customers, clients and competitors.

Thus these systematic distortions of relationships relieve the group of part of its anxiety. The 'outside' is commonly scapegoated or devalued in some way to preserve the 'inside'. De Board (1978) elaborates a similar concept of 'defence mechanisms against anxiety': people invest energy in repressing anxieties, or projecting their feelings onto others – energy which is then not available for productive work.

This framework can be developed and applied to common contemporary business characteristics and to the related concept of ecological abuse in the following way:

- The pressures of modern business (increasing competition, deregulation, takeovers, job insecurity, etc) are anxiety-provoking. Hutton (1994) reflects a common view when he suggests that 'the new structures in the labour market, with the increasing difficulty of securing and holding a full-time job ... are entering the very marrow of human experience – and impacting on our readiness and capacity to build and maintain networks of families and friends which are the prime source of human satisfaction' (p13). Thus the support systems (offered both by the state and by our informal networks of friends and family), all the more necessary in times of personal economic anxiety have been weakened. Many others (eg Handy, 1994) point towards the stressful lives and long hours of work now so common amongst the upper echelons of the professions and industry and the ill health and alcohol and drug abuse which so commonly occurs as a result of this.
- The issue of environmental sustainability is ultimately about the possibility of irreversible ecological damage and global destruction, and leads to further anxiety about what we are doing to the world and the hopelessness of the present situation. It is often seen that moving towards sustainability will be economically and personally threatening for those of us in the West, with serious implications for all occupations and sectors. Commonly, the perceived problem is so massive that people feel powerless to act and build a set of defences allowing them to retreat from dealing with the issues. Common defences revolve around rejecting the information pointing to ecological crisis, seeing things as not being as bad as the information predicts, a belief that technology will come to the rescue or a belief that nature will sort itself out in some way. Some may even convince themselves that governments will be able to sort out the problems as they occur.
- The more powerful or senior the organization members, the more they may have to lose by the fundamental changes which ecological information suggests as being necessary. Equally, the more powerful they are to influence the repression or denial of ecological information. We have already suggested that power is used to shape organizations to the psychological needs of (powerful) members. Similarly Menzies (1970) argues that '... socially structured defence mechanisms appear as elements in the structure, culture, and mode of functioning of the organization, the result of collusive interaction and agreement, often unconscious, between members of the organization ... old and new members must come to terms with (these mechanisms)' (p10).

In Figure 4.2, these factors are added in to the 'power, production and pollution' model represented in Figure 4.1. The anxiety (9) resulting from both economic and ecological threats (7 and 8) contributes to (10), information rejection or problem denial. Here, as we so commonly see, business leaders reject the idea that there is an environmental crisis, often challenging scientific evidence, and where environmental management strategies are followed they tend to be piecemeal, reactive and designed so as to be consistent with the more traditional objectives of business.

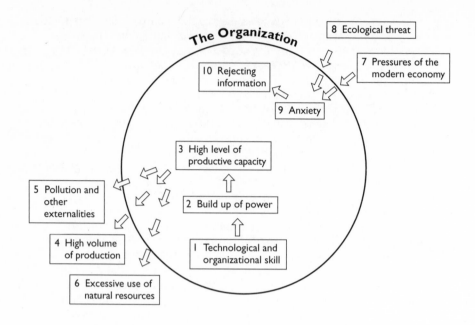

Figure 4.2 Organizational Psychodynamics and Ecological Abuse:
Anxiety and Denial

This theory leads to a number of predictions:

- Ecological information capable of causing anxiety is likely to be suppressed by the organization.
- Firms will adopt real and practical environmental management projects that do not ask challenging questions about the system which leads to ecological crisis. Any environmental projects which do exist will be there to serve as a social defence mechanism against anxiety and designed to show both insiders and outsiders that the company is responsible.
- The existence of anxiety about job security may lead to a range of other social defences. These are likely to include the devaluing or scapegoating of the external world consistent with a lack of concern for the environment. There commonly follows ecological abuse such as pollution and other externalities.
- The social defences employed by senior members will commonly include the devaluing or discounting of other organizational members, particularly lower status members.

Figure 4.3 represents the addition of these factors to the model. The social defence mechanisms used to combat anxiety in the firm lead to both external and internal discounting (11 and 12). The picture is therefore of an increasingly powerful, but anxious, organization. The model suggests that environmental damage pollution does not just arise because of the volume

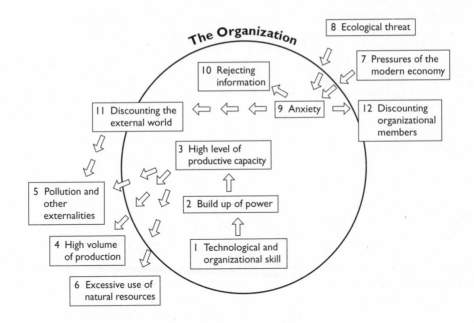

Figure 4.3 Organizational Psychodynamics and Ecological Abuse:
Anxiety and Discounting

and nature of production (arrow from 3 to 5), but because of a type of psycho-logical need to scapegoat (arrow from 11 to 5.)

To explore further possible consequences of unhealthy psychological functioning in organizations, we turn to another psychological school – family therapy. Gore (1992) referred to this school of thinking in developing the analogy between the dysfunctional family and the ecologically destructive society. Here we draw an analogy between the (un)healthy organization and the (un)healthy family.

Skynner (1995) citing the Timberlawn Studies, argued that a healthy family fosters higher level values, individual security within interdependent relationships, openness in emotional expression, clear boundaries on behaviour, hierarchal structure without extremes of laissez faire or autocracy. On the other hand the unhealthy family, according to Skynner (1992), tends to result in:

> *Unloved people [who] begin to suppress or ultimately to deny, even to themselves their need for acceptance-affection. This kind of freedom from pain is won only at the expense of hiding that part which makes life most worth living experience of warmth, tenderness, beauty of nature ... joy and delight ... More and more extreme and bizarre stimulation is needed ... even to get the same flat reaction, after progressing towards more anti-social activities.* (p8)

Thus when emotional needs are not met, either in the home or in the workplace, it is plausible to suggest that the consequences will include the ubiquitous insatiable consumerism (with obvious consequent ecological problems), or an insatiable need for power, 'fat cat salaries', ego and recognition (with the negative implications discussed above).

In particular, the view that excess consumption is a form of substitute for some other unobtainable satisfaction, is similar to that expressed by Gorz (1989) with his concept of 'compensatory consumerism'; or Seabrook's (1986) view of the production-consumption process described as 'a voracious and mobile process that never rests, so that even as more and more wealth is created, it is attended by the growth of subjective feelings of inadequacy' (p165).

Additionally, Marsh and Collett's (1986) study of the company car (described in Chapter 2) illustrates how consumer activities may play a part in, and reinforce organizational dynamics. The company car, which creates particularly high ecological costs in that it also stimulates a high volume of extra private driving (Moore and Hanton, 1995) is a symbol of status and acceptance within the firm. Indeed, other types of consumption are also linked with the desire for status and recognition. Those people who although poorly paid buy designer label clothes at very high prices do so because they need the recognition which is taken away from them by a system which discounts all but the powerful. Organizational discounting, itself the product of anxiety builds consumerism back into our model. In Figure 4.4, boxes 13 and 14

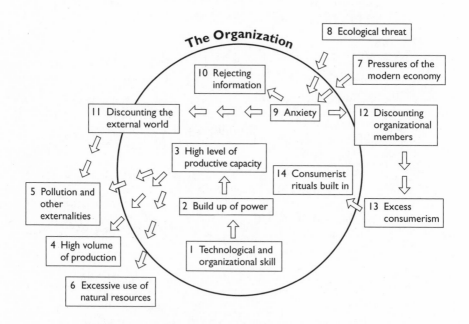

Figure 4.4 Organizational Psychodynamics and Ecological Abuse:
The Role of Consumerism

represent the integration of individual and organizational consumerist behaviour, respectively, into our model of the organization. But as Seabrook (1988) implies, consumerism and anxiety merely feed each other.

We might also make a distinction between a healthy and an unhealthy orientation towards power. Commonly, we see management hierarchy linked to decision-making power as a requirement for organizational effectiveness. The systemic family therapy school sees hierarchy as a requirement for a healthy social system. But hierarchy becomes dysfunctional (both to organizational effectiveness and to the welfare of individuals) when people identify their self-achievements in their power over, and relative to others: an attitude prevalent in the 'power culture' organization or in the high 'power-distance' organization discussed by Hofstede (1983) and also conveyed by Steiner's (1979) concept of 'power play'. So often, achievement and success is measured through power over others and as more individuals seek out the ego trips which are substitutes for satisfaction and happiness, so the search for power increases. The irony of the power culture organization is that it tends to be driven by those unhappy people for whom career and work is everything rather than those more rounded, more balanced and arguably more competent people who have a wider range of interests, experiences and understandings. Such people are capable of being much better managers and more effective leaders but are rarely interested in engaging in the rat race.

ORGANIZATIONAL LEARNING AND ENVIRONMENTAL RESPONSIBILITY

The work of Argyris and Schon (1978) has been a major influence on thinking about organizational learning. Their basic concepts can be explained with the help of Figure 4.5. On the left hand side of the figure we find 'espoused theory' – the policy and values espoused by the firm. The strategic policies of the espoused theory are elaborated into the more detailed 'implementation strategy'. 'Action' indicates the actual implementation by local managers and operatives. At this stage, members of the organization (ie staff, customers and other stakeholders) can act as learning agents, detecting errors in theory prediction, that is, differences between what is planned and what actually happens, and feed this information back into the decision-making systems, so that the errors are corrected.

Organizational learning can be either single or double loop. Single loop learning means the detection and correction of errors that lead to changes in implementation strategy, but without challenging the espoused theory or higher level policy. Double loop learning relates to the modification of the underlying policies, aims and objectives. In the latter, members detect and feed back more fundamental errors, especially information on discrepancies between espoused theory (what the organization says its policy is) and its 'theory-in-use' (the implicit or apparent policy that can be derived from its actual practice). In this way, flannel and hypocrisy is detected, and an organization learns to set more specific, and implementable, objectives.

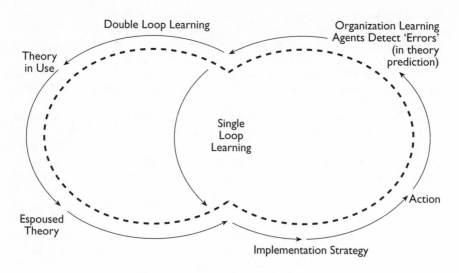

Figure 4.5 Organizational Learning

In developing this framework, Argyris and Schon (1978) comment:

> *Unless people acting as agents for organizations and societies are able to learn how to detect and correct double-loop errors, the survival of the society may be in doubt ... We begin to suspect that there is no stable state awaiting us over the horizon. Our very power to solve problems seem to multiply problems. Our organizations live in economic, political and technological environments that are predictably unstable. The requirement for organizational learning is not an occasional, sporadic phenomenon, but is continuous and endemic to our security. (p5)*

Even if they were not referring to ecological crises explicitly, these comments seem particularly relevant to this discussion – especially taking into account the point made by Gore (1992) that many ecological changes are too slow or gradual for the information to be readily picked up. Sophisticated learning systems are therefore required to pick up weak signals.

Argyris and Schon (1978) see the major barriers to organizational learning as the adoption by organization members of such defensive norms and strategies as:

- The protection of selves and others, unilaterally, from criticism, etc;
- keeping one's own views private and not testing out for differences in views;
- not trying to see the whole picture;
- the taking of unilateral action based on one's own private view of the issue in question.

This 'model 1' individual behaviour (referred to as defensive climate behaviour), is manifested in defensive group dynamics. Difficult issues become undiscussable, and that undiscussability itself becomes undiscussable. Model 1 behaviour leads to inaccessible, unclear or inadequate information systems: people protect each other by not confronting each other with difficult information. The result is an organization with a limited learning system, capable of single loop learning at best.

Considering environmental issues, it is easy to see that such a secretive, closed, protective and ill-informed culture is more likely to give rise to ecological abuse, per se. In addition, however, the anxiety provoked by worries over environmental issues will tend to activate barriers to learning and create a defensive climate, in which difficult questions are not asked. So even if the company mission statement (the espoused theory) is phrased in terms of 'stewardship for future generations', a defensive climate may create a theory-in-use more associated with not providing information on specific issues that challenge commercial interests or organizational dynamics. Thus environmental issues become taboo and ignored.

Such problems of accessibility of information are exacerbated by the characteristics of the power culture as Pedlar et al (1988) argue. If senior people discount less senior people and their information, and reward them only for information they want to hear, then the information in circulation is likely to be even more limited and distorted, as well as only representing limited interests.

The application of the organizational learning model in this situation therefore suggests that key cultural changes are required for an organization to make progress in the learning process required for a transition to sustainability. Such change must ensure that all members and their ideas, beliefs and feelings are taken into proper account. It requires the organization to move away from power and status preoccupation and to encourage the search for and dissemination of clear and accurate information relevant to the problems it identifies. Sometimes this can be a source of conflict, but managing and learning from such conflict is very much part of the learning process and is ultimately much more useful than bland adherence to norms set by the elite.

THE FLEXIBLE FIRM MODEL

We now move on to consider a model of the firm, economic in origin, which is very influential on current management thinking. The flexible firm espoused by many managers, talked of in uncritical terms by many academics and feared by most workers has, we argue, the potential to exacerbate such problems as power abuse, to reduce organizational learning and to increase ecological abuse.

The economic philosophy of flexibility is, according to Prowse (1990)

> to compete in world markets and react swiftly to changing consumer demand whilst reducing unit labour costs ... achieved by a deployment of tasks within the workforce, using a range of workers not required as permanent staff to cover peak work periods, a reward strategy for flexibility and acquisition of new skills. (p13)

Whilst recognizing the need for firms to respond to economic pressures, a key question revolves around what happens to staff at non-peak periods. A study by the US National Bureau of Economic Research (NBER) (Abraham and Houseman, 1994) suggested at least two alternatives: US-style flexibility, in which the number of employees is varied dependent on market conditions; and (continental) European-style flexibility, in which the hours worked per employee is varied with market conditions, but nearly all employees stay on the books. In the latter case (ie Euro-style flexibility) it was found, for instance, that investment in training was a lot higher, and that European employers have found it easier to nurture the kind of longer term relationships that are essential for real flexibility through a highly skilled workforce.

It is the US-style flexibility (also more popular in the UK), and the relationships or contracts it creates, that exacerbates the problems identified in this chapter. Firstly, it increases power differentials because it gives the core staff almost unrestricted power to hire or fire non-core staff. Secondly, it gives non-core staff very little incentive to share in any feeling of corporate responsibility. Thirdly, the insecurity of such short-term contracts discourages non-core staff from giving any critical feedback on organizational practice. Workers therefore commonly have no real commitment to the organization and the organization itself lacks any real participative element. These characteristics are an essential ingredient for an environmental management programme.

Additionally, US-style flexibility seems to militate against individual and organizational learning. There is less incentive for the firm to train individuals, as suggested by the Abraham and Houseman (1994) NBER study. For example, it cited a finding that the countries with the longer term employment relationships are also the countries with the better in-house training provision. The average tenure in France, for instance, was ten years whilst over 30 per cent received training, whilst in the US only 17 per cent of workers were trained and the average tenure was under seven years.

But a learning organization is not just about workers updating their skills: every member of a learning organization needs to be encouraged to pick up relevant information and feed it back into the organization's decision-making process, so that organizations both improve existing practice, and constantly review their fundamental objectives and policies (double loop learning). The insecurity of short-term contracts militates against the giving of such feedback. Commonly, workers are too scared of losing their jobs to complain about anything. Job insecurity seems to be leading to a type of 'freezing': people say nothing or espouse only what they think the power figures want to hear. Who dares to raise difficult questions about environmental responsibility in such a context?

Even more worryingly for the move towards sustainability is the fact that the application of this model of flexibility seems to increase the level of unemployment in society. US-style flexibility means 'de-hiring' people in recession or when public spending is cut. Commonly, these jobs are never fully reinstated in the up-turn, as the proponents of this approach to flexibility argue. Evidence suggests that in the US economic revival of 1993 average working hours went up to 41.7 hours per week, the highest since the war, as managers squeezed out more production without hiring new staff (Walker, 1993). Any measures which increase the levels of unemployment further increase social power differentials and further increase the ease with which employers can hire unquestioning employees and maintain compliance in their workforces. As Hutton (1994) argues, this concept of flexibility seems to be destroying social cohesion and damaging personal well-being.

POWER, ORGANIZATIONAL DYNAMICS AND THE LEARNING ORGANIZATION

Having discussed problems associated with power, organizational dynamics and learning individually, we must recognize that these problems taken together (a not uncommon picture) compound each other, make solutions more difficult and contribute to the evolution of unsustainable practices within and outside of the organization.

A high concentration of power internally seems to have been associated with the development of successful entrepreneurial organizations. The values and ethos of such a power culture are likely to have been reflected in production for luxury markets, in the externalization of costs and in the discount of powerless outsiders (such as future generations). This actually results in non-optimal economic behaviour when ecological factors are taken into account.

Internally, power culture values discount the views and feelings of less powerful insiders. One consequence is the limiting of information required for organizational learning and change, so that any challenge to ecologically abusive practice is less likely. A second consequence could be that the powerless, to compensate for the stress and the insult to their esteem, respond with irresponsible behaviour, such as wasteful or polluting behaviours, or excess compensatory consumerism. Psychological and organizational dynamic factors further exacerbate such tendencies. Pressures of modern business are anxiety creating. Contemplation of ecological disaster is the ultimate in anxiety creation; and information about what needs to be done to avoid it is threatening to many people.

Organizations (and their most powerful members in particular) respond to anxiety with various defence mechanisms. Commonly this includes denial of the problem and rendering it undiscussable. The job insecurity created by economic factors (particularly by certain interpretations of the flexible firm) further militates against discussion of difficult issues and challenge to the status quo; against the creation of a learning environment. In such a climate it is likely that company environmental management projects sometimes do not tackle the most ecologically significant and deep rooted issues, and just become 'defence mechanisms against anxiety' in themselves.

Implications for Action

We have highlighted the complexity of the organizational systems that are creating ecological unsustainability, and the mutually reinforcing nature of their elements and sub-systems. It would be easy to draw the pessimistic conclusion from this, that action at the level of the individual organization is futile. But an optimistic interpretation of systems theory is that even small changes, at the right time and in the right combination, may upset the equilibrium of the (unsustainable) status quo. We do not know precisely what these levers of change might be – but we suggest the following recommendations as a strategic guide as to where to look in the organization and what questions to ask. Additionally, of course, higher level political action by organizations and their members (eg through trade associations, professional organizations or trade unions) is a vital complement to within organization action. But we concentrate here on action within the firm, that might be considered by managers and consultants (or action researchers). This set of recommendations is not intended as a detailed recipe, but rather as a strategic guide as to where to look in the organization, and what questions to ask.

RECOMMENDATIONS

1) What can you do to help create trust and security, and reduce anxiety, the pre-requisites for both organizational and individual learning of new ways of thinking? You cannot ask confrontational questions effectively unless you are trusted. An intervention agent needs, as a key skill, to help create the climate in which people express their anxieties and face them, rather than repressing or projecting them. One way of reducing anxiety is to support moves to longer term contracts of employment, in accordance with the 'Euro-style' model of flexibility.

2) Check that the firm's environmental agenda is based on a clear analysis of the ecological problems being addressed, and of the behaviours in the organization that are most relevant and significant in contributing to these problems, quantifying the effects. Challenge the vagueness and evasion that serve as barriers to organizational learning.

3) Use a range of diagnostic approaches (as summarized in Chapter 2) to learn about organizational cultural factors and their contribution to unsustainable practices.

4) Adopt Critchley's (1994) principle: accept and acknowledge people by learning about their work, their history and their values, before explicitly trying to change them.

5) All firms are pluralist coalitions, with a variety of cultures; major change requires the identification of and working with them all.

6) Look particularly at power relations, reflected in the degree of devolution of decision making, in information flow and in the nature of contracts. Trace what happens to various pieces of information, relevant to environmental decision making; look at who is dependent on whom for their jobs to continue, and how that affects information flow.

7) There is a limit to the change that people and social systems can tolerate. Be aware of the problems associated with the flexible firm (or at least some interpretations of it).

8) Intervene to give people more security in their membership of organizations and reframe perceptions so that people see themselves as part of a wider organization or society which, if they devalue, they devalue themselves.

9) If people are locked into consumerist and organizational reward systems at the subconscious level (as suggested in this chapter) then participative democracy, as advocated by many environmentalists, may not lead to change on its own. Can more intrinsic and less material rewards be substituted, as a way of moving to a less materialist and consumerist culture?

10) Some benevolent paternalism may be required to create trust and security in the first place, whilst working to spread power throughout the organization. Senior management, as well as being discouraged from the 'hire and fire' mentality, and being encouraged to delegate and develop staff, may also need to (re)create various organizational rituals or functions so that they are seen to be caring.

Part 3

Developing Strategies for Managerial Action

Chapter 5

DEVELOPING AN ENVIRONMENTAL CULTURE THROUGH ORGANIZATIONAL CHANGE AND LEARNING

Minna Halme

INTRODUCTION

It is broadly recognized that the goal of sustainability or sustainable companies culminates with the question of profound change in organizational cultures (Shrivastava, 1995). In order to achieve the requirements of the sustainable development ideal, business enterprises must make considerable changes in their products, services and processes throughout the life cycle. The scale and scope of the necessitated changes are too big to be accommodated within the business-as-usual mindset (Schmidheiny 1992). Therefore, as several environmentally advanced companies have realized, we must look towards cultural change.

Organizational culture has been compared to an iceberg. Parts of it, such as symbols, customs, and traditions are visible, but most of it remains below the surface. Such elements include assumptions, beliefs, values, and norms that direct the participants' decision-making and behaviour, often unconsciously. Culture is a result of history. Certain solutions to organizations' internal or external problems have worked well enough, and, consequently, people have started to regard them as 'the right way to do things'. Gradually they have become taken for granted guidelines that are no longer questioned: they direct the organizational members' actions unconsciously. For decades one taken for granted assumption within many corporate cultures was that environmental questions were external to business operations.

This chapter will concentrate on how organizations can develop environmentally aware corporate cultures. First, it looks at the types of impulses which can trigger environmental change processes, and discusses factors that make some organizations more responsive than others. The chapter will go on to look at patterns of organizational culture shift. Traditional top-down models will be compared with other models such as bottom-up and middle-up-down change. Thereafter phases of organizational change will be focused. In many organizations environmental change process begins with resistance, followed by a period of 'unfreezing', where unlearning old assumptions and routines which exclude the environment will be important. As learning progresses, we see new organizational practices and principles being adopted and the cultural shift becomes profound, with organizational members developing new commitment to ecological improvements.

Factors facilitating and impeding cultural shift will be examined and the chapter ends by addressing the tools for developing environmentally aware corporate cultures. These include education and training, incentive systems, information dissemination, participation, motivation, performance appraisal, pilot projects and cross functional task groups. Throughout the chapter, examples will be used to illustrate the points made.

TRIGGERS FOR ENVIRONMENTAL CHANGE IN ORGANIZATIONS

Most often, various types of external pressure act as a trigger to environmental change processes in organizations, although occasionally it is possible for a change to start from an internal impulse as well. We shall first have a look at the external impulses that can trigger environmental change. Moving from business-as-usual mindsets, which exclude the environment, to environmentally aware cultures, usually requires a revolutionary or second-order change. Such changes are usually induced by the misalignment of external conditions and organizations' current strategic orientation (Bettis and Pralahad, 1995). A critical source of change triggers are organizational stakeholders (Dutton and Duncan, 1987).

Environmental legislation or regulation either at national or international level may trigger organizational change. In recent years we have seen a tightening of environmental regulations throughout the world, such as a ban on leaded gasoline in Switzerland, or the law on liability for environmental damages in some European countries. Threats of environmental organizations' demonstrations or consumer boycotts, or negative media attention may also be a catalyst to environmental change in a business enterprise. In recent years these sorts of boycotts and demonstrations, often coupled with media attention, have increased in visibility and influence on business decisions (we only need to think back to the Greenpeace campaign against the dumping of the Shell oil platform Brent Spar into the North Sea). Customers may demand improved environmental standards of operation as a condition for buying. Financiers may refuse to fund investments that pose an environmental risk or insurers may not provide insurance to such investments. The above examples of external triggers involve a threat of a negative outcome to a company.

But environmental change does not need to be triggered by a threat. For some companies, international agreements may act as a trigger of change. Agreements such as the Montreal Protocol in 1987 seeking to reduce CFCs changed operating conditions throughout a whole industry. Furthermore, green markets (customers wanting environmentally friendly goods) increasingly act as catalysts for environmental change in corporations.

PREREQUISITES FOR ENVIRONMENTAL CHANGE

External impetus for environmentally sound performance is often necessary for organizational change to begin. However, external pressure alone will not bring about culture change in a business enterprise. There must be a capacity for response within the organization.

What, then, makes some organizations more responsive than others? One prerequisite for environmental change can be, for instance, openness of the organization to allow its members' interaction with various other actors and organizations in society. If business decision-makers interact merely with other similarly minded business people, the interaction tends to reinforce and strengthen their old business-as-usual world views. They will not be disposed to different ideas. This is particularly true in an environmental context where various interest groups in society are important actors. These influential groups, such as environmental organizations, may have different perceptions about sustainability. Instead, if a company allows, or, even better, encourages its members to have contacts and interaction with, let us say, environmental groups, it may have better means to assess and anticipate future develop- ments, and, consequently, adapt early or innovate in order to be more successful in the future. In other words, this makes possible early recognition of weak signals. This interaction needs to occur through a dialectical process where each participant actively tries to make his or her world view visible, understand those of others, and, ultimately, broaden his or her own world view. In such a way, the array of potential solutions to achieving sustain- ability widens.

Not only openness and interaction but also allowing alternative opinions and ways of thinking in an organization, as well as acting upon them, may improve the organization's ability for environmental change (Halme, 1996, and see also Jones, 1995). Weick (1995) argues that the greater the variety of beliefs the organization has in its repertoire, the more fully any situation should be seen, the more solutions should be identified, and the more likely it should be that someone knows a great deal of what is happening. If an organization allows only one way of thinking, warnings or weak signals go unheeded. For example, in most business enterprises there are some members who are personally dedicated to environmental causes (Wolters et al, 1995). These people are likely to pay attention to early customer questions about environmental aspects of the firm's products and production, or to environ- mentalists' criticisms of industry practices. If these environmentally aware organizational members are allowed to voice their observations, and act upon them, the firm can respond early instead of waiting until the pressure increases and it is necessary to change practices. Early adopters have greater degrees of freedom in their response, and will also get the image benefit. A flat, non-hierarchical organization structure is more suitable to realize the above conditions. Such a structure is more likely to encourage flow of ideas and information within an organization (Callenbach et al, 1993).

PATTERNS OF ORGANIZATIONAL CHANGE

Organizational culture can be observed at different levels. The most visible level is that of artefacts, visible organizational structures and processes; in other words all the phenomena that one sees, hears, and feels when encountering a new group with an unfamiliar culture. At the next level are strategies, goals and espoused values. At the deepest level are basic assumptions and beliefs that are shared by members of an organization, that operate unconsciously, and that define a basic 'taken-for-granted' style for an organization's view of itself and its environment (Schein, 1992). In more everyday language, culture can be seen as 'the way we do things around here' comprising the internalized and unspoken beliefs and norms that shape the way the organization functions (Barrett and Murphy, 1995).

Culture change is a slow process. A change cannot convert an entire organization instantaneously, but rather begins with a 'nucleus' (Gersick, 1991). It is most common to assume that top management induces organizational change. According to the top-down view of environmental change in an organization, top management decides to incorporate environmental considerations into the corporate strategy, it establishes an environmental policy, guidelines, and principles, and then disseminates these throughout the company (Smart, 1992).

The strength of the top management environmental change is that it is most likely to guarantee top management commitment necessary for implementing a company-wide environmental strategy. On the other hand, it may appear that when the top managers are the key people promoting the environmental strategies, the changes end up being planned by the management group, and then pushed down in the organization. In such an instance, there is the danger that other organizational members will not develop an ownership of the issue, environmental efforts will remain as statements or credos, and practical improvements realized slowly if at all. For the top management approach to succeed, it is crucial that lower levels of management and workers are involved in planning the environmental programme from an early stage so that they will develop the necessary commitment, and so that the best possible expertise can be gathered with respect to all the operations of the organization.

However, there are other patterns by which an environmental change can happen, such as the bottom-up or the middle-up-down approaches. In the bottom-up model, middle and lower managers function as intracompany entrepreneurs. A bottom-up cultural change in an organization can begin with behaviour and an organization 'becomes what it acts' through recognizing the benefits of a new type of behaviour. This translates into a bottom-up approach, where people develop new patterns of behaviour and from their experiences come new attitudes, values and beliefs. In such instances, culture change often begins with the analysis of a specific business problem at a small unit level and response to this problem can trigger internalization of new ways of doing things through the process of 'learning by doing' (Hendry and Hope, 1994, Nonaka, 1994).

Culture change involves learning and a creation of new knowledge. According to Nonaka (1994), organizational knowledge creation related to the cultural change process can be viewed as an upward spiral process, starting at the individual level moving up to the collective (group) level, and then to the organizational level, sometimes reaching out to the interorganizational level. This cycle is shaped by a series of shifts between different modes of knowledge conversion. Knowledge is created through conversion between tacit and explicit knowledge. There are various triggers that induce the shifts between the modes. Once knowledge creation starts at the individual level, it moves up to the group level through a socialization mode. In the socialization mode of members of a 'team' or 'field' of interaction new tacit knowledge is created through shared experience. In the second mode of knowledge conversion, externalization, individuals exchange and combine their newly acquired tacit knowledge in successive rounds of dialogue, for instance through such mechanisms as conversations and meetings. To facilitate tacit knowledge becoming explicit, metaphors can be used to enable team members to articulate their own perspectives. Next, in the combination mode, the new knowledge is combined with existing knowledge. Through an iterative process of trial and error, concepts are articulated and developed until they emerge in a concrete form. This experimentation can trigger internalization through a process of 'learning by doing' (Nonaka, 1994).

Bottom-up change is not initially corporation wide. Instead, it begins through ad hoc initiatives on the periphery of the organization, and grows and moves gradually towards the core. It proceeds through the development of a shared vision of how to manage and organize towards solving that problem; grows through reinforcement of successful experience; and spreads through imitation in other units and, only after its success has been established, through the development of formal policies, systems and structures (Hendry and Hope, 1994).

In the bottom-up model, the change agents usually have less formal power than those within the top-down model. As a consequence, the manner of promoting change is more conservative and negotiative, and planning environmental management improvements becomes interactive. Interactive planning is well suited for generating motivation amongst organizational members.

The weakness of the approach is potential lack of support from the top. For a bottom-up approach to succeed, top management must at least legitimize the actions based on it. Namely, even when members lower in the organizational hierarchy have a lot, if not most, of the impact on the change in organizational culture and even when they initiate the majority of the change proposals, legitimization from the top is still needed. In other words, although leaders may or may not propose alternate perspectives themselves, they do shape the possibility and course of a cultural change by legitimizing (or not) the expression of particular perspectives (Bartunek, 1984). Even if leaders themselves do not propose new environmental policies and practices, they must nevertheless enable others to be expressed and allow actions based on them to be taken.

Both the top-down and the bottom-up model imply that the role of the individual as an independent, separate actor, is critical (Nonaka, 1994). It is true that change agents are crucial in promoting environmental changes in the organization, but occasionally the identification of environmental innovations with only one particular individual may prove counterproductive over time. If understanding and knowledge are confined to a single individual, then the whole project is at risk if that person leaves before the idea has taken root in the organization (Nielsen and Remmen, 1994, Barrett and Murphy, 1995).

It is also possible to combine the two alternatives of top-down and bottom-up change (Post and Altman, 1992). In contrast to them, a middle-up-down approach takes a view that organizational members work together horizontally and vertically, and puts more emphasis on collectivity. A major characteristic of this model is the wide scope of co-operative relationships between top, middle, and lower managers. In the middle-up-down management top management provides 'visions for direction.' Middle management translate these generalized visions into middle-range visions, which are to be realized in the field. Middle managers create their visions out of those from top and lower managers and materialize them. The gap between the two forms of perspectives, top managers' vision and lower managers' view of reality, is narrowed down by and through middle management. In other words, they work as a bridge between the visionary ideals of the top and the often chaotic reality of the frontline of business (Nonaka, 1994).

In an environmental management context a typical alternative is a change model where a number of organizational members form a group or a team that initiates environmental change in the organization. The members may represent different organizational levels and/or functions, and may come from different units of a corporation. This approach can be regarded as a variant of the middle-up-down or bottom-up model of change. Often the members of the initiating team are environmental experts or persons who otherwise are active in and aware of environmental issues (Meima, 1995).

There is no evidence of the superiority of any of the above models. They all have strenghts and weaknesses. To some extent, the suitability of the approach is dependent on the current organizational culture. The need to generate commitment to change and capacity for innovation through learning suggests a more participatory and negotiative approach than command and control practices. Yet in an authoritative culture, a self-organizing bottom-up approach may turn out to be impossible. In such a case, top-down can be the only reasonably workable approach. In any event, regardless of which approach is chosen to promote environmental change in an organization, it is crucial that there is a person or, preferably, a group of persons taking responsibility for the change, and that they are persistent. Cultural change is a slow process, and the road to an environmental culture, even if rewarding, is also rocky.

PHASES OF ORGANIZATIONAL CHANGE

Corporate culture is a set of beliefs and assumptions and typical patterns of ways of doing things that evolves from the accumulated shared learning of a given group. Shift from a traditional management culture to an environmental organization culture requires unlearning of certain old assumptions and customs that exclude environmental considerations from business decision-making, and, on the other hand, learning new ones that include the environment in the underlying value system of management. It is possible to distinguish different phases within the environmental culture change in organizations. Obviously, not all organizations follow the same phases in their change processes; the phases may vary from one organization to another. However, on the basis of previous studies on organizational change, and some recent studies on environmental change in organizations, it can be argued that a number of distinct phases can fairly often be identified (Halme, 1996, Jose, 1995, Wuori, 1995). This is illustrated in Figure 5.1.

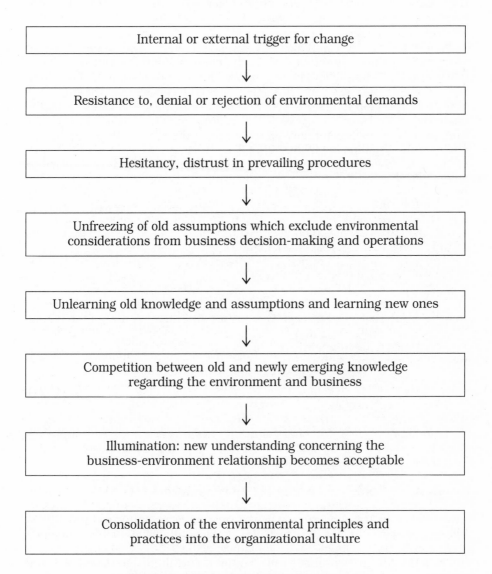

Figure 5.1 Phases of Environmental Change

When an organization encounters the demand or opportunity to make its operations more environmentally sound, it does not necessarily recognize these signals. Organizations are guided by sets of basic assumptions about how the world works, what counts, and what does not. Once a set of shared basic assumptions has formed, the culture can function as a cognitive defence mechanism for both the individual members and the group as a whole. Unlearning of the basic assumptions and ways of doing things is difficult and takes time, and, consequently organizations are tempted to rely on previous successful behaviours.

Culture also provides individuals and groups with stability and meaning. Thus, it contributes to a tendency to distort new information and ideas by denial, protection, rationalization or other defence mechanisms. Ecological considerations have been excluded from business decision-making for such a long time that many organizations simply do not acknowledge messages regarding ecology. The observed external changes are often first belittled, or they are looked upon as results of misunderstandings (Hedberg, 1981). It is typical to ignore the change and hope that it will go away, or to 'dig in' and hold on to the familiar. This resistance is mainly because taken for granted assumptions at the core of the corporate culture are a very powerful mechanism for rejecting new signals that do not fit into the prevailing organizational world view. If the trigger for change – whether external or internal – is powerful enough, or if there are persons in the organization who are capable of acting upon weak signals, then the resistance phase will be followed by a period of 'unfreezing' the organizational core assumptions (Bartunek, 1988).

Unfreezing will not happen simultaneously throughout the organization but occurs within a limited number of members first; there are pockets in the organization where the new thinking exists (Jennings and Zandbergen, 1995). In the beginning there is likely to be considerable tension between groups that hold different perspectives. Old and newly emerging assumptions, and actions based on those assumptions, compete, because the equilibrium has broken. Unlearning and relearning takes place. The period of unlearning and relearning is frequently turbulent. It proceeds through negotiation and often also involves conflicts. This is because the organizational members feel uncertainty, often accompanied by powerful feelings (Gersick, 1991). Substantial organizational uncertainty and chaos are involved when old core assumptions are unlearned so that new ones can come into existence. A profound shift in organizational culture occurs through a dialectical process in which old and new ways of thinking and operating interact, resulting in a synthesis, a new way of understanding. Because the process is dialectical, it involves a conflict between perspectives (Bartunek, 1984). Such a state of affairs is inherently painful and threatening. Apparent hostility to change among some organizational members may therefore reflect feelings of insecurity as well as genuine conflicts of interests (Barrett and Murphy, 1995). The aim, however, is not to remove the conflicts altogether: without conflicts there can be no development (Callenbach et al, 1993).

In order for an environmentally benign cultural change to proceed, it is essential that in the period when old and new ways of doing things compete, the organization gains positive experience from the environmentally improved actions. External reinforcement of the success of the new practices accelerates the cultural shift and, in many instances, may be necessary for the shift to proceed (Halme, 1996, Barrett and Murphy, 1995).

Emotions have an important motivational role in an environmental change process (Bartunek, 1984, Gersick, 1991, Halme, 1996). It is a stressful process and tension is bound to exist among the organization's members, and there will be a fear of changing the current modes of operating. The awareness of discrepant information that initiates cultural reframing typically includes negative feelings. During the shift period, it is important to be optimistic, because there is no way to prove that an idea will succeed. The change agents should inspire confidence and enthusiasm for the new direction. Ultimately, when the world view and standard operating procedures break down, the organization finds itself either paralyzed or busily relearning (Hedberg, 1981). Without an adequate combination of urgency and optimism there is a greater danger that relearning does not start, and the organization clings to old patterns (Tushman and Romanelli, 1985). In a successful case (Box 5.1), the learning proceeds, and consolidation of the new environmental principles and practices into organization culture begins. The final stage, when the new understanding is acceptable, is likely to be accompanied by sense of 'rightness' and satisfaction (Bartunek, 1984). If the cultural change is profound, organizational members will develop commitment to continuous ecological improvements.

Box 5.1 *Case Study 1* In the end of 1980s, a Nordic corrugated board firm encountered an impetus to change its environmental practices. A packaging decree that required producers and sellers to take back their packagings was going to be drafted in Germany. Some of its customers began to demand packaging that contained recycled fibre. Management first rejected the demands as unreasonable: they had always considered corrugated board an environmentally friendly material since it is made of renewable resources, it is biodegradable, and production does not cause emissions. Life cycle thinking did not take place. The pressures, however, accumulated and after a short while some changes were made with reluctance: recycled fibre use was increased and a collection system for used corrugated board was initiated. As a result of positive experiences from the compliance actions, a learning process began. The first step was unfreezing of the organizational core assumptions. Old and newly emerging assumptions, and actions based on those assumptions, were competing. During this period the organization gained positive experience of recycling and acquired new environmental skills. Positive experience reinforced the new behaviour. At the cognitive level, the firm learned that it could gain a competitive advantage by a proactive environmental response. Eventually, the learning process resulted in a shift in a number of assumptions underlying the corporate culture.

FACTORS FACILITATING AND IMPEDING CULTURAL SHIFT

Impediments

There are a number of factors that facilitate or impede the shift to an environmental corporate culture. Impeding factors can be, for instance, cognitive frameworks, motivational barriers, constraints created by obligations inside and outside of the system, contradictory goals, and deficient information flow. Cognitive frameworks of the organizational members may contain assumptions and beliefs which simply hinder the organization from even considering proactive environmental responses. Among such typical beliefs are that the environment is only a cost factor, that it is enough to obey the law or that environmental issues are a fad that will pass. Such beliefs often prevent managers and employees from perceiving the potential of even those environmental performance improvements that would be cost-efficient.

Motivational barriers may be raised by the perceived uncertainty about the future, which is usually related to change. Feelings of uncertainty often create hostility to change. In such a situation, a common human reaction is to seek ways of minimizing personal insecurity by putting pressure on senior managers to give the lead. When faced with the loss of old habits and practices, people need a sense of security in order to step down to the unknown territory (Barrett and Murphy, 1995).

Environmental performance improvements and scrutiny of values inherently imply criticism of past practice. Consequently, reluctance to 'admit having done wrong in the past' may raise motivational barriers (Box 5.2) (Halme, 1996). Furthermore, motivational barriers can be caused by the underlying concern that developing new processes and techniques may be used for rationalizing or at least making changes in the existing status quo of power and influence relations via changes in organizational structures and procedures (Box 5.3) (Barrett and Murphy, 1995).

Box 5.2 *Case Study 2* A paper manufacturer in Northern Finland decided to change its forest management methods. For several decades, large-scale Scandinavian forest management tradition had been followed. With the aim of small-scale forest management the following changes were made: reduction in the size of harvesting sites (average three to four hectares), favouring a mixture of trees instead of monocultures, shifting from the planting of pine by ploughing to natural seeding, leaving seed trees and buffer zones around small water courses. Considerable change resistance occurred for two reasons. In the beginning, resistance evolved because of the doubt that forest stocks and efficiency could not be maintained by small-scale forest management. In addition, certain methods within the large-scale Scandinavian forest management had already been under critique in the past, and from time to time the forestry professionals had had to defend them, even in public. Thus, some foresters were against the changes because they found that the change looked like admitting they had done wrong in the past. Later on, some years after these changes were started, environmental organizations began to demand protection of large areas of forests in Northern Finland. The company made the decision not to buy wood from areas that environmental organizations considered being comparable to old growth forests. Among the lower management and employees, the change of forest management methods and protection demands interwove together in the daily discussion, causing fear for a future where there would be no forest industry in Northern Finland. Thus, some employees feared that the forests in the area would be turned to museums and jobs would be lost.

Box 5.3 *Case Study 3*   In February 1996, in AgrEvon, a subsidiary of Hoechst, a German chemical corporation, one tonne of pesticide containing hazardous chemical, isoproturon, exploded and spread over an area of 50 hectares. The accident was not the first one: within the last three years, Hoechst has had 62 accidents. Information dissemination about the accident was slow: it took 40 minutes to call the fire brigade, and only after eight hours were the inhabitants of the area informed and asked to keep their windows and doors closed. The management commented on the delay in information dissemination by saying that the public cannot be informed until enough is known about the accident. A day later an intermediate product of an analgesic drug leaked into the rivers Main and Rein from another Hoechst plant. The leak occurred for three hours before it was noticed. An employee noticed that one chemical was missing and recorded the information. Neither the shift manager nor the group manager took action. Only a fourth person started to question why there was a particular chemical missing. When explaining reasons for the repetitive accidents, the chairman of the board considered the unskilled labour force the reason for the accidents, and said that it is difficult to get an educated work force committed to their work. He blamed the workers saying they belittle the seriousness of the accidents, because they do not record the mistakes. However, there is another side to the story. The workers face the risk of being fired if they make mistakes. This causes reluctance to record the mistakes.

Source: Ekholm, 1996

The task of management is to remove such impedients. The lesson of Box 5.2 is that the executive managers should consult with staff members with regard to what the changes mean for the future of the company, and thus also for the members of the staff. High levels of unpredictability and uncertainty related to environmental change can increase resistance if people are left in a state of anxiety about their own future within the new culture. Even if it is difficult to provide all the answers, when there is uncertainty about the feasibility of practical implications of alternative courses of action, the staff members' feeling of insecurity can be alleviated by openness. An open dialogue between different levels of management and the employees about various aspects and consequences of the environmental questions is necessary in order to deal with uncertainty and resistance. If top management decides everything and afterwards informs the staff, discontent and unnecessary conflicts will be created. In this case, the implementation of a decision often becomes slow and difficult due to internal resistance. Box 5.3 indicates that employees should be positively, not punitively motivated. Individuals should be rewarded for a job well done and receive concrete, constructive feedback and training.

Constraints can also be created because the impacts that environmental measures have on the contents of jobs vary according to the function and hierarchical position. The way in which, for instance, assembly line employees are confronted differs from that of administrative or sales personnel. The situation is aggravated if there are contradictory goals and communication barriers between different managerial or employee groups. Firstly, different groups can have contradictory goals regarding environmental issues which hinder finding environmental solutions that satisfy all. This is further enhanced by the fact that organizational subgroups often have their own vocabularies and style of communicating, which can create barriers of communication (Gersick, 1991). It may be easier for engineers to talk to engineers and sales persons to sales persons. It has occasionally also appeared that environmental management change may be easier for top management than for employees at lower levels of the organization. While environmental policy for top managers may mean vision and careful calculation, for operational level managers and workers it may mean only new rules, restrictions, and tasks to take care of: in other words, simply more work (Brauchlin, 1988, Halme, 1994b, Wolters et al, 1995). Occasionally, power conflicts appear when environmental issues that have traditionally had minor importance in organizational decision-making, gain more importance (Callenbach et al, 1993).

Another crucial motivational barrier to the rooting of environmental culture into the organization is the potential contradiction of economic and ecological goals in incentive systems. For example, traditionally incentives systems in the paper industry have been based solely on volume output. Thus, when there is a problem in the production process that causes an overload to the waste water treatment plant, the production should be stopped in order to make the necessary repair. Yet a stop reduces the volume of production and as a result also the salary of the employee. This demotivates the employees to stop production and take the repairing action. Deficient information flows may also impede environmental change efforts. Incentive systems as well as information dissemination will be considered in more detail later on in the chapter.

Facilitators

Good working conditions improve the staff's willingness to adopt environmental criteria into their job (Wolters et al, 1995). The internal working environment of a company is of critical importance to the physical and mental health of everyone who works there. If stressful conditions of bad lighting or ventilation, dust, noise, toxics or physical danger are not avoided, employees can hardly be asked to take creative interest in general environmental matters. The same holds true for social conditions. Low job security, punitive motivation systems or other unsolved problems within the relationship between employees and management can hinder environmental culture development. Internal and external environmental concerns are tightly linked, and need to be treated with an integrated approach. Employees' motivation can be improved by connecting working environment aspects to external environment aspects (Box 5.4) (Aldrich and Lorentzen, 1994, Callenbach et al, 1993).

Box 5.4 *Case Study 4* A fish filleting factory in Denmark wanted to establish an environmental management system. Within the fish filleting industry it is typical to send the employees home when there is no fish, and call them back when there is fish. The system furthers instrumental attitude to work. In addition, the industry is characterized by considerable working environment problems: the work is monotonous and repetitive, and employees suffer from cold and draught. At first the interest of the employees in establishing an environmental management system was low. It turned out that the employees' motivation in the project was related to an interest in their own working conditions. Moreover, they were more motivated to concrete improvements than a system (whether regarding the working conditions or the external environment). Eventually the employees entered into the project on the condition that solving working environment problems would be one of the goals.

Source: Aldrich and Lorentzen, 1994

A flat organization structure facilitates development of an environmental corporate culture. Holistic ecological performance can seldom be realized by orders from on high. It requires that every staff member recognizes ecological aspects of her or his work. In addition, interaction with external stakeholders such as environmental organizations facilitates the adoption of environmental thinking. Through such interactions it becomes possible for the members of the organization to make their core beliefs and assumptions visible, and also challenge them. Unless there is a contrast brought by another stakeholder group, it is often difficult to recognize how we think, why we think in a certain way, and what might be alternative interpretations and responses. Finally, personalized experiences and affective reactions to environmental questions are important in keeping the cultural change process ongoing (Dutton and Dukerich, 1991).

Public commitment to environmental protection and positive public attention can reinforce environmental culture in the company (Box 5.5). This is because of the tendency of human beings toward commitment and consistency: we tend to behave in ways that are consistent with the stand we have taken. Once a decision is made and an action started, the person/s tend to stand behind it, because the self-image of an actor is directed by pressure of consistency. This pressure is further aggravated if there is publicity. The tendency to try to appear a consistent person in the eyes of others directs the future behaviour. Whenever a stand is taken that is visible to others, there arises a drive to maintain that stand in order to look like a consistent person. For the actors of an organization, there is publicity within the organization (other organizational members' assessment), and also outside of the organization. For appearances sake, then, the more public a stand, the more reluctant we will be to appear inconsistent (Cialdini, 1988).

Box 5.5 *Case Study 5*   Tampere Hall, the largest congress and concert centre in Scandinavia, introduced an environmental programme in 1993, aiming at energy saving, waste minimization, and environmentally responsible purchasing. In the beginning there was resistance towards the environmental measures among some staff members, some were passive, and the responsibility for environmental performance improvements was mainly on the members of the environmental task force, a group of people who had initiated the programme. In 1994, the Hall won the EIBTM (European Incentive and Business Travel Meeting) environmental award. The award acted as a watershed for personnel commitment and cultural change. The recognition brought along by the award facilitated the acceptance of the environmental programme throughout the organization. The members of the organization felt that as the award had been won, they were doing valuable work, and should be an example to others.

Source: Aerschot and Heikura, 1995, Halme, 1995

TOOLS FOR DEVELOPING ENVIRONMENTALLY AWARE ORGANIZATIONAL CULTURES

One of the first steps when starting to take the environment into account in the company is information dissemination. Notice boards, company newsletters, company electronic mail networks, circulated material, an ecology library, regular reports (eg annual or environmental reports) and speeches for special occasions offer channels for ecological information dissemination (Callenbach et al, 1993). A more interactive, and perhaps also more efficient means are briefings and consultative meetings (Wolters et al, 1995). It is easier to inform and instruct in such a way, and provide the participants with reasons for environmental measures. Moreover, getting feedback and utilizing staff members' knowledge becomes possible. Information dissemination, however, has fairly limited potential for creating any true environmental culture change. It is a supplementary measure to several tools that will be presented next.

Education and training provide organizational members with the requisite environmental skills and knowledge and are among the critical components of incorporating ecology into the organizational culture (Milliman and Clair, 1995). Heightening the environmental awareness of the staff through education brings along two kinds of benefits. First, understanding environmental problems improves the staff's willingness to approve new environmental criteria even if these add to their work load. It is important to provide staff members with reasons why it should take the environment into account in their work (Linnanen et al, 1994). This is particularly true for expert organizations where the employees have a great degree of freedom, and where they are not used to taking orders without knowing the reason for it. Second, environmental awareness helps staff members to recognize where environmental improvements can be made (Wolters et al, 1995).

In the early stages of integrating environmental considerations into the company's operations, environmental education and training is usually arranged separately. In the longer term, however, all training programmes should be extended to include the ecological dimension whether in-house or through external continuing education programmes. A careful balance between economic and ecological effects should be established and maintained in all aspects of the training programme (Callenbach et al, 1993). Ecological training must not degenerate into a separate programme with no obvious links to occupational training, otherwise there is a danger that ecology would remain separate from or inferior to other objectives. Ecology training must have clear links to the practical work of participants.

Box 5.6 *Case Study 6*   Duke Power has developed environmental awareness training programmes that increase employees' awareness of the company's commitment to environmental protection in order to ensure that environmental issues are kept uppermost in employees' minds while they cope with daily business challenges, and enhance employee motivation to implement proactive environmental practices. It is considered that environmentally aware employees are more likely to perform their jobs in an environmentally responsible manner, to share their positive attitudes with others, and to provide more ideas and suggestions. However, after the environmental awareness has heightened, Duke Power is now adding performance-based training to knowledge-based training. Their instructors now teach environmental skills in the context of how employees will use them in the job. Skill-oriented training techniques at Duke Power include small group exercises, role playing, games, and case studies. In comparison, Allied-Signal Inc seeks to ensure the effective application of training skills to the workplace through the development of support groups and the selection of organizational problems and projects that are manageable.

Source: Milliman and Clair, 1995

When planning the training programme, the first step is to assess what knowledge and skills are needed to meet the training objective. The training objective should be derived from the overall environmental goals of the firm. The second step involves determining which employees are to be trained, and what will be the content of training. A third key step is deciding who will conduct the training, the location and length of training sessions, and what media and types of presentations (eg lectures, case studies, exercises, tours, etc) are most effective in promoting environmental learning for the different groups of organizational members (Milliman and Clair, 1995).

In order to create a culture change, environmental education should be given not only to those who are directly responsible for environmental issues, but for the whole personnel. Education should be on a continuous basis. If it is arranged as a one-shot campaign, there is the risk of slipping back to old habits as the lessons fade (Linnanen et al, 1994, Wolters et al, 1995).

Formulating and implementing environmental goals will be easier if management style is cooperative and systemic. Staff and middle managers ought to be involved in environmental management development at an early stage. A higher commitment can be achieved when staff members themselves have participated in developing the environmental programme for their company (Klinkers and Nelissen, 1995, Barrett and Murphy, 1995). They feel more responsible for achieving the goals when they have taken part in drafting and deciding about them. Additional benefits are realized from involving employees early. When employees participate in the preparatory review of environmental impacts and policy creation, it is possible to get a better and more detailed overview of the factory's influence on the environment and get an environmental policy which is deeply rooted in the organization (Box 5.7). Employees possess detailed knowledge concerning the firm's production processes (eg resource and energy consumption, emissions etc) as well as other, more indirect environmental impacts (Wolters et al, 1995). In addition, when employees participate in making the preparatory review, vital knowledge will remain with the company and not vanish with a consultant. Retaining the knowledge in the company means that it will be accessible in relation to initiating new pollution prevention activities. Furthermore, the awareness of the employees of environmental impacts of the company will increase (Nielsen and Remmen, 1994). Extensive participation of the organizational members in the change process also provides a means for reducing conflict, apathy and inaction (Barrett and Murphy, 1995).

Box 5.7 *Case Study 7*   A Finnish food industry company, Saarioinen, signed the ICC Principles of Sustainable Development. In order to make them operational, five project groups representing contract cultivation, breeding, buying, production, and end products, were formed. Members of the groups participated in environmental education seminars. Next, the groups surveyed the direct environmental impacts within their respective areas, and each group produced a report of the results. Thereafter, the managing director and the quality manager negotiated with each group about the objectives for reducing these impacts, and the measures with which to reach the objectives. The environmental objectives and measures were determined in co-operation with the groups and the top management. The measures were integrated into the (already existing) quality manual. Environmental education for the whole personnel was started, and a similar type of cooperative process for determining objectives and developing environmental improvement measures was spread to all sub-areas under the above mentioned five operational areas. Participants were the original group members and representatives of employees from these sub-areas.

Source: Halme, 1995

When seeking to achieve motivation, it will be useful to appeal to what motivates people professionally. To take an example, department heads and group supervisors are often bottlenecks: in order for environmental management to proceed to the respective department or group, it is important to get the heads motivated. Image and publicity motivate the marketing manager, reducing waste disposal problems appeals to the head of materials management, and with the finance manager cost savings can be emphasized. It will also help to appeal to whatever personally motivates the people, empathizing with their feelings and thought processes. For instance, focusing on pioneer work in environmental management may motivate managers and the staff (Callenbach et al, 1993).

Appealing to the employees' feelings to 'do good', ie to protect the environment, also provides a potential source for increased learning. Today, people increasingly have a desire to identify themselves with their job and they seek deeper value-based meaning in their work. Environmental care can be one of the things that gives the employees meaning to their work, inspires, and motivates them (Box 5.8).

Box 5.8 *Case Study 8* In the aforementioned Finnish paper corporation (Box 5.2), the adoption of small-scale forest management instructions for forest machine operators has meant finding new meaning in their work. Previously, during the intensive forest management era, they used to cut large areas mechanistically. In contrast, small-scale forestry requires more care, more knowledge about forest ecosystems and natural processes, and landscape considerations. The harvesting foremen cannot mark every bush, tree, a group of them, or a special area to be left uncut. This means that the forest machine operators are given far more decision-making possibilities than previously, and there is more variety in their work content. During the recent years they have been trained in small-scale forest management. Now they have more responsibility and decision-making power concerning the final result in the forest. A forest machine operator says: 'I'm glad we moved to a small-scale forestry. Now everyone can use his own brains. Previously it was too simple; I think most of us now find it more interesting. And it looks better; you feel better about the results in the forest'.

Yet involvement of the lower level managers and the employees is not a question of management motivation techniques only. Neither do all companies have preconditions for developing environmental management based on employee participation. But if there is genuine willingness to change the basics, for instance, of an authoritarian corporate culture, environmental management development can work as the first step towards that. At best, environmental change processes can act as a springboard for a sense of togetherness and 'we-spirit' in the organization and thus the effect reaches a far broader scale than environmental improvements (Callenbach et al, 1993).

The organization of environmental management is an important consideration when integrating environment into corporate culture. Many large companies have established positions such as Environmental Vice-President or have created corporate level environmental management departments. Several companies also have environmental committees that consist of corporate level managers. Some companies utilize technical committees whose members are drawn from all departments (Callenbach et al, 1993). In large corporations a variant of a technical committee can be an advisory committee consisting of environmental experts from different units. External stakeholders might also be included. These committees can, for instance, assist the environmental manager or conduct environmental audits within the company plants. In such a way, valuable knowledge and experience can be moved from one unit to another. In the first stages of environmental management development when the corporation does not yet want an external audit, considerable improvements can be achieved with an internal audit conducted by an advisory or technical committee. Again the great advantage is that the experience and knowledge remain within the company. Some companies have found that it is easier to be more open to an internal committee than to an external auditor. Independent of the exact task and nature of such committees, they should be set up on an ongoing basis, meet regularly and prepare periodic reports (Callenbach et al, 1993).

It is critical that environmental managers and committees are given funds and other resources necessary to carry out their tasks. Environmental managers and experts should not be used as alibi persons with minimal power. Their expertise should be fully utilized, and they should be part of a normal organization; they should be given enough power so that they can influence the decisions in the organization.

A second requirement is that where disagreements arise between environmental managers and line departments, they should be decided without delay. As mentioned before, conflicts should not be feared but recognized as signs indicating that neglected issues are being raised and change is being brought about (Callenbach et al, 1993).

A hierarchic, mechanistic organizational structure may be inappropriate for companies undergoing an ecological change. A flat organizational structure is usually better suited for holistic environmental management. Holistic ecological performance can seldom be realized by orders from 'on high', but requires that every staff member recognizes the ecological aspects of her or his work, and, moreover, is capable of working together with others to create environmentally benign solutions. Multiple layer hierarchy and bureaucracy are not appropriate for teamwork or for encouraging individual initiative. Flat organizations with organic structures are more efficient for conditions where new knowledge emerges constantly and environmental demands change fast (this is examined in more detail later in the book).

Factors such as performance measurement, appraisal systems, promotion systems, and qualitative and quantitative reward systems reinforce cultural values and norms (Kerr and Slocum, 1987). Measuring environmental performance and providing feedback are efficient means for demonstrating to the organization that ecological objectives count. Special care should be taken to ensure that ecological and environmental objectives are worked out with the same degree of thoroughness. Otherwise it will be in vain to hope that the environment can ever be integrated into corporate culture. Performance appraisal systems that are not aligned with environmental goals, work against those goals, and create frustration in those managers who are squeezed between the new environmental principles and old performance appraisal criteria. Earlier in this chapter an example was given of contradictions between ecological and economic goals. It is, however, perfectly possible to successfully integrate environmental criteria into the compensation system of employees.

Box 5.9 *Case Study 9*   Neste, the Finnish national petroleum company, has been using a production bonus system at its Porvoo oil refinery since 1986. The system is based on the chemical industry's international Responsible Care programme and on the central Total Quality Management (TQM) principle of continuous improvement. The levels of the reward system include:

- Quarterly follow-up of quality indicators;
- biannual assessment of the cleanness of the workplace;
- annual economic performance indicators.

The quality indicators measured include accidents; cases of unexpected fires; environmental incidents and quality of delivery. Environmental incidents refer to emission levels higher than anticipated. Each of the indicators carry equal importance when an employee's quarterly production bonus is calculated

Source: Linnanen, 1995

To measure environmental performance effectively, quantitative environmental goals are often included as key criteria in appraisals. However, including difficult quantitative measures in appraisals can create extensive pressure on managers such that they focus exclusively on numerical objectives and ignore the qualitative aspects of environmental initiatives. To prevent that, Browning-Ferris Industries (BFI) has developed an environmental performance appraisal system for its regional and facility managers that evaluates the following aspects of environmental management:

- Management systems;
- compliance programmes;
- government and community affairs;
- permit management;
- risk management/loss control;
- environmental training; contingency and preparedness; and
- environmental monitoring.

A diverse number of goals prevents managers from focusing on only a few aspects. Managers receive points in each of the above areas depending on the level of accomplishment. The BFI performance appraisals take into account external factors (eg delays in permit approvals) which are beyond the immediate control of managers (Milliman and Clair, 1995).

Rewarding employees provides further incentives for ecologically proactive performance. To date, organizations have developed both monetary-based and recognition-based rewards for environmental performance. Recognition rewards have been developed in many organizations including Monsanto, Dow Chemicals and ICI Americas. Important for the success of these rewards is company-wide public recognition. Such attention increases the organizational members' awareness of environmental accomplishments and sends a powerful message about the importance of the environmental effort throughout the organization. Recognition-based awards are a well suited means for building an environmental culture. Recognition awards should be offered at different levels of the company, and they can be given either to individuals or teams (Milliman and Clair, 1995).

So far only a few organizations have provided financial incentives. One reason might be that the development of performance-based environmental indicators is at an early stage. There are, however, exceptions. At BFI, for example, a facility manager's bonus is contingent on environmental performance outcomes and managers do not receive any bonuses if their environmental goals remain unmet. Monetary rewards for environmental performance can motivate the staff members, but they can also cause competition between employees and distort the overall environmental results. In contrast, team and plant-wide rewards are generally viewed as being better at motivating employees to share information and work together (Milliman and Clair, 1995).

One form of incentive system can be based on a suggestion system (rewards for initiatives). It has been tried and found particularly fruitful at the early stages of corporate environmental management development, although it is useful later in the process as well (Halme, 1995b). Xerox, for instance, has developed an 'Earth Award' to recognize achievements in innovations of waste reduction, re-use and recycling (Milliman and Clair, 1995).

Longer term aspects such as promotion should also be crafted into the organization's environmental performance appraisal system. The career development of managers or other organizational members with extensive environmental responsibilities is an important consideration. Working experience and achievements with environmental management should give merit similar to any other field. If environmental management jobs or responsibilities are a side track that never lead to higher positions in the organization, these jobs will not tempt the most capable and ambitious persons.

It should be emphasized that financial incentives alone cannot change the organizational culture or motivate the staff members to continuous environmental improvements. In a company with good physical and social working environments the employees can and will take initiative and they are prepared to reach the targets if they are given responsibility. However, for an environmental culture change to proceed it is essential that resources – both time and money – are allocated accordingly. In some companies, quality assurance managers have had environmental policy management added to their job descriptions without reducing any of the ongoing responsibilities. If new environmental tasks come in addition to other duties, such an accumulation of tasks may diminish enthusiasm in giving environmental management the priority it needs (Wolters et al, 1995). In many companies, new environmental managers have been hired. Both ongoing and newly created posts require new operational funds for improving environmental performance. Even a highly motivated new environmental manager with no budget for staff environmental awareness will not be able to implement environmental improvements effectively, let alone set off a cultural change process.

Earlier it was emphasized that all organizational members should take environmental responsibility in their jobs. Nonetheless, it is not enough for individual staff members or separate groups of them to work to create environmental solutions, if that happens in isolation. Due to the interconnectedness of environmental problems and their solutions, close co-operation is called for in order to develop the best possible solutions for the whole. Environmental sustainability appears to demand greatly improved co-ordination and integration across the traditionally isolated functions and staff organizations within the firm. Crossing the traditional boundaries between traditionally isolated corporate functions is necessary for a holistic environmental culture to come into existence, even if co-operation between different managerial and staff groups can first appear troublesome because of different job contents, professional identities, and language. It is easiest for people to talk to those who have similar educational background and work experience; they think and speak alike. But this tendency can be a real pitfall when developing environmental management. We only need to think of the typical boundary between marketing and production functions. In order for a firm to sell its more environmentally sound product alternatives, or inform its customers about environmental characteristics in its production processes and products, it is not enough to develop environmentally benign products and improve processes; they must also be communicated to customers. Furthermore, customers can give valuable ideas for improvements. Marketing personnel are the most likely staff to come across these demands first, but in order for them to be realized, there must be a channel to take these ideas further to product development and production (Halme, 1995b).

Thus, in order to solve environmental problems for the benefit of the whole firm instead of just finding the best solution for one part, cross-functional task groups (interdepartmental) or problem specific cross-functional projects should be established, and teamwork encouraged. Several firms have found this particularly useful in the running-in phase but it can be used continuously for instance in developing environmental product innovations. Different perspectives will be taken into consideration. Participation of different units and departments furthers the acceptance of environmental thinking in different units because they have had a stake in planning and decision-making.

Another solution is to arrange meetings or workshops for representatives from various functions. Klinkers and Nelissen (1995) give an example of workshops that consist of two sessions: a problem-diagnosis segment and a problem-solving segment. In the diagnosis segment, an inventory is made of the influence of production processes on different environmental aspects such as noise, energy, and waste. In the problem-solving segment, small groups address a range of identified environmental issues and discuss solutions. The suggested solutions are then collected and presented. After concluding the workshops, it is good to publicize the results to those who did not participate, for example in an environmental newsletter. Naturally, the solution alternatives must be worked on after the workshops, and the feasible ones put into practice. Otherwise the process will create an air of distrust amongst the participants.

Box 5.10 *Case Study 10*   Three Swedish companies, Perstorp Laminate, Gambro Lundia (produces dialysators), and BTJ Products (manufactures library furniture) participate in a Green Concurrent Development project. A researcher from the International Institute for Industrial Environmental Economics at Lund University co-ordinates the project. The project aims at developing environmentally integrated products with the help of cross-functional teams. The idea behind the Green Concurrent Development project is to build a team of such staff members that are involved in the same phase of the product's life cycle. These so-called 'Green Teams' consist of four to six persons, including the co-ordinating researcher. In Gambro the people involved are medical manager (physician), product manager, R&D manager, and an employee from plastic disposables production, and a production preparer. From BTJ, the marketing manager, production manager, industrial designer, and a purchaser are involved. The team work aims at firstly, collecting expertise regarding the product's environmental impacts from different parts of the firm, and simultaneously finding opportunities to reduce these impacts, and secondly making sure that the eventual solutions to environmental problems will not bring about new problems in another part of the firm or the product's life cycle. Different Green Teams can be built up at different levels of the firm, eg strategic/management, project and operative level. In some instances it may be appropriate to build a team at the product system level.

Source: Karlsson, 1995

However, as regards the composition of workshop participants, opinions differ. Some studies find that workshops in which participants are from the same department or with the same kind of duties (Klinkers and Nelissen, 1995), result in more focused and specific treatment and suggestions for actions toward environmental issues, whereas others emphasize that it is better to form mixed workshops (Servatius, 1992, Callenbach et al, 1993). These contrary views may imply that the best composition of workshop participants should be determined problem-specifically. If the intention is to identify and solve problems that only involve one department, then the workshop participants can be from the respective department only. Also in the first stages of identifying environmental problems and potential solutions, a unified composition may be well in place. However, as soon as the solution suggestions begin to touch multiple departments, participants from different locations should be gathered. In any event, the argument can still be posed that multiple perspectives in a workshop or task group will result in a more creative treatment of ideas.

Traditionally, different departments solve problems together at top management level. In the above ways, middle and lower level managers from different departments as well as staff members can also co-operate. Direct contacts at top management level only are not enough. In some organizations, there still exists the illusion that environmental change can be managed by reporting on environmental problems, solutions, and developments of different departments of the firm to the top management, who then disseminates information to other parts of the organization. Even if this is a good security measure, it is, however, insufficient. There are questions that can only be solved by interaction and direct contact. Moreover, cross-departmental and cross-level work for environmental management can also have a broader range of spin-offs. It can advance dialogue between management and employees, and between different occupational groups in other areas than environment-related ones.

Environmental pilot projects can be a good way to collect experience as well as reduce the barriers toward the integration of environmental criteria into company operations. A forced top-down environmental change can cause resistance that may slow down the implementation and harm the process. In order to avoid that, integration of environmental issues into the organization and culture can be phased in. Piloting the integration of environmental issues in a part or a few parts of the organization provides the possibility to test the workability and learn (before large-scale implementation), what works in the organization. Successful piloting encourages people to continue working towards the realization of environmental goals. A broader scale implementation is easier after piloting. Pilot projects and cross-functional task groups should have clear goals and timeframes, ie there ought to be well defined problems and a deadline for coming up with the solutions (Servatius, 1992).

Environmental management systems (EMS) are another potential tool for developing an environmental corporate culture. An environmental management system usually contains the organizational structure, responsibilities, practices, procedures, processes and resources for determining and implementing environmental policy (Netherwood, 1996). In recent years, EMS have gained popularity, and it has become possible to standardize EMS under BS7750 or ISO14000 schemes. Since 1995, European companies can receive the European Union's EMAS (Eco-Management and Auditing Scheme) approval. As environmental management systems are presented in detail elsewhere (Welford, 1996), they are assessed here only from the viewpoint of enhancing environmental organization cultures.

EMS can promote the transition to an environmental corporate culture. EMS organizes the environmental management tasks, and also gives credibility in the eyes of those organizational members who like to see management with systems. As EMS include the idea of continuous improvement, it provides a step-by-step framework for environmental management improvements. It systematizes the environmental tasks. Yet, for a variety of reasons, EMS may also fail to do so, or may even counteract environmental culture development. If, after developing an EMS, a firm relies solely on that – 'once the system is in place we can take it easy' – or if the system is built merely for reasons of competition, EMS will not further environmental cultures. Hence, EMS alone will not transform a company. Top management commitment, genuine interest, and knowledge are necessary.

The same goes for standardized environmental management systems such as ISO14001 or BS7750. These specify the structure of an EMS that an organization must have in place if it seeks to obtain certification of the EMS according to International Standards Organization (ISO) or British Standards Institute (BSI) guidelines. ISO14001 provides a framework for an organization to manage its environmental performance. It is generic in the sense that it does not set any absolute requirements, except for compliance with the laws. It does not require that an organization implement any particular environmental management strategies, it does not say anything about resource (either material or energy) use or emissions levels. It only requires that organizations have a commitment to compliance, continual improvement, and pollution prevention. 'Commitment' is not defined by ISO, but it is expected that an organization which makes a policy commitment will be able to demonstrate to interested parties that the commitment is in fact being implemented. Thus, the key in ISO14001 will be the environmental policy the organization commits itself to follow. This implies that except for compliance and commitment, the organization with an ISO14001 certificate may manage its environmental affairs in whatever fashion it chooses. It is up to the organization to determine what the content of the structure will be. The organization has to decide what it wants to do regarding the environment. Then the EMS organizes the tasks necessary to accomplish this.

EMS may be more appropriate for large corporations than small and medium-sized enterprises (SMEs). Documentation, costliness, and bureaucracy related to building an EMS may hinder its adoption and use in SMEs, or at least they need lighter EMS versions. The experiences of EMS are fairly limited in general, and, consequently, findings regarding their effect on corporate culture are even fewer. The next few years will show us if, and under what, EMS turn out effective in enhancing environmental corporate cultures.

The following model (Figure 5.2), which involves several of the tools presented above, has been proposed for promoting environmentally aware corporate cultures (Servatius, 1992). It suggests organizational and individual learning through a task-specific problem solution. The underlying idea in the model is that organizational learning in ecological issues happens in the course of action. With the aim of developing environmentally responsible corporate cultures, the model suggests binding a problem solving process to an organizational learning process. The idea is to first identify the environmental priorities, ie the tasks that need to be conducted in order to achieve the most significant improvements for the environment. After that, interdisciplinary project teams that will find solutions to the problems will be built. Ambitious environmental goals and deadlines for achieving them should be set for the teams. By conducting successful pilot projects, and by collecting and documenting their experiences, the results can be communicated to the organization, and used as an example for encouraging and developing environmental management within different areas of the company's operations.

Simultaneously, with regard to organizational learning, management should be given environmental education and training. If possible, it should proceed in rounds beginning from the top management and the project team members. The purpose of the training is to focus on the ecological connections of the company's activities. The aim will be that through concurrent educational and practical activities, a personal 'consternation' among the participants regarding the impacts of the business on the natural environment will happen. Also the creation of incentives for environmental performance will contribute to the thawing of traditional ways of thinking and thus cause a gradual change in attitude.

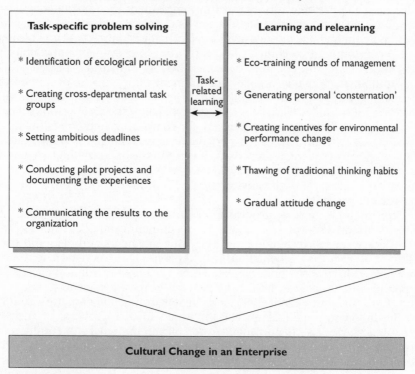

Task-related learning provides a setting for evolutionary cultural development process in a business enterprise

Task-specific problem solving		Learning and relearning
* Identification of ecological priorities		* Eco-training rounds of management
* Creating cross-departmental task groups	Task-related learning ←→	* Generating personal 'consternation'
* Setting ambitious deadlines		* Creating incentives for environmental performance change
* Conducting pilot projects and documenting the experiences		* Thawing of traditional thinking habits
* Communicating the results to the organization		* Gradual attitude change

Cultural Change in an Enterprise

Figure 5.2 The Evolution of Corporate Environmental Awareness

CONCLUSIONS

Organizational commitment is needed to integrate environmental aspects into all activities – from research and development to production and distribution. Strategies and action plans are required to change the corporation's processes and systems to align them with a corporate vision incorporating environmental sustainability principles. Responsibilities at the board of directors, management and operating levels must be clearly understood and reinforced by appropriate incentives. Without a critical mass of individuals a change in company's operations will not happen, but people must share a vision and commit themselves to act on it before an environmental change turns into living reality.

The road to a green culture is often rocky. Managers must take steps to orient, institutionalize, and sustain the corporate conscience or value system in ways that are as realistic as those that guide strategy formulation and implementation. Rhetoric and value statements are not enough. Rewards, incentives and audits, and clear leadership action are critical to this task. Management must be given permission to think and act environmentally. This condition affects organizations more deeply than statements and credos (Goodpaster, 1989).

The environmental change process in organizations is usually an evolutionary, on going learning process. Some companies, particularly those encountering serious external pressure in environmental issues, may go through radical shifts in their ways of thinking and operating, but even in such companies a cultural change to an environmentally sustainable company will not happen overnight: it is a long-term gradual process. It is necessary to have a vision and general targets towards which to move, but companies usually appear to proceed in an incremental way towards the targets; much will be learned by doing.

Companies do differ in environmental management as well as in any other aspect. It is possible, but not always applicable to copy a model or an approach from one industry or company to another. The environmental change programme in the corporation needs a tailor-made approach. The specific situation of the company must be taken into consideration.

Chapter 6

Reassessing Culture and Strategy: Environmental Improvement, Structure, Leadership and Control

John Dodge

INTRODUCTION

This chapter provides an overview of the links between environmental culture and the firm's environmental strategy formulation and implementation. The association between an organization's culture and its strategy, leadership, structure and control systems is explored to show how to elevate environmental values in the business priorities. An organization's culture has a profound impact on the creative processes necessary to develop a new environmental programme. The perceptions of governments and the demands of stakeholders are filtered by our values and our culture. The firm's ability to recognize environmental problems is all a matter of culture. The enthusiasm, commitment and expectations of the company toward their environmental strategy reflect their core greening values or beliefs. The selection of the optimum leadership style should reflect the needs and employee readiness of the organization. Culture also flows into the implementation of the structure, control, monitoring and administration systems. The manner in which environmental responsibilities are allocated and the progress of these organizational structures are affected and moulded by the organization's culture. The selection of monitoring and control methods and the overall acceptance of these methods and standards are all impacted by the corporate culture. Each of these issues will now be explored in more depth.

CORPORATE CULTURE

Actions of managers and employees are often guided by the unwritten rules or implicit forces within the work place rather than by the formal written procedures of an organization. In fact, it is these unwritten rules that often exert greater influence than do the formal control mechanisms. New employees seem to quickly learn informally from other employees that 'this is the way we do things around here'. It can affect simple codes of behaviours or even the way one dresses at work. It can, however, reach much deeper – it can shape the way an employee reacts to competition, customers or even greening pressures. These internal forces combine to create the culture of a corporation that seems to embody the mood, the stance and perceptions that employees use to shape future actions. An organization's culture is the sum total of these subtle, elusive and largely unconscious forces that shape the work place. Not wishing to get bogged down in terminology, corporate culture is sometimes called organizational climate, corporate style or even corporate ethos. Whatever the name, it can be a valuable tool or, in some cases, a hinderance to the implementation of strategic change and, in particular, greening strategy.

Corporate culture is shaped by significant events and can be strengthened and reinforced through time. In many instances, the founding owner imparted fundamental values and traditions within the firm. If greening values were very important to the founder, environmental issues are probably embraced as core values within the firm. Conversely, if the green values espoused by the founder were non-existent or negative, the organization would reflect non-existent or negative green values. As the organization matures it builds on this value base to build its own culture. These values are imparted on to employees through stories of individuals within the firm. The corporation may issue symbolic gestures, acts, rites and corporate ceremonies to further embed the culture. The rites may take the form of annual meetings or other public forums where individuals are implicitly honoured or dishonoured by the top management of the organization. The honoured employee becomes a symbol of important employees' qualities.

The rewards, maybe even the perks, are long established symbols for reinforcing the profit culture of an organization. The greening culture must share the stage with these long entrenched monetary views on what is important to the business. The very fact that companies don't focus on greening issues gives a significant cultural signal to employees.

How can a business manager judge the positive or negative impact the firm's culture is having on greening performance? It is easy to agree that culture exists but it is more difficult to understand its dimensions. According to Killman, Saxton and Serpa (1985) three aspects – direction, pervasiveness and strength – can be important dimensions for culture. We gain some very interesting insights as these concepts are applied to their impact on environmental improvement. Direction refers to the degree to which the corporate culture supports corporate greening, rather than interfering with the environmental programmes. Pervasiveness of greening cultures refers to the extent to which these traits are shared within the organization. A weak pervasive culture could be recognized when only small pockets or a few departments within the company have adopted greening values. In such a situation the business would find it extremely difficult to create a concerted corporate environmental strategy. The third dimension, strength, refers to the absolute pressure or commitment of the greening culture within the organization. It is fairly obvious that a firm with a very positive, strong and pervasive greening culture will have the least strain implementing greening programmes.

SHARED ENVIRONMENTAL VALUES AND ORGANIZATIONAL EFFECTIVENESS

The value component, one of the prime ingredients of an organization's culture, is worthy of deeper analysis. When employees share common environmental values and hold similar beliefs they form an integral part of an organization's culture. The establishment of common, pervasive shared values and beliefs helps to keep the business focused on their environmental programme. For an organization to sustain a long term commitment to environmental management it will require positioning the environment at a higher level within the organization's value system (Welford, 1992 and 1995). This requires the integration of concern and care for the environment into the firm's fundamental value system (Roome, 1992). Conversely, in extremely difficult situations, employees and management may share negative environmental views which will have significant adverse effects on the firm's greening performance. For these reasons, any environmental improvement programme should encourage the creation of positive environmental values throughout the business.

When a firm establishes a new environmental paradigm, it will disappear in the cultural foundations of the company just as the drive for profit has. Successful implementation of an environmental strategy will also require a shift in organizational values to increase the ranking of environmental values. Environmental issues affect, either directly or indirectly, all parts of the organization. Most organizations would say their production or manufacturing activities have the highest environmental impact, but all departments – marketing, finance, human resources, technology development – can significantly impact the firm's greening performance. Therefore, environmental values must become part of the total value system and pervade all departments. Organizations with these well developed integrated environmental values should behave in accordance with these values and thus act in a more responsive and caring fashion towards the environment. Value congruence amongst various departments and employees is required to sustain an environmental strategic shift – congruence meaning the condition where the values agree or correspond with each other.

A value is a type of belief (Rokeach, 1979). A value is a belief that is at the core of one's total belief system and influences how one ought to behave. Value congruence exists when one's personal beliefs or values are similar to the organization's. A link exists between value congruence and effective decision-making (Liedtka, 1989; Meglino, Ravine and Adkins, 1989) and also a link exists between value congruence and job satisfaction (Chatman, 1991; Meglino, Ravine and Adkins, 1989). The implications of these findings have a very interesting impact on work place morale. If employees value the environmental programme at the same level of importance as their employers they will tend to have higher levels of job satisfaction than if they do not. These shared values will have a positive impact on overall employee effectiveness, turnover rates and absenteeism.

Increasingly, business is recognizing the importance of environmental values and its relationship to effectiveness. Values can make or break a firm's strategic success. Strong cultures exhibit values with both intensity and crystallization (O'Reilly, 1989). Intensity occurs when all in the organization understand top management environmental values. Crystallization occurs when these values are viewed positively by all groups within the organization.

Therefore, it is important to examine and compare employees' green values with the values considered desirable by the organization. If these values are congruent then it could assist the implementation of environmental management strategies and move the firm toward sustainable development practices. Many organizations have discovered that green values are not part of the existing culture and that environmental values must be nurtured within the firm (Lublin, 1991). To change corporate cultures will require organizational members to know and share a common set of expectations or values. These expectations or values must be integrated across organizations, locations and layers. Environmental values should be intensified and crystallized as an organization moves to improve its environmental processes. Corporate culture becomes the foundation from which an organization establishes its corporate strategy, its structure and its administrative control systems.

CORPORATE STRATEGY – SHAPED BY THE ORGANIZATION'S CULTURE

All businesses have a defined corporate strategy. At times, it may be more implicit and covert in nature than one would like but it is always there, guiding the firm in some fashion. Many organizations have extensive formalized strategic planning processes while others tend to have informal fluid processes. What shapes these corporate strategies? Profit-driven strategies can be pushed through by the money-driven values and the investment culture of the principal owner and other shareholders. If all the organizational members share this money culture with the owners then the strategy is usually quickly implemented. If, on the other hand, all the organizational members do not accept the owners' views then this will resist and slow implementation. This analogy can be directly applied to greening strategies. If the owners and the other organizational members share positive green values and culture then it would be expected to generate a successful and quick implementation of a proactive environmental strategy. It is all a matter of culture. Much of the academic literature has hotly debated the factors that shape and deliver strategies. Is it more dependent on the external demands from outside the organization or is it the entrenched values and culture of the shareholders and the organization? It is obvious that both play a role but clearly internal cultural factors shape the processes in a significant way. Why do two firms in the same industry choose different environmental strategies?

Case Study 1 – The Recycling Device – Two Corporate Strategies

The following case is a summary of an interview with an executive of XXTECH Inc, a fictional name for a real North American company that manufactures instruments to contain toxic substances. Some of the facts have been disguised to present the case.

This struggling small high technology firm developed a device to capture and recycle a very toxic substance which will be called 'Toxicfume'. The chemical is used to fumigate imported goods to kill insects and other health contaminants. The fumigant is an ozone depleting substance that has been selected as a 'Montreal Protocol Listed Product'. Given this background, it is understandable that Toxicfume chemical was under significant pressure from Greenpeace and other environmental groups who were pushing to have it banned. The current practice is to place the contaminated goods into a large sealed building and inject Toxicfume into the building. After a set period of the time, roof hatches are opened and the fumigant is fanned into the atmosphere. This procedure is commonly accepted as having a negative impact on the environment. The small, high technology company, XXTECH Inc, developed a device to capture and contain the fumigant and recycle it for the next use. Although not a complete solution, the device was expected to extend Toxicfume's life and permit Toxicfume's continued production.

Two major producers, one in North America and one in Europe, dominated the world's supply of Toxicfume. Both companies competed aggressively on a world wide basis. The North American firm was the sales leader in its home market but was second place in world production. The other main player dominated the rest of the world but competed in second place in the North American markets. XXTECH Inc expected to reach cooperative agreements with these producers to market and sell these devices. Both chemical suppliers faced the same two basic strategic alternatives:

1) 'Co-operate and Promote the Device': they could view this new recycling device as a positive environmental breakthrough and as a profitable recycling opportunity. This strategy would provide an added benefit by exhibiting product stewardship leadership for this environmentally sensitive chemical.
2) 'Bury XXTECH Inc': the opposing strategy would view the device as a threat to the traditional sale of the virgin fumigant because the recycled fumigant would reduce the need for new raw chemical. This strategic approach would lead to resistant behaviours by a chemical company to block the introduction of the new recycling device.

The two companies, making the same product, approached the situation with entirely different business and environmental strategies. The North American Company was offered a strategic partnership to bundle the recycling system with the sale of the fumigant. This would generate new profit from the recycling business as the sale of the virgin fumigant fell. However, the company took the second stance: 'We will bury XXTECH Inc'. The corporation did everything in its power to bury and destroy XXTECH Inc. They tried to influence buyers, fumigators, the USA Environment Protection Agency and Department of Agriculture to discredit XXTECH and limit sales of the recycling device.

The European company on the other hand had a completely different approach. They sought out XXTECH Inc voluntarily, at their own expense and asked to be a partner in the commercialization process. They offered help, co-operation, money and assistance with the regulators to get the device approved. They also offered XXTECH access to their world wide distribution system. This chemical company wanted to be perceived as a green company while also thinking the recycling could be profitable. They believed that if their company exhibited exemplary product stewardship, the chemical would not be banned and the product's life cycle would be extended. The company did not want Toxicfume to be banned since it made 60 per cent of the world's production.

These two companies had different environmental values and cultures which led to two quite different corporate strategies. One displayed very resistant environmental strategies while another exhibited very proactive environmental strategies. The fundamental differences can be traced to each organization's culture. Clearly the development of a corporation's environmental strategy is linked to its culture.

The strategic management process is the relationship and fit of internal factors of the organization with the external forces on the organization. Many business and academic strategists have argued that external forces – mostly market driven – are much more important in shaping strategy than an approach based on internal organizational processes and cultural factors (Ansoff and McDonnell, 1987; Mintzberg and Quinn, 1992; Buzzell and Gale, 1987). Others argue that strategy implementation is fundamentally driven by internal organizational processes and culture (Mintzberg, 1985; Pettigrew, 1977; Pettigrew and Whipp, 1991). It also has been argued (Grant, 1991) that internal resources and capability (Hofner and Schendel, 1978) provide the basic direction for a firm's strategy. From this case example of the two chemical companies it is interesting to note that both companies had very similar external environmental factors. Both competed head to head in all markets, had similar products and nearly similar market positions. Each developed very different environmental approaches to recycling, based on their corporate and employee values. Internal cultural factors not external market factors appear to be the determining factor for their environmental strategies.

An organization's greening culture, the glue that binds and shapes the firm's environmental characteristics or processes, is one of the prime strategic drivers. It provides an organization with attributes that separate it from others. It provides the unwritten rules or codes of conduct for employees. It will have a profound effect on the firm's ability to respond and change as greening forces increase on the firm. It will significantly impact on the success and effectiveness of the greening strategy.

Business must assess and mobilize its many resources to succeed in environmental actions. Organizations possess both balance sheet and non-balance sheet resources. They can be tangible or intangible. Resources can have many dimensions including financial, human, technological, reputational and organizational. The most fundamental intangible asset a firm needs is an organizational capability to learn and change. Certain cultures are more adaptable to change. Organizational values towards personnel, technology and reputation can have a profound effect on the ability of the company to mobilize these for greening purposes. A firm that has been efficient at mobilizing these is more capable of changing and will have a competitive advantage over other firms in the same industry. The ability to change and the ability to take advantage of increasing environmental forces will impact the long term competitive strategy of these companies.

A key ingredient in the relationship between resources and the capability to change, or the facility to capitalize on change, is the ability of an employer to achieve co-ordination and co-operation among staff members and teams. Those firms that have, or create, cultures that foster co-operation traits will be in a better position to create new profitable environmental strategies. Conversely, those firms that have an unco-operative style among employees will probably not succeed in proactive environmental strategies.

A corporation's environmental strategy is closely linked with its culture. The firm's outlook, the perceptions it has of its external environment and the assumptions it makes in building a strategy are all rooted in the corporation's culture. The business style that evolves is based on these ingrained attitudes and perceptions. The ROAST Scale of Environmental Performance (Figure 6.1) was developed to measure and describe these corporate cultural stances that tend to produce similar environmental strategies (Dodge, 1995).

Environmental Factor	Code R1 Stage I	Code R2 Stage II	Code R3 Stage III	Code R4 Stage IV	Code R5 Stage V
	R	O	A	S	T
INTERNAL RESPONSE	←— UNRESPONSIVE/REACTIVE		RESPONSIVE/ PROACTIVE ——→ TRANSFORMATIONAL		
Organization's ATTITUDE	←——— ENFORCED		——————→ VOLUNTARY		
GENERAL STANCE	RESIST	OBSERVE & COMPLY	ACCOMMODATE	SEIZE & PREEMPT	TRANSCENDENT CHARISMATIC
	R	O	A	S	T
Culture, Values, Leadership Environmental Response	unchangeable	reactive to change forces	recognize need for change & its opportunities	seize change in strategic shifts	unchangeable on importance of environment

Figure 6.1 ROAST Scale of Environmental Performance: Strategic Responses and Organizational Culture (Summary only)

The ROAST scale can be used by managers to understand and anticipate an organization's response to environmental programmes. The ROAST scale is a five point scale ranging from Stage I, unresponsive or resistant environmental strategy, to Stage V, a transcendent strategy that displays extremely proactive traits. The earlier case example of the chemical fumigant suppliers placed the North American producer as a ROAST Stage I with its obstructionist and resistant strategies. The European producer, who proactively sought out change and recognized opportunity in the environmental changes is demonstrating Stage III and IV ROAST Environmental Performance characteristics. The study of an organization's culture will assist in anticipating future strategic environmental responses to greening problems. If the firm's culture is rigid and unchangeable, it will tend to continue to display the same strategic response traits in the future. If the culture is a learning and co-operative one, its strategies will be less predictable and more flexible.

Older, well established companies, may be more resistant to new environmental initiatives. The history of an organization's ability to change or innovate has an impact on the way it responds to new external greening pressures. This sense of history becomes a cornerstone of the firm's culture. Organizations go through a series of life cycle stages as they mature over time. The level of innovation and change within the organization tends to diminish as the company matures and gets a more ingrained sense of culture. After maturity, a firm must either maintain or increase its rate of innovation or it will decline (Greiner, 1972). If a strong rigid culture becomes entrenched in the early stages of a business then as a mature organization it will be less innovative and less receptive to greening change and innovation. Older companies with these qualities would be even less likely to possess the capabilities to develop a proactive environmental strategy.

The formulation and implementation of an environmental strategy may require the business to change its culture. Each corporation has an established culture with its established direction, pervasiveness and strength. These characteristics help to define the initial ability of the business to develop a greening strategy. In some instances the culture may be very supportive of environmental programmes but in some corporations that culture establishes a very resistant organization. Therefore, as a company develops its greening strategy, it must understand its own cultural characteristics and begin to modify those that are not supportive of environmental programmes.

A green organizational culture, with an ability to learn and adapt, is the key to successfully implementing a progressive environmental strategy. Factors such as organizational structure, administrative systems, and management's leadership styles can also have a profound effect on the rate of implementation. The following sections will explore the links between these factors and greening culture.

LINKING ORGANIZATIONAL STRUCTURE AND CULTURE

Environmental structures, both formal and informal, reflect the organization's culture. The manner in which environmental management activities are structured will have a significant impact on the effectiveness of the programme. Typically, an organization groups its activities and responsibilities together in an effort to achieve the chosen strategy in an efficient and effective manner. This formal structure tends to be revised as a firm encounters problems with the implementation of this chosen strategy (Chandler, 1962). These revisions to the organization stem from the recognition of a problem that must be corrected. Subsequently, as problems increase, changes are made to the structure to overcome these difficulties. This process of problem recognition and corrective action is affected by the organization's culture.

Management's and staff's perceptions of environmental problems are shaped by the organization's culture. The basic operating assumptions used to explain problems are shaped in some fashion by the organization's experiences and history – which again is linked to culture. Some firms recognize environmental problems and react – others do not. The first step in the process is the recognition of the problem. The next step is the implementation of a solution by organizing the activity in a different fashion and structure. The following examples might be useful in demonstrating the impact of culture on structure.

Model 1 – A Firm With No Environmental Structure

This model provides an example of a business without any formal environmental structure. This occurs when a firm does not recognize an environmental problem as an important issue because it is void of a positive and pervasive environmental culture. The fashion in which management and staff screen and filter environmental pressures is strikingly affected by the firm's culture. Since the firm has not recognized the environmental issue, it will not structure the environmental strategy within the organization. This lack of structure reflects the ostrich nature of the firm. This phenomenon can occur throughout the corporation levels or within individual departmental units. When a deficient environmental structure exists it can be directly linked to the low corporate value placed on greening and subsequently a low priority issue within the company.

The following compressed statement from a Canadian mining executive reflects this case very well:

> *The number one problem is culture. People need to see the environmental issues as problems. We are in a bit of an ostrich mode and we tend to ignore the environmental threats and problems. We think the environmental issues are only temporary issues.*

Model 2 – Informal Structure Controls the Environmental Strategy of the Firm

A resistant environmental culture uses the informal organizational structure to control environmental strategy. Formal structures refers to the declared official reporting relationships of subordinate to supervisor with the attendant responsibilities. The informal structure is the unofficial, casual relationships within the workplace. Model 2 occurs when a firm provides a formal structure to deal with environmental issues but the informal structure takes over as the entrenched culture guides the continuation of resistant environmental behaviours. Unfortunately, the end results probably do not produce the desired improved environmental performance. The organization recognizes the problem and reorganizes the activities and tasks to achieve an improved result but something seems to go wrong. Employees and some of the management personnel reject the formal structure and continue operating with the old ways. This means the organization's informal structure, its old communication links and habits, are more powerful than the new formal structure. Why does this happen? An organization with entrenched values and culture will continue to resist change and cling to old communication and environmental habits.

These behaviours can be demonstrated by an abridged statement from a production department manager who stated:

> *There is a debate in our company on who is responsible for environmental management. This production department does not accept any responsibility for environmental management.*

This statement reflects a departmental manager not accepting the announced formal organizational structure for environmental responsibilities. He continues to operate using the old structure without accepting the changes. Management and workers appear to openly accept the resistance and debate as a legitimate one. This process of debate and delay demonstrates the lack of acceptance of a proactive environmental strategy. The debate process can lead to an improved environmental performance if the organizational cultural consensus is supportive of the environmental programme. Alternatively, the discussion can also lead to the hardening of negative environmental culture if the traditional values are not supportive.

Model 3 – A Firm With a Traditional Centralized Structure

The design of an organizational structure requires the manager to decide which functions should be broken up and distributed throughout the organization. Tied to this decentralization issue is the level of effort required to keep these functional activities co-ordinated and unified (Lawrence and Lorsch, 1967). As environmental units or functions are decentralized it becomes more difficult to maintain consistent action in all departments. Another factor arises when an organization is operating within a very volatile market or turbulent environment where quick decision-making is required. Increasing environmental pressures may require the local department to react immediately, which it may or may not be capable of doing. If these environmental pressures are unique, the department may also require cognitive power to solve these problems. This would indicate that a firm, with volatile and changing environmental conditions, should possess a decentralized organizational structure. This raises some interesting implications for businesses with their existing organizational structures. The best structure to solve green problems may not be the best structure for running the core business. The following cases highlight situations when existing organizational structures encounter new greening demands.

The optimum structure for managing environmental activities may be in conflict with the existing structure in the firm. As an example, let us explore a firm with an entrenched, tightly controlled organizational style which has been formed to suit the nature and tradition of its core business. All functions report to a central unit, with most decisions emanating from the centre. This structure is typically found in a business with repetitive functions with few changes in product or its environment. This firm believes that efficiency, command and control are the best way to achieve objectives. This structure's effectiveness comes under considerable pressure as the firm is faced with unique, volatile and unpredictable environmental issues. These organizations tend to react slowly because the core decision-making unit is removed from the external influences. This centralized structure relies on a few people making decisions. The central unit must assimilate this new environmental information and react with new greening initiatives, while still under the day to day pressures of running the core business. If the existing lines of communication do not react to these environmental anomalies, it may be a very long time before the environmental issue is perceived important enough for new greening responses.

Volatile greening issues may call for a decentralized structure to deal quickly and effectively with local environmental pressures. In this example, this would require a structure that is inconsistent and in conflict with the entrenched traditions of the firm. It is unlikely the leadership would be able to tolerate a unit making its own environmental decisions without approval, nor would employees have experience of making their own environmental decisions. It can be concluded that the best structure to handle environmental issues may conflict with the best organizational structure for the business. The traditional culture of this centralized organization has trained workers and managers to react consistently. A new responsive decentralized environmental structure will require a shift in worker and leadership attitudes toward decision making and environmental issues. It is reasonable to conclude that the entrenched culture sets constraints on the selection of a structure for environmental management.

Model 4 – Firm With Established Internal Co-ordination and Communication Patterns

The existing communication and coordination patterns formed to manage the core business are components of the firm's integrated cultural style. The links become reinforced over time and are reaffirmed by the organizational structure. The reporting lines and the level of decentralization have an impact on the level of co-ordination effort required. Firms with responsibilities distributed throughout the organization require open communication between departments and high levels of co-ordination to develop consistent behaviour from all departments. The introduction of an environmental programme must tap into these existing lines of communication and co-ordination. If the lines do not exist or are functioning poorly, the greening programme implementation will be slow and unco-ordinated. The communication patterns may make sense for the current business practices but might be inadequate for improving environmental practices. If the existing communication patterns are supportive of environmental improvements then the programme implementation could be very rapid and consistent. Therefore, for management to launch new environmental initiatives and structures, it must understand the communication component of the corporate culture. To change these patterns, a new structure may be required to break the inertia to change. If the organization is extremely resistant it may require the reassignment of employees to different supervisors and workplaces to break up the established informal and social communication patterns which are part of the negative environmental culture. The resistance to change is definitely affected by the ability of an organization to establish an environmental communications culture with open co-ordinated styles and ready to accept innovative change.

To introduce a new environmental programme, leadership is required to implement the changes to the culture and structure. The next section introduces three leadership concepts applicable to the process of launching a new environmental programme.

LEADERSHIP AND CULTURE

Leadership has been described as a seemingly vague and esoteric concept that is an essential element of strategy implementation (Pearce II and Robinson, 1991). With a greening strategy, the leadership skills and styles of the key managers are of particular importance. The leader's style is strongly linked to his/her values. The issues surrounding leadership will obviously play a role in an organization as it responds to greening pressures. Many competing leadership theories and conflicting research has evolved, particularly in the North American literature (Bass, 1985; Blake and Mouton, 1985; Fiedler, 1967; Fiedler, 1986; Fiedler and Garcia, 1987; Hersey and Blanchard, 1988; Mintzberg, 1983; Pfeffer, 1981; Tannenbaum and Schmidt, 1973). Given the extent of the controversy, this chapter chooses not to slip into academic debate but rather to apply portions of these theories to leadership of the environmental process within an organization. More specifically the general leadership theories described within the Management Grid by Blake and Mouton (1985), the Situational or Contingency Leadership Model of Hersey and Blanchard (1988) and the Transformational Leadership Model of Bass (1985).

Environmental Management Grid: Relationship Between Environmental Performance and Profit/Production

The Environmental Management Grid (Figure 6.2) illustrates the relationship between increasing production and profit at the expense of environmental management. These could be considered to be on a linear or bipolar scale where either ecology or profit is sacrificed to benefit the other. These two competing values, that become part of the culture, can be created or modelled by the organization's leadership. In effect it is possible to categorize the environmental leadership style of any manager by constructing a nine by nine grid. The vertical axis shows the degree of concern for environmental performance and the horizontal axis shows concern for profit/production performance. The scale ranges from one representing a weak concern to nine representing a strong concern. A manager can fall anywhere on the grid. A leader exhibiting a weak concern for environment and production and profit is defined as having a *Destitute Management* style. These attributes indicated that minimum effort would be exerted by this manager to either increase profit or environmental performance. A *Transcendent Manager* has a strong concern for environment with weak concern for production and profit. This manager, in extreme cases, would not be able to sustain the economics of the

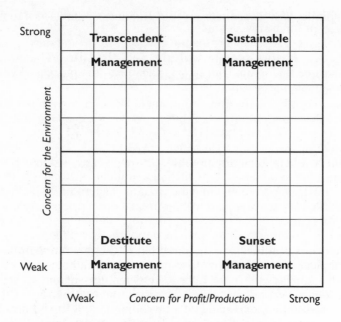

Figure 6.2 The Environmental Management Grid

business. The manager showing both a strong concern for environment and profit performance would be classified as a *Sustainable Manager*. The fourth quadrant represents the *Sunset Management* style which shows weak concern for environment with a strong concern for production and profit. The Environmental Management Grid is a useful tool to define the existing leadership style within an organization. When change is needed it will help to show the leadership and values required to attain the desired environmental and general management goals.

Environmental Leadership: Fitting Employee Readiness and Corporate Culture

The situational theories of leadership are particularly applicable to environmental leadership because greening leadership is closely related to the culture and the readiness of employees to implement greening strategies. Employee or follower readiness to launch environmental initiatives is a combination of ability and willingness. Ability includes the employee environmental traits that represent the established ability, skill, knowledge and experience the employee has to manage the environment. Willingness comprises the commitment, confidence and motivation to complete the greening task. This theory builds on the non-environmental work of Hersey and Blanchard's (1988) Situational Leadership Theory. This concept breaks leadership into four styles, telling, selling, participating and delegating. Situational leadership principles promote the belief that leadership styles should be tailored to the situation, particularly dependent on the readiness of employees to follow the leader:

- Telling style may be used in situations of low employee readiness where the followers are unable and unwilling to take responsibility for the greening tasks.
- Selling style may be used in situations of low to moderate readiness, where followers are unable to take environmental responsibility but are willing.
- Participating leadership style may be used in moderate to high readiness situations, where followers are able to take greening responsibilities, but are unwilling to do so.
- Delegating leadership style may be used for high readiness situations, where followers are able and willing to take appropriate environmental responsibilities.

If the employee's readiness or the direction of the environmental culture is low, the employees are less likely to follow greening initiatives unless directed to do so. The directive style (or telling style) requires minimal efforts by the leader to pressure the firm to better environmental improvement. As the employee readiness increases and environmental culture becomes more positive and pervasive, they become receptive to the selling and training messages of the leadership. As the greening culture becomes stronger and employee readiness increases even more, the empowerment process begins to take root. At this stage employees participate in the decision-making and implementation process under the guidance of management. This participation process will require a significant effort and time commitment from the organization's leaders. With the delegating style, followers are ready and have a strong and pervasive environmental culture. At this stage, the unwritten cultural rules are sufficiently strong to allow the leader to step back from the process and delegate the decision-making and implementation to the employees. This type of process is mapped out in Figure 6.3.

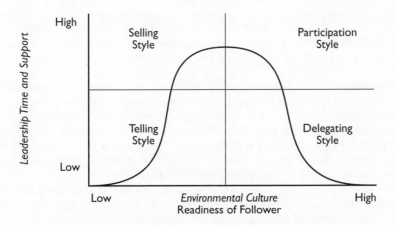

Figure 6.3 The Development of Environmental Leadership Styles

Most managers establish a dominant leadership style. An interesting situation arises when this historical style may not be the optimum style for the introduction of a new environmental programme. Let us explore, for example, a manager who is successfully managing the core business using a delegating style of management. The workers are experienced in running the business without much guidance from their leader. Now the manager wishes to introduce a new environmental programme. Should the manager immediately delegate the implementation of the new programme as just another business task? The decision depends on the environmental readiness of the employees and the environmental culture within the organization. If the greening culture and employee readiness is low, the manager may need a telling, selling or participating style to get the programme started. At a later date, the manager may be able to fully delegate the implementation of a new environmental initiative. However, the manager may not be capable of altering his/ her leadership style. The manager may be unable to tell, sell or participate with workers to achieve the desired ends. In this situation, additional assistance may be required from central environmental units, outside consultants or trainers. It is therefore important to select an environmental leader or champion who has the appropriate management style to fit the stage of the firm's environmental development.

Environmental Leadership: Transformational Versus Transactional Leadership

Some leaders bring about major change and inspire followers to pursue extraordinary levels of environmental effort beyond the normal expected levels. How can we explain why some managers are capable of this while others fail? The differences can be interpreted by distinguishing leaders as having transactional or transformational characteristics (Bass, 1985).

The transactional environmental leader motivates subordinates to perform greening activities at expected levels or at the required compliance levels. These leaders seem to help employees recognize their greening responsibilities and goals. The leader assists the employees in acquiring confidence to achieve the desired greening performance levels. The good transactional manager will organize the firm to achieve its minimum environmental performance levels – but the manager is seldom able to motivate workers to exceed the compliance levels.

The transformational environmental leader motivates individuals to perform greening initiatives *beyond* expectation and compliance levels by inspiring employees to focus on broader environmental missions that transcend their own immediate self-interest. These leaders concentrate on intrinsic high-level environmental goals rather than lower-level environmental programme and system goals. They give followers the confidence in their abilities to achieve the extraordinary environmental missions articulated by the leader. Transformational leaders have charisma. Charisma is the ability to inspire pride, faith, and respect in their followers. These leaders can effectively communicate a sense of environmental mission or a vision of the desired. Transformational leaders develop followers' environmental capabilities while paying attention to each individual's needs. They can stimulate followers to be innovative by offering new environmental ideas and intellectual stimulation. This encourages employees to look at problems from multiple view points and create breakthroughs to overcome environmental obstacles.

An organization wishing to transform itself to an environmental performance culture – going beyond required goals – will need some elements of the charismatic transformational leadership style. Obviously, if these traits are lacking, the organization is probably limited to only achieving the minimum environmental expectations set by the corporation.

ADMINISTRATIVE CONTROL SYSTEMS AND CORPORATE CULTURE

As business organizations implement an environmental strategy they usually select monitoring and control mechanisms to shape and guide the process. The choice of control systems ranges from controlling outputs to controlling behaviours. These systems are categorized into four main styles: market control, output control, bureaucratic control, and clan/culture control (Table 6.1) (Hill and Jones, 1992; Ouchi, 1979). The actual choice of which control system to use can be very dependent on the management style of the leader and the established control norms within the company. These four controls can be used individually or together, depending on their appropriateness to the situation and the culture of the organization. On occasion, these controls are linked to employee compensation through reward and bonus arrangements.

Table 6.1 Environmental Control Systems

Market Control (changes due to environmental performance)	Output Control (controls on emission and other environmental outputs)	Bureaucratic Control (rules to perform tasks and control behaviour)	Clan/Culture Control (control through the embedded culture)
Stock Price	By Divisions	Rules and procedures	Norms
Return on Investment	By Function	Budgets	Values
Market Shares	By Individual	Standardization	Socialization

An environmental market control system occurs when the business's environmental performance is monitored, evaluated and controlled by the market, such as stock prices or market acceptance. For example, when the market value of a firm's stock declines because of an environmental spill, the firm responds with improved environmental performance and the stock subsequently improves in market value. The same could happen if a firm's product acceptance and market share is reduced because of environmental implications. These external market controls can be very effective if management compensation is directly tied to market share and stock price changes caused by environmental performance. In practical terms, this monitoring and control method can be very ineffective if other economic and competitive factors are more important in the determination of market share. Nonetheless, if salaries and bonuses are tied to market controls, the organization will be very sensitive to market changes caused by these external events.

Another control is the environmental discharge or output control system. This is commonly used by governments and companies to set emission limits. These goals or targets can be set by geographic area, division, function or individual operating units. This system has been used to establish benchmarks for a variety of gaseous, liquid and solid discharges or for internal material usage. These outputs are monitored and subsequently used to control the process. The minimum standards are usually set at the legislated compliance levels but the environmental culture plays an important role in goal-setting. If the culture is resistant and not caring for the environment, the firm will set production output controls that defy environmental regulations. In a more positive case, the pervasive and strong environmental culture may take extreme pride in setting standards well beyond compliance levels. This demonstrates that culture establishes the formal environmental control standards of the company. If the organization sets its formal benchmarks at compliance levels but does not care if it meets or exceeds these targets then the formal output control system is worthless. The main advantage of the output control method is the ease of monitoring results. The primary weakness, however, is the possibility that the system is monitoring the wrong items, overlooking the real source of environmental non-performance.

Bureaucratic controls are based on a comprehensive environmental system driven by rules and procedures to direct the actions and behaviours of divisions, functions and individuals. The bureaucratic control is intended to lay out, in step by step form, the exact system to follow. The implementation of these steps and procedures becomes the environmental goal (rather than a discharge goal). If the business follows these procedures it feels it is achieving the desired behaviours. However, the procedures may not lead to satisfying environmental performance. Common bureaucratic controls include rules and procedures, budgets, and standardization of inputs, activities and outputs. This control style is particularly useful for employees performing repetitive tasks and where employee readiness is low. Established rules and procedures seem to give the legal fraternity and government inspectors comfort. Unfortunately, if the procedures are wrong or if an unusual situation arises, the procedures may actually inhibit environmental performance. Once the procedures become entrenched they are difficult to change, which subsequently may restrict innovation and positive improvements. Organizations without the necessary environmental culture tend to rely heavily on bureaucratic controls to quickly establish a minimum standard of behaviour. However, if the organization has very little experience in using procedures and rules in the workplace, it might find it very cumbersome and difficult to write the procedures, train workers and monitor the procedure. The system can carry a very significant cost as it requires significant human resources to construct the system, monitor and audit the procedures, and take the expected corrective action.

Clan and culture controls, in pure form, would use the organization's environmental culture to control and monitor the environmental performance of the company in the absence of any market, output or bureaucratic control mechanism. This control mechanism is very lasting and requires little extra administrative cost to support. Environmental cultural controls require a long time to develop when compared to the output or bureaucratic controls. Businesses requiring strong initial results may resort to bureaucratic output control, but over time, as the environmental culture is developed, they can begin to relax the bureaucratic control in favour of environmental clan controls.

As a firm's greening strategy is proactively implemented, it may be integrated into the control and reward systems of the company. Many firms choose to use a different control system in progressive steps. Early stage controls would begin with measurement and control of pollution discharge outputs. The next stage would be to see the introduction of bureaucratic controls with environmental procedures, audits and budgets. The next stage would be represented by clan controls with the integration of environmental values and norms. The environmental compensation system would follow, as reliable standards of performance were achieved. The last control system stage would see the use of market controls to judge the organization's performance based on both economic and sustainable development criteria. Obviously, the rate of acceptance of these control procedures will be very dependent on the direction, pervasiveness and strength of the environmental culture. As the dimensions of environmental culture are intensified and crystallized, the need for expensive monitoring and audit control diminishes. An organization with a strong environmental culture may not require output and bureaucratic control systems. Market controls, in the long run, will establish the environmental criteria for the firm.

MONITORING AND MEASURING YOUR ENVIRONMENTAL CULTURE

From the previous sections it is obvious that environmental culture has a significant impact on the choice of strategy, organization structure and administrative control systems used to manage the firm and in particular the environmental services function. If the wish is to advance the environmental agenda in an organization, the greening values in its culture must be repositioned to a higher elevation. The use of strategy, structures and control will not be enough to establish an environmental programme that has its own energy and momentum. This requires a shift in values.

As managers monitor the progress of an environmental programme, they would typically audit the actual procedures and systems and verify employees assuming their defined responsibilities. In a technical audit, considerable effort would be set to verify the pollution outputs, inputs and ecological impacts of the organization. These monitoring programmes are valuable tools in the progress toward defined environmental goals. Why not confirm the shifts in environmental values? We know that if the values have not shifted, the organization is always susceptible to recoiling to its old environmental habits.

The auditing of environmental values can be a very valuable tool to identify resistant departments and progressive departments. Since long-term strategy will not be sustained without value congruence, an environmental culture audit can identify which areas of an organization need the most training, encouragement and participation to ensure a sustained effort. One way to start this process is to undertake a values survey that coincides with the technical output measures. Shifts in values can be precursors to sustained technical environmental improvement.

A simple one to two page survey can yield some rather informative results. These surveys, although customized to the organization, must be adequate to define the environmental values characteristics within various locations, departments and employee levels. The dimensions used to define these characteristics will be direction, pervasiveness, strength and congruency. Information needed can be derived from the following kinds of questions:

- Are environmental values positive or negative?
- Are environmental values found through the organization?
- How weak or how strong are the environmental values?
- Are environmental values of employees congruent with management?
- Are personal environmental values congruent with the company's?
- Are values congruent across departments, locations and levels?

It would be inappropriate to create a standard survey or questionnaire for all companies and all situations. The following simplistic example (Box 6.1) is intended to display the audit design principles.

- **Part 1: Personal and Demographic Information.** These surveys are reliable only if the identity of the respondent is kept confidential. One section defines the demographic characteristics of the employee. Characteristics such as location, job classification and department are used later to compare values from one department to another and one level of the organization to another. If the organization has undertaken environmental training courses it would be useful to verify the employee's attendance. This allows managers to monitor the impact of training to promote positive environmental values within the organization.
- **Part 2: Employee Values.** This section is intended to quantify the environmental personal values of each employee. This section can be tailored to specific value statements thought to be important in the corporation. These will be compared to Part 3 which is the employee's perception of the company's values.
  Part 3: Company Values. This section asks the same questions as Part 2, only the respondents are asked to answer them based on their perceptions of company policy.

Sampling should follow the normal research protocols. Care should be taken to generate a random sample of sufficient size to give reliable information at various levels in the organization, locations and departments. Response rates for the survey can vary widely, from 30 per cent to 80 per cent, depending primarily on the credibility of the surveyor, questionnaire design and support from supervisors to permit time to fill in the information. It is suggested that an independent group such as a consultant or an educational institution undertake the design, collection and analysis to provide independence and improve the credibility of results.

The data contained in the returned questionnaires is then coded directly onto a computer spreadsheet or statistical software package. The routine statistical tests are used to compare the average environmental values across levels in the organization, locations and departments. Because the same questions are asked throughout the firm, the actual questions become less important than the relative response of different parts of the business. For example, by comparing the average response from one production department to another we are able to rank the department's values. If the appropriate questions are asked, the ranking will approximate the environmental culture of each department.

The analysis will produce results showing the leading and lagging departments. This helps environmental managers to focus on areas needing more work and to recognize departments where quicker results can be anticipated without much support. This information should help to direct the educational and skill development programmes in a more effective way. Over time, as the organizational surveys are repeated, they should yield data that can give concrete evidence of shifts in values.

The quantitative data can add a concrete dimension to the discussion of environmental values and culture. It allows managers the opportunity to use the survey data to develop concrete action plans.

Box 6.1 Sample Environmental Questionnaire

The following questionnaire is designed to study environmental factors in the workplace. The research is undertaken by Laurentian University with the support of Mr. Top Brass, President of Anycompany Ltd. Your help in completing this questionnaire is greatly appreciated. Your responses are anonymous and confidential.

PART 1 – PERSONAL DEMOGRAPHIC INFORMATION

1. (i) Please indicate the department in which you are employed.

    ____ Finance
    ____ Manufacturing
    ____ Human Resources and Public Affairs
    ____ Sales
    ____ Others (indicate) _____

   (ii) Please indicate at which Location you are employed.

    ____ Halifax
    ____ Montreal
    ____ Sudbury
    ____ Other (indicate) _____

2. In which category is your job classified?

    ___ Level I manager (job class a to b)
    ___ Level 2 employee (job class b to c)
    ___ Level 3 employee (job class c to d)

---

3. Have you completed the following training programmes offered by our company?

   ____ yes   ____ no   Spill Reporting and Emergency Response programme
   ____ yes   ____ no   Recycling and Reuse programme
   ____ yes   ____ no   Community Environmental Workshop
   ____ yes   ____ no   Sustaining our Ecological Environment

PART 2: EMPLOYEE VALUES INFORMATION

4. Please indicate how important the following factors are **to you** by circling the appropriate number.

How important is the following to <u>YOU?</u>	Not Important	Less Important	Neutral	Important	Very Important
Oil spill containment	1	2	3	4	5
Employee safety	1	2	3	4	5
Recycling	1	2	3	4	5
Protection of animals	1	2	3	4	5

5. Please rank (**in your own opinion**) the importance of the following factors.
   (1 = last choice – least important, 5 = first choice – most important)

   ____ **Creativity** (refers to willingness to accept new ideas)
   ____ **Environment** (refers to the natural environment)
   ____ **Product Quality** (refers to degree of defects)
   ____ **People** (refers to the degree of integrity)
   ____ **Profit** (refers to financial position or 'bottom line')

6. Should Anycompany Ltd. change its response to environmental issues? (choose one only)

   ____ be more environmentally responsive
   ____ keep the same environmental response
   ____ be less environmentally responsive

PART 3: COMPANY VALUES INFORMATION

7. Please indicate how important the following factors are **to Anycompany Ltd.** by circling the appropriate number.

How important is the following to <u>our company</u>	Not Important	Less Important	Neutral	Important	Very Important
Oil spill containment	1	2	3	4	5
Employee safety	1	2	3	4	5
Recycling	1	2	3	4	5
Protection of animals	1	2	3	4	5

8. Please rank the following factors in the order you think **Anycompany Ltd. (Senior Management)** would rate their importance.
   (1 = last choice – least important, 5 = first choice – most important)

   ____ **Creativity** (refers to willingness to accept new ideas)
   ____ **Environment** (refers to the natural environment)
   ____ **Product Quality** (refers to degree of defects)
   ____ **People** (refers to the degree of integrity)
   ____ **Profit** (refers to financial position or 'bottom line')

SUMMARY AND CONCLUSIONS

The links between environmental culture and the firm's environmental strategy formulation and implementation must be understood if a company is to successfully sustain a proactive environmental management programme. The association between an organization's culture and its strategy, structure, leadership and control systems shows how to elevate environmental values in the business priorities. The enthusiasm, commitment and expectations of the company toward their environmental strategy reflects their core greening values or beliefs.

Therefore, it is important to examine and compare employees' greening values with the values considered desirable by the organization. If these values are congruent then it could assist the implementation of environmental management strategies and move the firm toward sustainable development practices. To change corporate cultures, which is more than the summation of individual values, or the introduction of new positive environmental values into the existing culture, will require organizational members to know or intensify and share or crystallize a common set of values. These values must be integrated across organizations, locations and employee levels to improve its environmental processes.

The corporation's environmental strategy is closely linked with its culture. The firm's outlook, the perceptions it has of its external environment and the assumptions it makes in building a strategy are all rooted in the corporation's culture. The business style that evolves is based on these ingrained perceptions and assumptions. The study of an organization's culture will assist in anticipating future strategic environmental responses to greening problems. If the firm's culture is rigid and unchangeable, it will tend to continue to display the same predictable strategic response traits in the future. If the culture is a learning and co-operative one, its strategies will be more flexible and less predictable in the future.

Environmental organizational structures, both formal and informal, reflect the organization's culture. The manner in which environmental management activities are structured will have a significant impact on the effectiveness of the programme. The optimum structure for managing environmental activities may be in conflict with the existing structure. The organization of environmental activities will be affected by the existing structure of the business. The historical centralization or decentralization, the level of communication and co-ordination within the firm become the starting points for the new environmental programme. What is appropriate for the core business may not be appropriate for environmental management. If they are in conflict from the beginning, the greening process may be doomed to failure because the core business culture will be much more powerful than the new environmental beliefs. Alternatively, if the structure, communication and co-ordination are supportive, the environmental programme would be expected to succeed.

Leadership is required to implement the changes to the environmental programme. The selection of the optimum leadership style should reflect the needs and readiness of the organization. The Environmental Management Grid (Figure 6.2) illustrates the relationship between increasing production/profit and environmental concerns. This helps to define the shift in leadership and values required to sustain the desired environmental and general management goals. Successful environmental leadership is closely related to the culture and the readiness of employees to implement green strategies. If the organization's environmental direction and readiness is low, the employees are less likely to follow greening initiatives unless directed to do so. As the employee readiness increases and the organizational culture becomes more positive and pervasive, they become receptive to the selling and training messages of the leadership. As the greening culture increases in pervasiveness and strength, and employees improve their readiness, the empowerment process begins to take root. At this stage employees participate in decision-making and implementation under the guidance of management. In the final steps of the process, the followers or employees are most ready and have a very strong and pervasive environmental culture which allows the leader to step back from the process and delegate the decision-making and implementation to employees. Therefore, the strength of the environmental culture has a significant impact on the effectiveness of the leader because it defines the readiness of the employees to respond to the new initiatives. Organizations wishing to transform themselves to an environmental performance culture – going beyond established goals – will require some elements of the charismatic transformational leadership style. Otherwise the organization is probably limited to only achieving the minimum environmental expectations.

The selection of monitoring and control methods and the overall acceptance of these methods and standards are also impacted by the corporate culture. Many firms choose to use different control systems in progressive steps. Early stage controls would begin with measurement and control of pollution discharge outputs. The next stage would see the introduction of bureaucratic controls with environmental procedures, audits and budgets. The next stage would be represented by clan controls with the integration of environmental values and norms. The environmental compensation system would follow, as reliable standards of performance were achieved. The last control system stage would see the use of market controls to judge the organization's performance based on both economic and sustainable development criteria. Obviously, the rate of acceptance of these control procedures will be very dependent on the direction, pervasiveness and strength of the environmental culture. As the values are intensified and crystallized, the need for expensive monitoring and audit control diminishes. An organization with a strong environmental culture may not require output and bureaucratic control systems. Market controls, in the long run, will establish the environmental criteria for the firm.

As managers monitor the progress of an environmental programme, they would typically audit the actual procedures and systems and verify employees were assuming their responsibilities. The auditing of environmental values can be a very valuable tool to identify resistant departments and progressive departments.

Chapter 7

CULTURE CHANGE, PLURALISM AND PARTICIPATION

David Jones and Richard Welford

THE AGENDA FOR CHANGE

Throughout this book we emphasize the importance of the human dimension of environmentalism. Without the co-operation and participation of all involved in a programme of change, such a process is likely to be unsuccessful. Any change process therefore needs to involve the whole workforce in a move towards a sustainable model of the business enterprise. How to achieve that requires much more thought however. We need to find a vehicle to put creative, imaginative and, at times, radical solutions in place. Here, we argue that that vehicle is a culture change programme centred on the re-evaluation of global, organizational and individual values in the business organization, stressing the need for participatory arrangements.

Corporate culture may be defined as a cohesion of ideas, values, norms and modes of conduct, which have been accepted and adopted by a company. That culture then constitutes a distinctive character of the organization. The challenge facing the modern business is therefore how it can redefine and change its corporate culture in such a way as to be consistent with a programme of environmental and social action leading towards sustainable development. Culture change within the organization will require everybody within that organization to reconsider their own roles, perceptions and values. The strategy will have to be participative but senior management will have to take the lead.

The concept of sustainable development, which goes far beyond incremental environmental improvement, cannot be successfully achieved at the firm level through prescriptive strategies involving traditional environmental management techniques (with an emphasis on management systems) alone. The system may be necessary but it will not be sufficient to bring about sustainable development. It is however, through developing real commitment within all individuals and by emancipating the worker, encouraging him or her to play a full role within the workplace, that we can begin to make the more radical shift towards a sustainable economic model. But without ensuring an individual's understanding and real commitment to sustainable development, each individual's potential contribution will be overlooked in favour of a more traditional management system and piecemeal approach to the problem. A prime example of this inadequate approach is that enshrined within the concept of eco-efficiency which is too often considered to be the most proactive method of achieving sustainable development (Welford, 1997).

Participation is at the heart of sustainable development and this means that the empowerment of workers and the introduction of more democratic arrangements within industry are fundamental requirements of any change process. However, all too often the extent of this empowerment is management controlled and individual participation in decision-making is limited and thereby stifled. Moreover, corporate vision and corporate culture is often narrowly linked to specific products, markets and modes of operation. Any attempt at culture change in this type of business setting is ultimately dependent upon the manager being able to persuade, to insist or to cajole others into accepting (or sharing) the managerial goal or vision (Plant, 1987). At worst, this approach can become synonymous with an attempt to exert and retain managerial hegemony. In other words, it is an approach where workers have to recognize and then fall into line with what is considered legitimate to change by senior management. Therefore, there is a tendency to introduce innately restrictive measurements throughout the business process, to produce a conveyor belt of incremental targets for the work force and to maintain a top-down hierarchy.

The starting point must be a programme of change which is much more democratic, egalitarian, creative and participative than traditional approaches to corporate environmental management. Considerable research has shown that when change is through choice (ie is self-determined) people are not only more intrinsically motivated but they are more creative, display greater cognitive flexibility and conceptual understanding, have a more positive emotional tone, are healthier, and are more likely to support the autonomy of others (Deci and Ryan, 1985). Therefore, a new corporate culture needs to be developed by a firm which captures a real sense of commitment from all its employees.

If people are given a worthwhile goal then the need for paternalistic, autocratic management becomes an anachronism. Business, it should be recognized, is as much about human relationships as it is about outputs. The tasks organizations set cannot be specified simply in terms of actions, but require adherence to sets of values held in common between people and with the organization. The time has gone when people will tolerate subjugation and dependence. Nor will people tolerate isolated independence. Community, in every sense of the word, calls for many different forms of solidarity and interdependence based on the common theme of sustainable development.

We must recognize that people will only comply with the ethics and practices compatible with the aims of sustainable development within the work place, when they are persuaded that it is right and necessary so to do. This means that they must have sufficient incentives to change their behaviour and must obtain the required knowledge and skills to act according to new principles. This requires environmental education linked to social education. The former helps people to understand the natural world and to live in harmony with it. The latter imparts an understanding of the values and behaviour that are required to achieve such a state.

We can identify eight areas where we might start to readdress ideas, values and behaviour:

1) Inter-generational equity: the next ten years is a critical decade. The quality of life and even the actual survival of future generations are at stake because global problems have reached a stage where much of the damage already done is irreversible.

2) Interconnectedness of problems: none of these global problems can be seen in isolation because they are systemic problems – interconnected and interdependent – and need a systemic approach to be understood and solved.

3) Shift from objects to relationships: the shift from the perception of the world as a machine or resource to be used, to the world as a living system is a key characteristic of a new ecological paradigm. We must move away from seeing reality as a collection of separate objects to an inseparable web of relationships.

4) Shift from parts to the whole: living systems comprise individual organisms, social systems and ecosystems, all of which are integrated. Although we can discern individual parts in any system, the nature of the whole is always different from the sum of the parts. The nature of any living thing, including a business organization, derives from the relationships among its components and from the relationships of the whole system to its environment.

5) Shift from domination to partnership: the shift from domination to partnership is also central to the ecological paradigm. In the business world this translates to a shift from competition to co-operation and from managerial hierarchy to participative arrangements.

6) Shift from structures to processes: systems thinking is process thinking and every structure is a manifestation of underlying processes. In order to understand and change systems we must understand processes.

7) Shift from individualism to integration: in a culture associated with materialism and consumption we have tended to overemphasize individualist perspectives of competition, expansion and quantity, and have neglected integration which relies on co-operation, conservation and quality.

8) Shift from growth to sustainability: the blind pursuit of unrestricted growth has been the main driving force of global environmental destruction. Within the business organization, sustainability must replace the drive for growth and this means constantly re-examining the very ways in which the organization conducts itself.

Strategic management begins with a vision of what the firm is and what it will become. This strategic vision which needs to encompass the principles of sustainable development will be based on a set of core values and is essentially an image that guides the firm's decision-making processes at all levels. The achievement of this sustainable vision relies on every individual participating in strategic decision-making rather than being involved in marginalist changes through improving current processes and systems. In order to induce this type of decision-making a thorough examination of an organization's capability, personnel and existing culture needs to be undertaken. Because the nature of the business, its processes and its marketplace of the future are going to be very different, then the new investment in developing appropriate capability, organizational values, culture and appropriate individual behaviour is very important and will only happen if it is part of an overall strategic plan. This vision and its accompanying strategy to change culture is one which does not attempt to predict the future or even to identify specific environmental market opportunities way in advance. It allows a general competence to be nurtured based around individual commitment, production and service flexibility and an ultimate goal of creating a sustainable organization. This provides an organization with a clear identity along with the satisfaction of being able to realign products, processes or systems.

THE CULTURE CHANGE PROGRAMME

Post and Altman (1991) provide some insight as to how formidable the cultural barriers are for implementing sustainable strategies in organizations. In their research of a range of firms, they conclude that long-term adoption of sustainability strategies will require a 'third-order change' in the culture of organizations. First-order change (developing new ways to reinforce current objectives, values, norms, structures, etc) and second-order change (purposely modifying current objectives, values, norms, structures, etc) are the normal focuses of a traditional organization's change efforts. A total quality management (TQM) approach to change would clearly fall within the second-order change bracket. However, third-order change is a different story. It requires the organization to adopt a completely new culture. First-order and second-order changes are linear in nature, requiring that organizations do basically the same things they are currently doing, only better. However, third-order change is discontinuous change that requires the organization to achieve an entirely different qualitative state (Bartunek and Moch, 1987). In order to invoke a creative tension to change, everybody within the organization must be either dissatisfied with the current strategy or have a clear vision of how things could be better. But to introduce a new order of things is difficult and requires a considerable amount of bravery on the part of owners and managers.

It seems logical to think that the power and status gained by top management through implementing current environmental strategies have such an extrinsically motivating addictive effect that people do not want to give these up readily. Managers who understand the concept of sustainable development know that the concept is synonymous with participation and co-operation. But, in turn, these often alien concepts remove a degree of power from managers and can question their very existence and it is no surprise that this should lead to inertia. Managers therefore need to be convinced in the first place that a radical change in corporate culture and in the ultimate goals of the organization are in their best interests. The question remains as to who precisely is going to undertake such an evangelical task.

To an extent therefore, managers have to rethink their own perception of reality and their role in a new corporate order. Ornstein and Ehrlich (1990) contend that people need to take advantage of the flexibility and trainability of the human mind in order to achieve the necessary changes to their mental pictures of reality. Arguably, humans are the most adaptable of species and they have the potential to synthesize large amounts of information. Education about the problems faced by humankind is important, but education about the way people think may be even more important. If people could learn how they learn, if they could understand how their perceptions influence their view of the world and their reactions to it, and how the very language they use is restrictive, then they would be better equipped to modify their cognitive structures to fit the demands of their current environment. Changing cognitive structures, of course, means changing values. Adequately including sustainable development into the mental pictures that people use in making strategic decisions can only be achieved by refocussing their perceptions on gradual, long-term processes.

Asking a basic question such as 'What do you stand for?' simultaneously with 'What business are you in?' provides an indication to the individual/ organizational/global purpose, and as such, it forms a direct link between ethical reasoning and strategic reasoning (Freeman and Gilbert, 1988). Philosophically, when an individual or a firm asks itself what it stands for and then consciously searches for the answer, it has an opportunity to gain a clear, in-depth understanding of the extent to which principles of, and values associated with, sustainable development form the foundation of his/her/its own ethical system. Our argument here is that significant clarification and modification of values will be necessary for most firms (including TQM organizations) that wish to develop and implement true sustainability strategies and intents.

Strong cultures are identified when the values expressed by individuals throughout the firm are well defined and are the same throughout the organization or congruent both horizontally and vertically (Deal and Kennedy, 1982). Most people are aware of environmental issues but few organizations have given their staff the opportunity to share their perceptions, to test the accuracy of their opinions and to relate their concerns to their business. This will provide a more clear understanding of the effectiveness of company policies and practices towards sustainable development. Without this kind of initiative, staff are likely to arrive at their own conclusions which will influence what they say to their work colleagues and to their family and friends. At best any negative views they may have will effect morale adversely, and at worst could, through time, damage the corporate image and the ability to recruit and retain good people. Therefore, the clarity, relevance and holistic focus of culture is crucial to the likelihood of producing a commitment to change.

Figure 7.1 derived from the work of Stead and Stead (1992) provides the basis for examining the culture change process. In order to achieve a commitment towards this vision, a change programme must consider values at three different levels. Starting initially with the global and ending with the individual, it is important to note that as each layer's values are considered, the depth of understanding that is required increases. Moreover, this is a building process, where the ease of understanding becomes easier and more relevant to the individual as he or she moves from level to level. As soon as all three levels are understood, the process of decision-making needs to be examined. This process links values to behaviour. A re-examination of values and the very ways in which decisions are made are therefore at the heart of

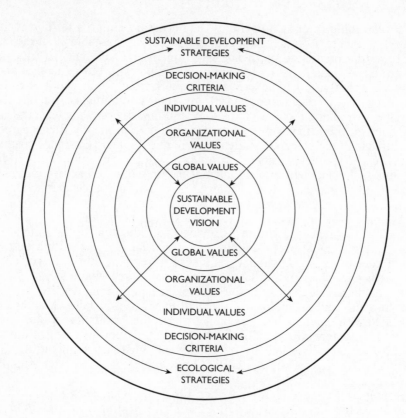

Figure 7.1 The Culture Change Process

the culture change programme. This provides the vehicle for all other ecological and sustainable strategies which can be seen as encapsulating the move towards the sustainable organization.

Global Values

Although sustainable development seems to be universally thought of as a good thing, nobody seems to agree on a universal definition for sustainable development, never mind its associated values. The term has been criticized as ambiguous and open to a wide range of interpretations, many of which are contradictory. The confusion has been caused because 'sustainable development', 'sustainable growth' and 'sustainable use' have been used interchangeably, as if their meanings were the same. They are not. 'Sustainable growth' is a contradiction in terms: nothing physical can grow indefinitely. 'Sustainable use' is applicable only to renewable resources: it means using them at rates within their capacity for renewal. This ambiguity is perhaps one reason why industry has applied only one ingredient to the recipe of sustainable development, which is environmental protection. This term itself is however ambiguous, thus compounding the problem to one that seems to industry to be too complex to devise a whole cultural change programme around. However, global values must consider a wider definition of sustainable development and this must incorporate the environment, equity and futurity (Welford, 1995). An excellent model for reconsidering our global values is provided by Agenda 21.

Agenda 21, the global plan of action adopted at the Earth Summit in Rio de Janeiro, recognizes that given the nature of the problems which now confront us as a community of nations and peoples, we are now more than ever bound together by a common destiny. Solutions to these problems will have to be found at an international level. The solutions to the global problems require action at a local level, including the level of the firm. We therefore need to consider our values and attitudes toward global problems and make a transition to sustainable forms of development and lifestyle.

Agenda 21 explains that population, consumption and technology are the primary driving forces in environmental change. It shows that there are significant roles to be played by everyone: governments, business people, trade unions, scientists, teachers, indigenous people, women, youth and children. Agenda 21 does not shun business although it makes us think about the ways in which we do business. A full consideration of the message of Agenda 21 must therefore be at the heart of a reconsideration of global values.

A major theme of Agenda 21 is the need to eradicate poverty by giving poor people more access to the resources they need to live sustainably. By adopting Agenda 21, industrialized countries recognized that they have a greater role in cleaning up the environment than poor nations, who produce relatively less pollution. Whilst Agenda 21 recognizes that sustainable development is primarily the responsibility of governments, these efforts require the broadest possible public participation and the active involvement of businesses.

Agenda 21 lays out a seven point plan for business and industry and this provides only the starting point for changing values and perception within the organization. It argues that business and industry should:

- Develop policies that result in operations and products that have lower environmental impacts;
- ensure responsible and ethical management of products and processes from the point of view of health, safety and the environment;
- make environmentally sound technologies available to affiliates in developing countries without prohibitive charges;
- encourage overseas affiliates to modify procedures in order to reflect local ecological conditions and share information with governments;
- create partnerships to help people in smaller companies learn business skills;
- establish national councils for sustainable development, both in the formal business community and in the informal sector, which includes small-scale businesses, such as artisans;
- increase research and development of environmentally sound technologies and environmental management systems.

Agenda 21 also recognizes that it is workers who will be most affected by the changes needed in industry to bring about a sustainable future. Trade unions, which have experience in dealing with industrial change, will therefore have a vital role to play. Governments, business and industry must foster the active and informed participation of workers and trade unions in shaping and implementing environment and development strategies. These strategies will affect employment policies, industrial strategies, labour adjustment programmes and technology transfers.

Unions and employers need to design joint environmental policies, and set priorities to improve the working environment and the overall environmental performance of businesses. Trade unions should develop their own sustainable development policies and take a wider perspective than the simple protection of their own members. For labour to fully support sustainable development, governments and employers should promote workers' rights to freedom of association and the right to organize.

Organizational values

The basic assumptions people make about the world determine the things they value, the things they pay attention to, and, ultimately, the things they do. In other words, human consciousness rests on the basic assumptions that people make about the world around them. The basic assumptions people make about business form the foundation for an organization's culture (Schein, 1985). Thus developing consciousness towards sustainability in business organizations means changing many of the basic assumptions on which businesses are founded (Stead and Stead, 1992). An understanding of global values outlined above gives rise to three closely related organizational values: 'profits out, ethics in'; 'smart growth'; and 'equality and democracy'.

Profits Out, Ethics In

Sustainability has to be seen as within the intrinsic business concepts like profit and loss, debt and equity, capital and cost, that make our system work. What many believe to be the most significant transition from the old to the new sustainable management paradigm is the shifting perspective from the profit motive. However many executives are motivated by short-term profits through some combination of selfishness, greed and power-seeking. Whether driven by such motives or trapped in old fashioned capitalist ideology, such people seem unable to realize what are actually their own long-term interests, as well as those of their fellow humans and of the planet. They need to become aware that it may be necessary to sacrifice considerable short-term gains in order to secure long-term benefits. One difficulty, that more progressive business managers face today in trying to shift to a longer-term approach, is that it could place them at a temporary competitive disadvantage in relation to their more selfish business competitors who persist in a short-term approach. Therefore, more public encouragement is needed for public-spirited business managers (Burrows et al, 1991).

Serving the varied, often conflicting, needs of multiple stakeholders requires the organization to develop multiple goals formulated in social and political as well as economic terms. Due to this need to develop multiple goals for multiple stakeholders, the management focus of organizations has become more strategic (Halal, 1986). Ansoff (1979) argues that because the strategic problems facing organizations are being complicated by increasing customer sophistication, expanding global markets, increasing environmental and social awareness, changing technology and escalating turbulence, management processes in organizations must become more strategically focused. Halal (1986) argues that strategically managed organizations are not just companies with strategic plans. These organizations don't just have a strategy, they have a philosophy of creating strategies, adapting to the environment through innovation and entrepreneurial activity.

Ernest Bader, who founded the successful Scott Bader Ltd, took a multiple stakeholder focus almost 50 years ago, and he believed that employees were the most important of a firm's stakeholders. He argues:

> *The classes of persons entitled to their ... satisfactions are the owners, the customers of the products or services, and the workers. Between these three is a constant jostling ... The stake of owners and customers in a business are temporary, transient, and partial, but the employee normally gives all his working time to one business and therefore seeks in and through it a much wider personal satisfaction.* (Hoe, 1978)

Today this philosophy has been adopted by many organizations. For example, General Electricity (GE)'s new organizational philosophy focuses on the human being as the key to future productivity (Rose, 1990). Indeed, quality of work life has become a primary focus of business organizations all over the world. Freeman and Gilbert (1988) believe individual worth should be the value that forms the foundation of an organization's principles. Their basic premise is that an individual has the basic right to pursue his or her own projects free from coercion and interference from others. Individuals are ends and never mere means to someone else's ends.

Ethics have become another dimension of the new management paradigm that focuses attention away from the profit motive. Cavanagh, Moberg and Valasquez (1981) espouse that human rights and justice must be as much a part of organizational decision-making as utilitarian concerns. Freeman and Gilbert (1988) point out that all business strategies have an ethical foundation regardless of whether management is aware of it. They believe that organizations should apply ethical reasoning to their strategic decision-making processes, analysing who is affected by the decisions, how they are affected, what rights the parties have, and so on.

All of this leads to the realization that organizations that serve the needs of the greater society in which they exist are more likely to prosper. The narrow economic niche in which business organizations once resided has expanded into a much broader societal niche (Zenisek, 1979). It is generally understood today that social performance cannot be separated from economic performance. As well as earning a profit, organizations today are expected to contribute to social welfare. Halal (1986) argues that the key to restoring economic vitality today is to recognize that social goals and profit are not only compatible, but so interdependent that the firm cannot succeed unless it unifies these two sets of concerns.

Smart Growth

Another dimension that could be included in this new sustainable management paradigm is the concept of smart growth, discussed most completely by Halal (1986). He presents convincing arguments that changing economic trends (such as the decline of materialism) and increasing environmental problems are rapidly rendering hard growth (growth achieved via increases in physical commodity production) unfeasible. Smart growth involves turning today's economic and environmental problems into tomorrow's business opportunities. Economic growth in the future will occur within organizations and industries that contribute to improving the quality of life. Industries such as day care, waste management, pollution control, educational services, and information processing are likely to grow, while basic manufacturing industries will continue to decline. Thus values are changing, people in advanced economies are becoming disenchanted with growth as an end in itself, material consumption is often unsatisfying, many distrust the complexity of technology, and they fear the insidious effects of pollution. Instead, they are becoming interested in social relationships, satisfying jobs, and other aspects of the quality of life.

Halal (1986) contends that the transition from hard growth to smart growth has been a three-decade evolution that began with challenges to unlimited material progress during the student activism of the 1960s, continued during the self-examination and inner growth period of the 1970s, and was solidified by the hard economic realities of the 1980s. This transition has led to a new, more thoughtful dream that balances the advantages of economic growth with its social costs. Halal calls this a transition from more, to better, to less. Peters (1990) agrees, suggesting that the great economies of the world cannot expect to continue to grow through greater commodity production and that the battleground has shifted from 'more, more, more' to 'better, better, better'.

Equality and Democracy

We have argued earlier in this book that truly democratic values must be universally incorporated for a sustainable culture to exist. This new organizational co-operative form of politics must build on a broad consensus of basic altruistic values, social justice, and decent standards for all. This new democratic form would start by considering the true basis for democracy.

According to Burrows et al (1991) a democratic order needs to have an adequate conceptual framework that would be provided by a holistic political philosophy including the following objectives:

- Unite people with a common purpose;
- care for all people, share resources fairly, and provide everyone with a decent quality of life;
- develop and use constructively, the abilities of all citizens and enable them to fulfil their creative talents;
- establish a just organization, with a proper framework of employee rights and employee responsibilities;
- carry out political functions at whatever scale or level is appropriate;
- decentralize, devolve and avoid bureaucracy wherever possible.

Individual Values

Any acceptable vision of sustainable development must include fair treatment of today's population through an appreciation of their individual aspirations to achieve a better quality of life, defined widely. Sustainable development as yet, has not been articulated in terms of what each employee in an organization can aspire to (self-determination, individuality, quality of life), how they are going to achieve these individual aspirations (unleashing creativity) and the mechanisms to achieve such a situation (participation, co-operation, empowerment, etc).

Understanding of global and organizational values gives rise to five closely related individual values: smallness, wholeness, posterity, community and quality.

Smallness

Schumacher (1979) promoted the concept of 'small is beautiful' and suggested that modern industrial society was living under three dangerous illusions:

1) Unlimited growth is possible in a finite world;
2) there are unlimited numbers of people willing to perform mindless work for moderate salaries;
3) science can be used to solve all social problems.

To him, these illusions were paths to resource depletion, environmental degradation, worker alienation, and violence. Large organizations inhibit freedom, creativity, and human dignity. The only way to reverse this in vast organizations is to achieve smallness within the large bureaucracy (Schumacher, 1973). This is precisely what organizations are accepting as they move towards ever more flexible organizations (Welford and Prescott, 1994). Peters and Waterman (1982) argue that small in almost every case is beautiful and that small, quality, excitement, autonomy and efficiency, are all words that belong on the same side of the coin.

Economic scale is ultimately defined by the amount of energy and resources that are transformed from their natural state into outputs, including wastes (Daly and Cobb, 1989). Thus valuing smallness has implications for every aspect of the economic cycle. At the production end of the cycle, smallness helps managers account more accurately for the value of the scarce resources that form the foundation of all economic capital. Smallness encourages strategic decision-makers to implement policies aimed at using as little as possible of the Earth's non-renewable resources. Expanding on the concept of smallness for organizational decision-making, Morgan (1986) proposes that co-ordination should be based on the development of shared values and shared understanding, with managers developing skills of remote management, such as 'helicoptering' and 'managing through the umbilical cord'. In other words managers must become skilled in designing and managing systems of small decentralized parts that are self-organizing and have a large degree of independence and self-determination. Management must become much more concerned with empowerment than with close supervision and control. Organizations applying smallness with a systemic perspective of the whole to their strategic decisions, are more likely to focus attention on searching for ways to save energy and to use more renewable energy sources in the production and distribution of their products and services. Smallness will also encourage organizations to look for ways to reduce the materials that go into their products, including packaging.

Valuing smallness in the production of goods and services has tremendous implications for the technologies used by organizations. Renewable energy technologies would obviously emanate from such a value. Peters and Waterman (1982) repeatedly found that the efficiency provided by smallness was consistently profitable for the companies they investigated. Organizations are discovering the economic benefits of small work teams, energy efficiency, and smart growth; industries (such as waste management) that deal with the deleterious effects of bigness show promising opportunities for the future. The premise of smallness is what Schumacher (1973) bases his five point strategy on:

1) Large organizations should be divided into 'quasi-firms,' small, autonomous teams designed to foster high levels of entrepreneurial spirit.
2) Accountability of quasi-firms to higher management should be based on a few items related to profitability. Decisions are to be made by team members in an ad hoc fashion without interference from upper management; upper management only steps in if the profitability goals are not being met.
3) The quasi-firms should maintain their own economic identity; they should be allowed to have their own names and keep their own records: their financial performance should not be merged with other units.
4) Motivation for lower level workers can be achieved only if the job is intellectually and spiritually fulfilling with ample opportunities to participate in decisions; this can only be achieved in small, meaningful groups.
5) Top management can balance the need for employee freedom with the need for organizational control by setting broad, strategic performance targets and allowing the quasi-firms to make their own decisions within these targets.

The structure of a company organized around these principles resembles a helium balloon vendor at a carnival with a large number of balloons for sale. The vendor (who represents top management) holds the balloons from below rather than lording over them from above. Each balloon represents an autonomous unit that shifts and sways on its own within the limits defined by the vendor. Organizations should be structured, like nature, into little cells. Therefore, organizational structures should be based on a broad network design that would be stimulated by advancing communications and computer technology.

Schumacher (1979) argues that business is not there simply to produce goods, it also produces people. Organizations have the responsibility to provide quality work for employees, work that is enjoyable and that satisfies the creative and spiritual needs of employees. Schumacher goes even further:

> *How do we prepare young people for the future world of work? ...*
> *They should be encouraged to reject meaningless, boring,*
> *stultifying, or nerve-racking work in which a man (or woman) is*
> *made servant of a machine or a system. They should be taught*
> *that work is the joy of life and is needed for our development, but*
> *that meaningless work is an abomination.*

Quality work can only be found in organizations that allow human dignity and freedom to flourish in small autonomous groups like those described in his model. The lack of available good work in our bureaucratized, mass production society is the primary contributor to inflation. When there is no intrinsic fulfilment from their job, the natural tendency is for employees to focus on getting more compensation (money) for what they do. But to change the nature of work will also mean changing the nature of education which prepares people for work. Education will have to deal more completely with traditional questions such as: What is (wo)man? Where do we come from? What is our purpose? Only when people find their own answers to these questions will they be able to identify what type of work provides them with their path to fulfilment.

Wholeness

Wholeness helps people remember that survival depends on successfully interacting with other living systems on the planet, because the whole cannot survive if its parts are destroyed. Further, because the whole is defined by how its parts interact with one another, valuing wholeness helps people to better perceive and attend to the relationships with other elements of the environment.

In his sixteenth century essays, philosopher Michel de Montaigne (1958a) elegantly appealed to the need for decision-makers to adopt wholeness as a value. He believed that people could comprehend the true impact of their decisions only if they accounted for the wholeness of the Earth and their role in it. On this point, he said:

> *Whoever calls to his mind, as in a picture, the great image of our*
> *mother nature in all her majesty; whoever reads in her face her*
> *universal and constant variety; whoever sees himself in it ... like a*
> *dot made by a very fine pencil; he alone estimates things according*
> *to their true proportions.*

Montaigne also believed that decision-makers needed to realize that when they made decisions, their actions would always have an influence (usually negative) on someone else and/or something else. Again quoting Montaigne (1958b):

> *No profit can be made except at another's expense ... As I was*
> *reflecting on this, the fancy came upon me that here nature is*
> *merely following her habitual policy. For natural scientists hold*
> *that the birth, nourishment, and growth of each thing means the*
> *change and decay of something else.*

Thus Montaigne captured two reasons as to why valuing wholeness is advantageous for strategic decision-makers wishing to achieve a sustainable balance between economic success and environmental protection. Firstly, a value of wholeness is of tremendous benefit to novel, creative efforts. New products, new services, and new methods can all spring from the value of wholeness. Thus valuing wholeness can contribute significantly to a firm's economic success in a very competitive world. Secondly, wholeness develops an understanding of where the organization fits into ecosystems, and that most organizational actions have some negative effect on other systems of the planet. Wholeness can give managers an ecological perspective on which to base their decisions. They will be more likely to examine the impact of their decision on other people, communities, societies, and the Earth. No doubt, wholeness is a value that, if adopted by decision-makers in organizations, would contribute significantly to sustaining the Earth's ecological balance.

Posterity

'We didn't inherit the Earth from our parents; we borrowed it from our children.' This well-known Kenyan proverb clearly describes why posterity is an important value in order to achieve sustainability. Valuing posterity, believing that future generations of human beings are prominent factors in strategic decisions, can be instrumental in attaining a sustainable economic and ecological balance. According to Speth (1990), sustainability can be achieved only if society can attain economic development that meets the needs of present generations without compromising the ability of future generations to meet their own needs.

The future does not look as bright for the younger generation of children as it did for the previous one, and the environment is a major reason why. An image of society based on unlimited economic growth has caused humankind to fall into ecological traps, raising serious concerns about the quality of life, for our future generations. Assuming social scientists are correct in concluding that a positive image for future generations is critical to the health of a society, then there is every reason to be concerned. Ornstein and Ehrlich (1990) make it clear that people's picture of the future will have to change drastically if they wish to develop a positive view for their children and their children's children. It may help if people realized how old (or young) humankind really is. The Earth is 4,500,000,000 years old, but human civilizations did not appear until 10,000 years ago, written histories began only around 5,000 years ago, and the industrial age has barely reached 300 years. Milbrath (1989) effectively demonstrates the significance of these time periods by envisioning a one-year film encompassing the Earth's entire history. If the film began on January 1st, dinosaurs would not appear until December 13th, mammals would enter the scene on December 15th, and Homo sapiens would make their film debut at 11 minutes before midnight of December 31st. Civilized human activity would not emerge until the last two minutes of the film, recorded history would begin one minute before the curtain comes down, the industrial age would dominate only the last one and a half seconds, and our own lifetimes would flicker by during the final half second of the film. Maybe this film can put what is called long range planning into its proper perspective.

Valuing posterity is an important ingredient in effectively managing the change and turbulence that all organizations now face and will continue to face in the twenty-first century. Adopting posterity as a value encourages business organizations to develop a vision of what they are and what they want to be. Having a clear vision of the future has proven to be a critical factor in successful organizations. Visions serve as common denominators around which strategic decisions are shaped and implemented. Shared visions in organizations encourage employees to think strategically; when strategic thinking is a part of organizational culture, the company is better prepared to manage its opportunities and threats in ways that are advantageous to its survival and prosperity (Ernst and Baginski, 1989).

In addition to supporting economic sustainability, posterity is also important in order to achieve ecosystem sustainability. In strategic decision-making, taking future generations into account significantly influences a wide range of choices. If managers believe that clean water, clean air, abundant resources, and natural beauty are the birthright of all generations, not just their own, then the decisions they make are bound to better reflect a concern for the Earth. The Iroquois Indians of North America had a seven-generation planning horizon; they try to predict the effects of their decisions for the next seven generations to follow. This type of long-range planning by business organizations would tremendously enhance the sustainability of our small planet.

Community

Communities are not simply groups of people occupying patches of land. They are complex social systems composed of diverse individuals and organizations. Communities share at least three characteristics:

1) The members are conscious of their relationships with others in the community;
2) the members are conscious of the limits of the community; and
3) the members are conscious of the differences between themselves and those who live outside the community (Daly and Cobb, 1989).

Thus, although communities usually share a common geography, the essence of a community lies primarily in the complex cognitive networks that form around the values and expectations of the individuals and organizations that comprise it. As Etzioni (1991) says, communities are identified by their 'sense of we-ness'.

Because communities are more cognitive than physical, they exist in many forms. Terms like local community, business community, religious community, and European Community all fit into the definition of community. In this sense, there is no need to differentiate between the terms community and society; communities simply represent the underlying social form on which societies are based (Daly and Cobb, 1989). Etzioni (1991) argues that communities exist like Chinese nesting boxes, in that smaller ones (eg families) are embedded in more encompassing ones (eg villages) and these in still more encompassing ones (eg counties) and so it goes on.

The shared values and expectations that make up the essence of communities lead to their strongest influence, establishing ethical standards.

Heisenberg (1985) contends that ethics is the basis for the communal life of people. Communities themselves have no power to coerce people to behave in socially acceptable ways (communities may have police forces with coercive powers, but the powers of the police result from shared community values for law and order, public safety etc); however, the moral codes of communities serve as public barometers by which the behaviours of individual members are judged and controlled (Etzioni, 1991).

Many ecological problems stem from the belief that serving one's self interests necessarily results in the collective good (the neo-classical doctrine of radical individualism). The opposite notion is subscribed to here. Individuals, organizations, and economies are parts of a greater community; thinking only of themselves leads to individual actions that are detrimental to the encompassing systems of which they are a part. Daly and Cobb (1989) argue that in the real world the self-contained individual does not exist. They reject the idea that organizations are like Robinson Crusoe, earning their way solely on their own guile, in favour of the belief that organizations are integral parts of interlocking communal systems composed of individuals, families, towns, cities, nations, international coalitions, and ecological systems bound by a common desire for quality of life.

Thus managers who value the greater community are better equipped to make decisions compatible with achieving sustainability. Those who adopt a value for community will better understand that the survival of their organization depends on their ability to serve the needs and follow the ethical standards of the more comprehensive communities to which they belong. Managers who value community will also be aware that the community's survival depends on business organizations that contribute to a viable economy. Thus, they are more conscious of the interconnections between their decisions and the quality of life in the communities in which they operate. They recognize that their organizations can prosper over the long run only if the community can maintain a balance between a healthy natural environment, ample opportunities for human development and fulfilment, a meaningful code of ethics, and a healthy system of economic activity. Accordingly, managers who value community are likely to benefit from numerous economic advantages such as customer loyalty, positive public image and employee commitment as well as contributing to the protection of the natural environment.

Quality

As a value supporting sustainability, quality is essentially the corollary of smallness. That is, changing from valuing bigness to valuing smallness dictates a value change from quantity to quality. Once organizations adopt the philosophy that how well products are made and how well customers are served is more important than how many products are produced and how many are sold to customers, then the proper scale of their operations can be defined by something other than physical growth: it can be defined by an overriding image of quality based on the perceptions of customers. As organizations learn that they cannot be all things to all people, smallness will very likely result from a focus on quality. When quality is the nucleus around which organizations revolve, they are likely to adopt a scale of operations small enough to focus on developing individual relationships within their stakeholder network. Further, as the United Kingdom has learned (often painfully) from the Japanese, improved customer loyalty, more stable supplier relationships, more participative interactions among organizational members, and improved operational efficiency are all possible outcomes for organizations that adopt quality as a key value in their strategic decision-making processes.

The value quality, best supports sustainability if it includes three basic dimensions:

1) Quality of products and services: quality products and services also support ecological sustainability because they last longer, are worth repairing, and can be exchanged more readily in second hand markets. Furthermore, high conformance quality (quality based on carefully and precisely conforming to internal specifications) reduces costs because of lower scrap, less rework and less time responding to complaints. Therefore ecological benefits are reduction in wastes and end user disposal. A preponderance of durable, long lasting products in the economic system will help to reduce the perception that constant style changes are necessary.

2) Quality work: quality products and services are simply not possible without quality work. As discussed earlier, structuring jobs around the concept of quality work, work that satisfies human needs as well as organizational needs, can improve the quality of products and services. This is because quality work encourages employees to be creative and to contribute their best efforts to accomplishing the organization's economic goals and objectives. Further, the psychological satisfaction that people derive from quality work often reduces their desire to consume more and more goods. Satisfaction derived from work is of equal importance with satisfaction derived from consumption.

3) Quality of life: achieving sustainability via quality is also enhanced by valuing the quality of life in general; valuing the quality of life encourages managers to recognize that all of their stakeholders have rights to physical well-being, long-lasting happiness, personal fulfilment, and a hopeful future (Milbrath, 1989). Such a value focuses the attention of managers on how intricately interwoven economic sustainability and ecosystem sustainability really are. Valuing quality of life brings a wide variety of economic and environmental issues to the attention of organizations, including job design, organizational reward systems, employee health and safety, shareholder wealth, community economic development, pollution, waste control, and so on.

Putting all the components of global, organizational and individual values together allows us to redraw our culture change process diagram. Figure 7.2 therefore maps out the actions required to change to values consistent with sustainable development. Having considered the need to readdress values within the organization we need to move on to consider the important issue of decision-making.

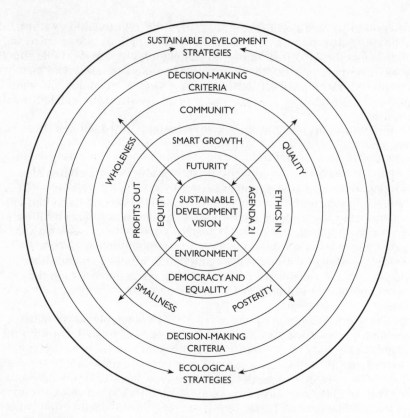

Figure 7.2 Principal Elements in the Culture Change Process

DECISION MAKING CRITERIA

Decision-making founded in systemic thinking represents a shift in the way that managers think about the problems they face. According to Senge (1990) the old management paradigm was dominated by linear thought processes that dictated that managers view organizational problems as cause and effect chains. He argues that linear thinking in organizations leads to seven organizational learning disabilities. These include:

1) Thinking in terms of individual jobs rather than in terms of the whole organization;
2) blaming problems on people or things that are outside the organization;
3) believing that organizations can always solve their problems by taking aggressive action against whatever external force they believe is causing problems;
4) becoming fixated on specific, sudden events;
5) being unable to perceive threats that result from slow, gradual processes;

6) believing that they immediately experience the consequences of their decisions; and

7) operating under the myth that management teams interact cross-functionally to solve problems when, in reality, these teams often spend tremendous energy defending the self interests of individual members.

Such outcomes are piecemeal, waste resources and lead to sub-optimal decisions being made. Yet they exist in many organizations and we all have experienced them at some time. Linear thinking must therefore be replaced with holistic, systemic thinking in order to allow organizations to see the broad, dynamic, recurring processes that underlie organizational problems. Systemic thinking allows organizations to understand that circular rather than linear relationships are at the heart of most organizational problems. Senge (1990) contends that reality is made up of circles. In systems thinking it is an axiom that every influence is both cause and effect. Once organizations begin to think about mutual causality rather than straightforward cause and effect lines, then identifying the true value of relationships among the key variables and agents involved in a situation becomes possible.

Senge (1990) provides a simple example of how this circular pattern works in business. A company produces a superior product that leads to satisfied customers; the satisfied customers pass the word about the high quality of the product to others; demand for the product then rises; the company produces more products, which leads to more satisfied customers, which leads to more word of mouth about the high quality of the product, and so on. In this way, the firm grows rapidly. However, if the firm does not recognize the circular relationships among the variables, then demand could begin to exceed the firm's ability to produce the demanded number of products and still continue to meet its high quality standards. If this occurs, then the firm may cut corners on quality in order to meet demand, and the cycle will reverse itself. Customers will buy the lower quality products, become dissatisfied, and spread the word that quality of the product is below par. All of a sudden, sales will begin to fall. The key to avoiding this problem is recognizing the circular, holistic relationships among quality, customer satisfaction, positive image, and sales.

In a similar way systemic thinking, helps people recognize that all the Earth's living systems are parts of a supranational ecological system. It drives people to better perceive and attend to the relationships with other elements of the environment.

Therefore, systems thinking provides managers with the broad perspective they need to remain competitive in today's living, global network of complex, dynamic business activity. Thinking of the world as an interconnected whole provides a much clearer understanding of the co-operative, participative relationships that organizations need to develop with their employees, customers, suppliers, and other stakeholders.

Systemic approaches to environmental improvement are fundamental therefore. As an approach to decision-making we need to put a renewed emphasis on creativity, action, consumer awareness, ownership, and a talent to perceive common interests and turn them into alliances. Let us deal with each of these in turn.

Creativity

Creativity is important in all areas of management but the particular challenges inherent in moving towards sustainability require creativity to be encouraged and supported at both the individual and group levels. This approach means that we must recognize that it is systems that control events. When we fail to grasp the systemic source of problems, we are left to treat symptoms rather than eliminate underlying causes. It is important to not focus on snapshots of isolated parts of the system, wondering why our deepest problems never seem to get solved. Raising the ecological performance of a business and its products needs constructive invention, not the common piecemeal approach of eliminating suspect ingredients or consuming less. The real environmental quality improvement delivers more performance from less energy and raw materials.

Individual creativity can be developed. Many techniques of creative thought have been devised, and some of them have been outlined by Koestler (1964), Mayne (1965), Rickards (1974) and Ochse (1990). Various techniques for developing group creativity, are to be found by reading Jungk and Mullert (1987) and Drambo (1988).

Action

It is often argued that business must have a proactive stance on the environment. This means approaching challenges actively rather than passively. But still, so many companies drive towards the future whilst looking through the rearview mirror. This must be overcome by adopting an attitude of anticipating and confronting future challenges rather than to manage in relation to events that have already occurred.

Awareness of the needs of consumers

Close awareness of the needs of customers and consumers is required and this must be an integral part of market research. Support from outside organizations, most notably local conservation groups and national pressure groups increases the credibility of the organization, as this shows an understanding of the intensity of consumer's concern about the environment. An 'outside-in' management philosophy is needed where managers relate to the environment in terms of what is necessary to meet the challenge of new technologies, and the evolving demands of external stakeholders, especially customers and potential customers.

Ownership

All employees must be encouraged to feel ownership of the company's environmental behaviour and environmental strategy. Changing a company's environmental behaviour cannot just be a separate, staff function. Senior management has to set environmental quality high on every middle manager's priority list. Then these individual managers will find the opportunities, and go after the necessary action steps with the same vigour that they pursue product improvements, marketing, volume, and profit opportunities.

Making Alliances Through Community Action

Environmental improvement often needs the combined effort of several companies, a whole industry and government. In particular, sustainability cannot be achieved if appropriate environmental strategies exist in only a few companies, industries, or nations. Managers need to use the community instrumental value, understanding that individuals, organizations, and economies are parts of a greater community (thinking only of themselves leads to individual actions that are detrimental to the encompassing systems of which they are a part). Daly and Cobb (1989) argue that in the real world the self contained individual does not exist. They reject the idea that organizations are earning their way solely on their own guile, in favour of the belief that organizations are integral parts of interlocking communal systems composed of individuals, families, towns, cities, nations, international coalitions, and ecological systems bound by a common desire for a high quality of life. It is not enough for a company to change its own products and processes. Success depends on a management's ability to mobilize other organizations to change their thinking and their actions.

Technology co-operation between firms, with benefits for all parties, is an effective way to enhance both productivity and environmental quality. Working with suppliers to ensure quality control and improved environmental performance can help purchasing firms as well as the suppliers. Industry trade associations can also act as catalysts to help an entire industrial sector.

MOTIVATING CHANGE THROUGH PLURALISM AND PARTICIPATION

Throughout this book it is emphasized that a move towards more sustainable ways of doing business requires the participation of everyone associated with a company. If there exist members of management or the work force who are not convinced of the need for ecological management strategies then they must be motivated to change. Unless there is a personal commitment to change, then the culture change programme can only fail.

Formulating and implementing change will ultimately be the responsibility of management, but they will find their task easier if they adopt systemic thinking and a co-operative and participatory style with employees. The focus should be on empowering individuals and harnessing their individual energies for change. This means recognizing people's full potentials, respecting their ability to make sound decisions, trusting their skills and experience, emphasizing intuition and increasing flexibility. Human relations need to be emphasized and managers should develop their powers of empathy.

When it comes to decision-making, not only should as wide a constituency as possible be involved, but they must also be provided with sufficient good quality information for those decisions to be quality decisions. People like to feel valued and needed and this will always be the case in a sustainable organization. Such respect for the individual is a critical motivator in its own right. When a decision generates positive results for example, this should be widely reported and the due recognition given to all those people who were part of that decision-making process.

Cultural development research has shown that for practical reasons associated with employee acceptance, even the most committed 'strong culture' companies, need to attend to participation and pluralism (Bate, 1994). Therefore, whilst representing for many people, a vision of what an organization ought to be like, the traditional hierarchical company fails to value workers and maintains a degree of alienation. Central to Agenda 21 are calls for workers (and their trade unions) to be more involved in the industrial change which will be necessary to achieve sustainable development. Businesses are called on to foster dialogue with workers, forming a partnership capable of shaping and implementing environment and development strategies at local, national and international level. This can only be achieved with increased participation of the work force within a more pluralist framework.

The challenge in maintaining order or ensuring sensible and controlled development is not to ignore, suppress, gloss over or eliminate differences between people (actions that were likely at best to enjoy only a limited and temporary success), but to develop greater sensitivity towards multicultural differences, accepting and welcoming, and continually looking for ways of expressing, accommodating and reconciling them. In short, companies need to realize that they need to manage the inherent 'pluralism' within and external to their organization. Thus if management is to be successful, rather than cosmetic or deceptive, it will have to comprehend comparative values and belief systems. The starting point here is for managers to understand themselves, first, and then go on to recognize the value of diversity.

This view substantiates research on environmental management and business level sustainability. Gray (1994) points out that the very critical nature of the environmental and social problems that one is seeking to address plus the sheer complexity of the issues and the increasing level of ignorance of humanity's interaction with the biosphere do not lend themselves to the assumption of 'rational', allocative decision-making by selected groups of the privileged. He argues for decision-making to be democratic, in the widest sense of the term, because it is society as a whole which must make the choices and trade-offs that are essential in the path to sustainable development. Welford (1995) argues for new forms of industrial organization as part of the equity dimension of sustainability. This would involve seeking to increase employees' decision-making powers, to increase democracy in the work place and to share profits with the work force, alongside improving environmental performance. This revolves around respecting the values of everybody associated with a firm or organization and the need for more open procedures and less hierarchical bureaucracy in decision-making to be developed within firms. Similarly, employee participation is first and foremost a question of recognizing the individual and collective interests of the employees, of the quality of working life and the nature of the relationship between management and employees: the social constitution of the firm.

Furthermore, a research exercise by Welford and Jones (1996) has pointed out the importance of empowerment strategies in moving towards sustainability, arguing that it is by empowerment that we can begin to challenge and change traditional balances of power. The logical next step must be to implement participation measures: participation in decision-making as well as financial (profit-sharing) participation and other non-financial rewards. Essentially we are searching for evidence of an equitable distribution of benefits. Ultimately the sustainable organization will be able to demonstrate that it is moving towards systems which provide for increased levels of industrial democracy.

With a more pluralist strategy, differences and conflicts of interest between individuals and groups are the order of the day and no amount of wishful thinking is ever going to change that basic fact. Nor could any single group ever hope to be able to impose its will unilaterally on the others or to be able to count on undivided loyalty, because power in the modern organization is too diffuse, and rarely coincides with formal authority structures. We have to accept the existence of different sources of leadership and attachment. The challenge for management in a pluralist organization is not to unify, integrate or liquidate sectional groups and their special interests in the name of some overriding corporate existence, but to control and balance the activities of constituent groups so as to provide for the maximum degree of freedom of association and action for sectional and group purposes consistent with the general interest of the organization. The aim is to provide leadership, not direction. But leadership is only possible where there exists a 'followership'. Thus, more co-operative, interactive and participative management is always likely to prove more successful in moving the organization forward.

An important point to note is that there is some evidence that organizations can not only tolerate many subcultures, but also benefit from the discourse about values which they inevitably spawn (Sinclair, 1993). Indeed organizations which embrace pluralism tend to be learning organizations, rather than structures driven by dictat. Therefore, rather than pursuing the strong corporate culture, the task for managers becomes one of understanding and unleashing the commitment of subcultures towards goals which are consistent with, or ideally advance, those of the organization (Martin and Siehl, 1983). Pluralists argue that the unitarist strategy is the antithesis of individual ethics, that such a culture demands a 'surrender of individual integrity' to the organization (Silk and Vogel, 1976). They argue that by relinquishing power to subcultures, communally mediated control is effectively increased, by sponsoring autonomy, commitment can be nourished, by encouraging connections between organizational subcultures and wider community groups, the organization's reserves are enhanced.

For a pluralist, the essential steps in the process of management are firstly, self scrutiny, weighing up individual obligations and responsibilities, secondly, weighing up professional and organizational responsibilities, taking personal responsibility for a decision and critically analysing the underlying assumptions of each course of action to better understand value choices, before finally applying decision standards and deciding. A key ingredient of this kind of more ethical management is the process of self awareness and self scrutiny that precedes it. Thus this puts weight on the process of thought that precedes action, to qualify behaviour before proceeding with action.

Because such thought requires a level of reflexivity and ongoing self-inspection, it is not enough to adhere single mindedly to simple standards of behaviour prescribed by others. For example, being ethical may require doing the opposite of what is comfortable, acceptable or expected by the culture. Managers must be wary of simply doing things which represent the continuation of accepted norms and practices. Such an approach does not impose a corporate culture, instead, it aims to stimulate more ethically aware behaviour of members of subcultures by collaboratively surfacing an awareness of subcultural differences, competing and common values and their effects on outcomes.

The pluralist strategy does not rely on management as the architects of the moral code, but works by encouraging individuals to understand and challenge the ethics and values they bring to the organization. This view has been confirmed by Post and Altman (1991) in their study of companies moving towards sustainable development. They base their methodology upon research done by Bartunek and Moch (1987), who argue that a change agent must not prescribe a particular value system, but instead be responsible for helping employees to self reflect and develop the capacity to change one's point of view, and therefore to explore one's own situation through a different light. Similarly, research on the implementation of environmental management techniques (Callenbach et al, 1993) suggests that people of different colour, women, labour, and other groups affected differently by company actions can be the eco-manager's best allies in bringing unique insights and solutions to problems. Ecological transformation is limited and likely to prove fragile without diverse participation, perspectives, and bases of support.

CONCLUSIONS

The thrust of any culture change consistent with the aim of creating a sustainable organization lies in a shift of business style from a management controlled, short-term, planning philosophy to one which bases its strategy on a long-term, democratic, creative, systemic form of decision-making based on the recognition of values at the global, organizational and individual levels. The scale and nature of this third-order culture change is such that the strategic approach can only be adopted successfully if staff at all levels are involved. It may take some time to build the understanding and commitment of all employees but without it, the achievement of the desired goals remains an illusion. In order to gain a true commitment to sustainable development strategies, a culture has to be defined, through an examination of the instrumental values required to be owned by each employee. It has been postulated that sustainable development global values need to move beyond the usual environmental concerns, into the realms of equity, environmental protection and futurity. They then need to be expressed in both organizational and individual senses for people to understand the collective gain but also their own individual gain (quality of life, individuality and self determination).

Culture change is not a once and for all process however. Most people require time to think through the implications of a more sustainable future. They need to come to terms with what is involved for them personally and to relate this to how they work with others. This cannot be done in a didactic way, it is unlikely to have any real effect. Culture change comes about through involvement and experiencing what it is like to live and work in accordance with the culture that is desired for the future health of any business.

Sustainable development at the level of businesses is going to be achieved, not through piecemeal approaches, but through a much more radical form of organization that uses its people to their full potential. This can only be achieved through a new culture based on clearly defined values which produce self determined creative behaviour. Managing to bind people together around a common identity and sense of destiny is one of the major factors for success. All too often, a company's shared vision has revolved around the charisma of a leader, or around a crisis that galvanizes everyone together. Sustainability must become an individual's vision as well as being a shared vision.

There is a clear need for a systematic framework to involve employees in top level dialogue and decision-making. There is also a need for strong leadership but this is only possible with a solid 'followership'. In the move towards sustainable development at the level of business activity we have made the case for a participatory strategy. But employees must see the point of participating. It must be more then mere lip service. Strong views from the work force (and indeed, other stakeholders) must be acted upon and positive outcomes from participatory arrangements may need to be rewarded. Over time, within the participatory framework, certain staff will become instrumental and they will become a powerful resource for education and awareness raising. Whilst their views are only as valid as anyone else's, one should not forget that they will often be able to synthesize and communicate the feelings and views of people around them. Therefore, the case has been made for a more pluralist, democratic strategy, which more fully respects diverse goals, values and aspirations. But it is not only internal structures which matter. As a powerful social actor the business has a responsibility to respond to and, where appropriate, influence its external stakeholders as well as its internal ones.

Chapter 8

Human resource management, strategic organizational capabilities and sustainable development

Tony Emerson, Ralph Meima, Romney Tansley and Richard Welford

INTRODUCTION

Human resource management (HRM) has an important role to play in corporate environmental management in supporting the success of environmental policies and programmes. Indeed, the sorts of changes advocated in this book are unlikely to succeed without the full support of human resource managers. Equally environmental initiatives and culture change programmes will not succeed without the full co-operation of all employees. One of the critical roles for the HRM function is therefore to motivate and include staff in the changes taking place.

The term HRM is used here to incorporate both traditional personnel management and the more contemporary concept of human resource management. The former is mainly concerned with cradle to grave (ie recruitment through to retirement) procedures in the employment of staff, whereas the newer concept of HRM is concerned with strategy and planning, and with the integrating of personnel policies with other policies (Clark, 1993; Blyton and Turnbull, 1992).

According to Wehrmeyer (1996) the role of HRM in environmental management can be argued on the grounds of:

- The importance of people in environmental success generally;
- the origin of environmental values inside companies;
- the f   technology alone is less relevant to success than the way
              eract with it;
              plex nature of environmental issues requiring special
              communication skills;
              that since environmental management should be
              ll business activities, it requires special negotiation and
              ls to support others in their implementation.

In this chapter we first develop a model for HRM involvement in environmental management: human resource managers can integrate their function into environmental management strategies by being part of the vision for the environmental dimensions of the firm, and through training, performance appraisal and reward setting. We look at the role of HRM in designing and implementing culture change programmes, in particular. We then consider the broader and longer term concept of sustainability, and suggest another (three level) model for HRM involvement in the transition to sustainability. We develop the concept of 'concursors' of sustainable development, and 'tracking' progress towards sustainability, suggesting a framework for a form of qualitative accounting. The central idea of this framework is that sustainability-oriented strategic management should equip firms with the knowledge, skills, experience, practices and other assets required for sustainable economic development – thus ensuring a major role for the HRM function.

A MODEL OF HRM INVOLVEMENT IN ENVIRONMENTAL MANAGEMENT

Adapting a model of HRM practices first suggested by Milliman and Clair (1995) we can see the role of HRM in the implementation of environmental management as having four main elements (see Figure 8.1). Firstly, the

Figure 8.1 A Model of HRM Involvement in Environmental Management

organization must develop a vision of how it can be environmentally responsible and translate this vision into effective policies and goals. As we have argued previously in this book, that process may involve culture change strategies. Once the broad framework and philosophy is in place there is then a need for effective training to communicate the message and develop the skills necessary to implement the policy. Thirdly, the process of employee appraisal must take into account environmental performance making employees accountable for adherence to the environmental policies. This is a two way process involving feedback and consultation about the environmental goals set. Lastly, there is a need to implement reward schemes that provide the incentives to accomplish environmental objectives. In other words, pay and other recognition·must be related to environmental performance at the individual, team and corporate levels. This process of involvement provides much of the information needed for the company to assess its overall environmental strategy and to refine and set new goals. Let us now consider these four elements in a little more detail.

The Strategic Context

Top management commitment is often seen as the essential driver for a number of strategic dimensions of the firm. That is also the case here but it is also vital that employees are involved in the environmental initiatives taking place. Senior management are responsible for ensuring that the company's policies are translated into action but the real change process will occur where those people responsible for individual processes are involved in that change.

A clear environmental vision must nevertheless be the starting point because it provides the direction and call to action that can energize all employees to implement effectively the environmental programme planned. This vision needs to be translated into goals and those goals broken down into changes in practices and procedures which will produce the performance required. The role of the human resource manager must be to ensure that people are aware of the new demands being put upon them and to match job specifications to the new ways of working. Everybody must be clearly aware of their own roles and responsibilities and the part which they play in the overall corporate plan. But this is not something which can be handed down 'from on high'. It requires careful negotiation, consultation and must allow employees to be involved in the change process. Two way communication strategies will be most effective, allowing employees to be involved in goal setting at the process level and encouraging suggestions for further improvements.

The interest of the HRM profession in strategy is relatively new. Clark (1993) describes a view of HRM in which the various components of personnel activity are integrated with business policy to improve overall organizational performance, a view that requires a level of strategic vision and influence beyond the personnel department. Indeed, a people management strategy needs to recognize that the core competitiveness of organizations is rooted in people and while systems are important, human resource practitioners need to relate their work to business objectives and strategy.

Another, relatively new, strategic level concept is that of organizational learning. The human resource development branch of the profession in particular now sees its role as promoting organizational (as well as individual) learning and development. This approach emphasizes the importance of human resources, as against material resources. Indeed, since the price of environmental resources will rise relative to labour and capital, this provides an advantage to businesses which replace dependence on environmental resources with more investment in human resources.

HRM as well as having specific decision-making responsibilities in relation to the employment of staff, has a traditional concern for organizational culture and the human side of management. It now sees itself as having a strategic organizational role, with a vision of a skill-intensive, learning organization of the future; and of a powerful role for HRM in guiding the firm in that direction. This is central to the fundamental changes in culture and strategy required for sustainability.

The whole environmental drive within the organization must be firmly embedded in the company's values and culture. Often that will require a change in the way business is done, in the way the company is organized and in the general corporate culture. The rhetoric of environmentalism must be translated into effective action. As a starting point this will require human resource managers to look closely at their training programmes.

Training

The key here is to ensure that the company vision for environmental improvement is translated into effective plans and procedures and that these are, in turn, implemented. Training programmes involving general environmental education can provide employees with the basic tools and information required for the implementation of new programmes of action. But more specific training will often be required where process changes are demanded. Here, there will be a need for the human resource manager to identify the precise environmental training needs in the organization.

Essentially, there are three steps in the needs analysis approach. Firstly, it is important to determine the extent to which environmental skills and knowledge already exists in the organization. Those employees already committed to environmental issues and possessing valuable skills can be effectively used as catalysts in the change process. Secondly, it will be necessary to identify where the knowledge and skills gaps are and to determine who will receive training and what the content of that training needs to be. Thirdly, the training programme delivery needs to be planned to ensure its effectiveness. Questions relating to who will conduct the training, where it will be held, how long it will last and how it will be presented need to be addressed.

The successful implementation of the training will be crucial. If it fails then the whole environmental programme of the company is in jeopardy. Training must deliver knowledge and skills but it must also enthuse employees so that momentum is ensured and the effective implementation of new practices follows. Stress must be placed on two way communications, the need for continuous improvement, goal setting, measurement and monitoring. The human resource manager must take on a leadership role, ensuring that each and every employee is committed to the environmental improvement process and feels able to make an effective contribution in the work they do.

Change programmes often fail when momentum is lost and commitment begins to dissolve. Management must ensure that initial enthusiasm built up during the training process is maintained. Part of this leadership role will see the human resource manager integrating environmental issues into regular performance appraisal.

Training probably needs to start with some work on general ecoliteracy and a recognition that environmental considerations must be fully integrated into all aspects of any business's activities. A real impediment to progress remains a low level of understanding about the inevitable, but often unpredictable, impact that physical environmental issues have on the way we run and develop our lives and our businesses. The ecoliteracy of those working in a business therefore needs to be improved.

Training then needs to move to the issues affecting the particular business under consideration. Here the vision of the firm needs to be considered and the most significant impacts addressed. Training on environmental management systems and particular programmes in the business will be essential. Teams working on particular processes must be trained to improve the way they carry out those processes. However, many of the most serious environmental impacts in a business are often unplanned. Training individuals to carry out certain procedures and act in accordance with a particular system alone are likely to be insufficient. Training must help individuals understand the potentiality of problems and the ways to deal with them. Giving individuals more responsibility and accountability for their actions is important here. Skills need to be developed enabling the employee to take appropriate action where required and to communicate up and down the organizational hierarchy their worries, ideas and solutions.

Performance Appraisal

If environmental management programmes are to be successful then they must involve everybody and each person must be able to play a part in the change process. Employees have rights, but they also have responsibilities and here each employee must be aware that they can be held accountable for their environmental duties in performance appraisals. Equally, the appraisal process must be a two way process, allowing the employee to make comments and suggestions relating to both individual programmes and the company's overall vision.

Methods of appraisal will vary from organization to organization and from task to task. Appraisal is likely to be linked to both quantitative performance measures and qualitative evaluations of effort, commitment and the like. Employees need to know in advance how they will be appraised, the basis of that appraisal and the sort of feedback which they can expect. The appraisal process will also involve negotiation relating to expected future attainment targets and discussion relating to how these will be achieved. Where performance has not lived up to expectations there must be an opportunity for dialogue relating to the reasons for poorer performance than expected. Appraisal must therefore be a two way process allowing the individual employee to be fully involved in the process of setting attainable yet ambitious targets.

Environmental audits and reviews of environmental management systems must be designed so as to produce some of the information which can be used by the human resource manager in the appraisal process. He or she must therefore be involved in designing such evaluations and outlining the sorts of information which will be most valuable. Thus the HRM function must be seen as integral to the ongoing evaluation of company environmental performance. Unfortunately, in many organizations the environmental audit is seen as a somewhat technical ecobalance type exercise with few links to the efforts and performance of individual employees.

Rewards

The final step in the model of HRM involvement in environmental management must be to consider the development of reward programmes which will help to maintain commitment and momentum and which demonstrate the importance which the company attaches to the environmental dimensions of its business. Reward systems are likely to be closely linked to performance appraisal and contingent on the attainment of at least most of the goals set. The system must be a combination of rewarding past efforts and providing an incentive to continue to make environmental improvements.

Rewards will, of course, take many forms. Financial bonuses (paid to individuals or to teams) for improving environmental performance will be just one of the ways to generate employee involvement and commitment to environmental programmes. Other approaches include having recognition schemes for individuals, teams and divisions, as well as extra holiday allowances, sabbaticals, gifts, time off to engage in local community projects, access to further training and, of course, promotion. Of all these various modes of award, recognition schemes are perhaps the most popular. Such an approach enables the company to push its environmental message by rewarding individual or team effort and then communicating these achievements in company newsletters, environmentally related events and external corporate relations activities.

HRM AND ORGANIZATIONAL CULTURE

We have argued throughout this book, that a transition to sustainability requires a fundamental change in organizational culture and psychology. Here we explore the role of HRM in designing and implementing the culture change programmes required for effective environmental management.

Staff attitudes and organizational culture are clearly in the domain of HRM. According to Burgoyne (1995) interventions to understand and influence culture are traditional HRM territory. Payne (1991) also notes the role of personnel in the development and change of organizational culture and in creating the processes which help senior management develop and nurture a culture suitable to achieving their goals. Payne distinguishes between explicit culture (the behaviour and artefact level) and implicit culture (the beliefs, values, norms which underlie and determine the explicit behaviour). Argyris and Schon (1978), and Stacey (1993), argue that these implicit beliefs and norms are often 'undiscussable' in organizations and that such undiscussability militates against the questioning of fundamental aims and norms. Skilled (inter-personal) intervention is required to overcome such barriers. Given the major changes in aims and norms required for a transition to sustainability, very major and very skilful interventions in organizational culture seem to be required.

HRM and Eco-Efficiency

Eco-efficiency is necessary (although not sufficient) to bring about sustainability. Closed loop cycles and technology will not deliver superior environmental performance alone however, and eco-efficiency will also require employees to be centrally involved in environmental management systems which put programmes of action in place. Thus moves towards giving greater responsibility for environmental issues to employees at all levels will be important. Teamworking, clear communications strategies and relevant employee reward systems are central here.

Empowerment and Developing the Skill of Individuals

Eco-efficiency means producing 'better from less'. That implies investing more in the training and development of people who work with physical resources, including manual workers and office workers. Many training officers and trade union representatives would support such a priority, while many environmentalists would recognize that the skilful and economical use of resources is preferable to recycling wasteful or unnecessary products. Investment in training also gives a message of valuing the people being trained.

A programme of environmental action requires the education and motivation of all staff. It necessitates the empowerment of workers and the development of their communication skills in line with the operation of the environmental management system approach proposed above. This suggests ecological awareness and inter-personal communication skills training for workers and the inclusion of such awareness and skills in the personnel specifications for these new posts.

Environmental Education

Environmental education should be seen as central to the development of individuals' skills as well as part of a wider discussion of ethical issues in a business. Managers (of all types) can contribute by supporting environmental education initiatives from wherever they come in the company. For instance, they can help publicize the events organized by energy conservation or other environmental specialists, and advise them on training methods and materials.

Educational and development measures to promote environmental awareness, and to aid the substitution of human skill and technological ingenuity, might include:

- Promoting the creation of databases and communication systems that help everyone understand the environmental impact of the company;
- providing induction/refresher training on environmental policies;
- promoting discussion about the impact of individual decisions and the identification of company-wide environmentally abusive practices;
- feeding back staff concerns and ideas to senior managers in order to foster debate about environmental issues.

Developing a Culture of Care and Trust

Wallace (1995) in his study of environmental policy in different countries noted how the Japanese business commitment to long-term employment seemed to foster trust and communication, and therefore to help firms tackle environmental problems. By contrast, the prevailing climate in most Western countries seems to be one of insecurity with fears about downsizing and job loss. People facing possible redundancy will be less than motivated by their employers' environmental programmes.

Helping Reframe Perspectives on Motivation and Reward

Given the likely constraint on material rewards, the great challenge for management will be to motivate people to, and through, personal development, and to the use of their energy, skills and ingenuity. The firm needs to build intrinsic motivation, opportunities for peer group acclaim or other means of reward and valuing people. This will only really be achieved by addressing the culture of the organization and implementing culture change strategies as advocated in earlier chapters of this book.

More specifically, the principles of the reward strategy we are advocating might be implemented through the following pay and benefits and/or staff appraisal measures:

- Rewarding innovative ideas and setting sustainability standards and targets in relation to team and individual performance;
- promoting the use of eco-auditing of the business and linking recorded performance to reward;
- building a degree of environmental performance evaluation into all employee assessments;
- greater security in work contracts.

HUMAN RESOURCE MANAGEMENT AND SUSTAINABLE DEVELOPMENT

There is a need to explore a range of HRM or personnel decisions that impact on sustainability-related decisions. Firstly there are the direct personnel decisions relating to issues such as recruitment, training, education, work practices, equal opportunities, management style and participatory arrangements which have been discussed throughout this book and which will all be important in various ways. Secondly, HRM has a less direct, but nevertheless important, influence on other organizational activities such as production, service delivery, marketing, distribution and supply acquisition, that result in environmental problems. The importance of training and staff development, of appraisal systems, and of pay and benefit systems, in support of environmental management programmes generally, is well recognized. The International Chamber of Commerce (1991), and Milliman and Clair (1995), argue that these processes should support or facilitate the attainment of environmental goals.

Thirdly, many commentators including Welford (1995), Fineman (1997), and Hutchinson (1992) argue that a transition to sustainability requires very fundamental changes in both the culture and strategy of the organization. The major changes required will include a radical rethink of the very existence of certain industries, and of certain practices common to all industries and services. Ultimately, green business could mean less business, as is argued by Elkington et al (1995) – less transport, less fashion, less non-seasonal fruit and vegetables and less energy.

McLaren (1995) however argues that sustainability does not necessarily require a reduction in standards of living. He suggests two broad strategies. Firstly, by increasing efficiency in the use of environmental resources, a smaller resource flow can maintain the same or higher levels of consumption, with improvements in product design and durability. Secondly, by applying the concept of 'sufficiency' it is possible to identify where we already have enough and where reduced consumption would improve our quality of life. This is something that both individuals and businesses must think about.

What the HRM profession has to offer would seem to have potential relevance to such fundamental changes. Personnel and training practitioners have a traditional concern for culture and the human side of management. But the new HRM profession sees itself as having a more powerful, strategic organizational role. Pedlar et al (1991) argue for a wider range of responsibilities for the HRM function including ensuring that all staff are informed about, and involved in, ethical issues and major business decisions. Indeed this involvement must spread to a consideration of how to move towards more sustainable industrial development. The human resource manager will have a leading role to play in encouraging and tracking this (see the following section). The ongoing ethical debate needs to include the ecological implications of the functions, processes and products of the organization. Staff at all levels will need an understanding of such questions as 'true environmental impact' and the implications for business. In addition, HRM is concerned about the motivation of staff and reward systems. Money is the primary means of reward, and money is a means to the consumption of goods and services. If intrinsic reward and/or non-material reward systems replaced extrinsic and/or material rewards, to some extent, could this help to reduce ecologically damaging consumption?

TRACKING PERFORMANCE: CONCURSORS OF SUSTAINABLE INDUSTRIAL DEVELOPMENT

Because sustainable development is such an imprecise term, open to wide interpretations, it is not possible to quantitatively measure positions and rates of change in terms of objective sustainability goals and targets. It is however, possible to qualitatively assess practices, competencies, capabilities, and other intangible assets to see whether they generally line up with sustainable development principles. Such assessments can serve as generally correlated indications, companion variables, or concursors of positive performance toward sustainability. The word concursor has been coined here to communicate a compound meaning: it is a thing which occurs with – runs alongside – something else, but where there is no clear way of knowing whether it is a cause, an effect, a characteristic, or simply a separate but related companion of that thing. The intention of this meaning is to de-emphasize concerns about causality and measurement, and to emphasize the naturalness and reasonableness of the association between the thing and its concursor. It is our assertion that the human resource management function is inextricably linked to the tracking of performance and therefore linked to the definition of concursors.

Concursors are not to be seen as indicators, they are not intended to be used as ways to literally sense the firm's environmental performance either directly or through some causally related, time lagged derivative variable (eg training programmes, reward systems, management commitment, information for suppliers, etc which have all been considered earlier in this book). The idea of concursors is different. They are to be regarded as 'fellow travellers' of sustainable development, although not necessarily causes or reflections of it. At a common sense level, it is possible to imagine them as things which, given wide enough application, will either lead to sustainable development or at least equip companies with an enhanced ability to survive and prosper in conditions which sustainable development might give rise to. However, the main point here is to avoid trying to rely on clear goals and coherent indicators of one's position relative to those goals, and to instead focus on action which is reasonable both with regard to current business realities and likely future trends. A number of concursors of sustainable industrial development are proposed below.

Action Comes First: Doing the Right Thing

A common formulation of the distinction between strategy and tactics is: 'Strategy is doing the right thing. ... Tactics is doing things right' (Michaelson 1987, p4). Even if it is very difficult for firms to know whether they are doing things right with relation to sustainability thresholds in a qualitative sense it is possible to draw conclusions about whether the right things are being done. Although the inventory of 'right things' will likely evolve quite rapidly and dramatically as we learn more about sustainable development, for the moment a list to encourage improved environmental performance might include:

- A well developed environmental mission statement or policy;
- an effective corporation-wide environmental management function;
- the implementation of standardized environmental management systems, which include auditing programmes;
- the publication of annual environmental reports;
- effective internal training programmes;
- corporate programmes to investigate and encourage the use of tools such as design-for-environment (DFE), cleaner production, industrial ecology, and cleaner production; and
- an active engagement in extended producer responsibility, product stewardship and life-cycle assessment.

A variety of frameworks of greater or lesser specificity have been developed to help managers explore the extent which such an inventory might encompass, such as the environmental value chain (ADL, 1991), an organizational model for environmental issues (Hutchinson, 1992), a 'strategic star' for environmental management (Steger, 1993), and a 'metabolic chart of a prototypical company' (Callenbach et al, 1993).

Beyond questions of advanced environmental performance, it is more difficult to know how to include the right things as far as social equity, futurity, human rights, and the other non-ecological aspects of sustainable development are concerned. Corporate practices would have to be examined more broadly to analyse concursors of the social dimensions which appear to be tightly bound with ecological degradation. However, some attempt at defining indicators of sustainability has been made by Welford (1996).

Sincerity and Authenticity

If it is not possible to foresee where one will end up, nor to know where one is at any given moment, then hard, sincere, focused effort will produce useful results, and moreover, since one cannot do any more in such a situation, and assuming that no competitor has superior information, this is a competitively optimal policy as well. For an external stakeholder it may be very hard to assess whether such a policy is actually leading anywhere or whether it is simply a surrogate for performance. However, if we choose to consider this a valid form of sustainability-oriented performance – given that the right kinds of efforts are involved – then a key indicator will be the sincerity and authenticity of the effort. For example, we can ask whether a company's efforts with environmental management systems are genuine or whether they appear primarily designed to obtain certificates to hang on walls. Or, we could ask whether overall attempts to reduce direct and indirect environmental effects over a broad array of product lines, regardless of barriers, competitive considerations, and institutional inertia, are genuine. One way of demonstrating sincerity and authenticity is to make all actions accountable, transparent, and credible.

Embracing Paradox

Sustainability-oriented strategic management is fraught with conflicts, contra-dictions, difficult trade-offs, and paradoxes. Examples of these include: the persistently recurrent incompatibility of investments in environmental quality with short-term business performance; the paradox that the state, supposedly the guardian of public needs and the interests of the weak, the unborn, and the non-human, can be co-opted by private interests; and, the apparently common tendency of managers in companies to overlook investments in cleaner production which can be shown to offer attractive returns on investment. Trying to develop clear quantitative systems of indicators may eliminate such realities on paper, but it does not resolve them in practice. Acceptance of this in a spirit of proactivity as opposed to resignation could also be an important concursor of sustainable industrial development.

Equipping for Higher Level Learning

A great deal has been written during the past decade or two on the subject of organizational learning (Senge, 1990) with much of it based on work such as March and Olsen (1976) and Argyris and Schon (1978). While this subject can become very detailed and arcane, a central concept is the idea that organiza-tions as a whole can learn new approaches to solving problems and balancing their internal integrity (demanded by the need to be efficient) with their flexibility (demanded by the need to adapt to a dynamic environment). While organizations do not possess 'group minds' disembodied from the brains of the individuals which make them up, they are characterized by fairly stable patterns of thinking, communication, and behaviour as they are repeatedly performed by their members. Changes in these patterns can be seen as a reflection of collective, collaborative learning.

Most theories of organizational learning divide learning into spectra that range from, at one end, simpler changes in certain patterns that do not require changes in more basic assumptions, to, at the other, broad changes in fundamental ways in which the organization works. ADL (1996), for example, classifies learning in connection with sustainable industrial development into three different types: incremental learning, redesign, and rethinking. Incremental change focuses on picking the low-hanging fruit of environmental performance improvements. Redesign requires basic reformulations of products and processes, an example being the elimination and replacement of CFCs in many industries. Rethinking is described as 'most radical,' and involves a complete revolution in frameworks of thought and action.

A concursor of sustainability-oriented strategic management might be, given the complexity, ambiguity, and uncertainty of its context, an active commitment to engage in processes which can lead to higher levels of learning, with the understanding that new and vital areas of organizational capability may result. This could involve, for example, experiments with new forms of environmental management, collaborative ventures with stakeholders with which there has been little interaction in the past, and novel forms of internal environmental training which use techniques like simulations, role-playing, and outdoor adventure-based experiential learning.

Collaborating

As already suggested, collaborative or co-operative relationships with, for example, customers, suppliers, or regulatory authorities is a likely concursor. New capabilities might emerge from such contacts, especially if a company has historically had little stakeholder interaction beyond simple commercial transactions, and one capability which would certainly develop is a better ability to manage such relationships in a way which preserves and enhances competitiveness. Collaboration can take the form of expanding the exchange of information, as in the case of public disclosure of environmental reports, as well as pursuing projects together and jointly sponsoring activities.

Finding the Right Map Among the Archetypes

The way of seeing reality which members of an organization use in common can be called a shared mental model or map. Comprehending the ecological reality in which a firm operates, from which many other compelling realities like environmental regulation and the prices of natural resources might be seen as derivatives, requires the use of mental models. Such models may often differ markedly from the ways in which members of an organization have traditionally viewed their own activities, their industry, their market, etc. Much of the present debate surrounding environmental management and sustainable development, and from which are emerging, among other things, calls for quantifiable indicators, obtains its energy from the fact that older mental models have become inadequate.

Interestingly, there does not seem to be an infinite number of distinct mental models. Instead, the models being proposed appear to spring from a limited number of archetypal models (many incorporated into the language of systems theory). They include the idea of circular flows of materials and energy, the idea of hierarchies of organization or aggregation in nature and society (which can be imagined in terms of pyramids or concentric circles), the idea of closed versus open systems, and the idea of networks of relationships (of which the stakeholder model is only one variant). In firms developing strategic management in which sustainability is systematically considered, one would expect people to be critically and open mindedly exploring the ecological and social models available and those which might be appropriate.

Not Forgetting that a Map is Only a Map

'The map is not the territory.' An additional aspect of the previous concursor is this maxim, commonly used in discussions of management and organization. Regardless of which mental model we adopt to evaluate our position, set goals, make strategic and tactical decisions, or measure progress, it will always be a representation of the territory in which we are operating, rather than the territory itself.

Sustainable industrial development is, as Gray (1993) suggests, a territory of presently very obscure topography and landmarks. A danger in hastily adopting systems of indicators based on our present rather incomplete knowledge is that, when implemented and codified into widespread practice, they can begin to become the territory in people's eyes, instead of merely aspects of a map. Such danger exists with all instruments of environmental policy and management when they become incorporated into company practices. For example, a great deal of emphasis is currently being placed on the life cycle concept as a tool of strategic environmental management. This naturally leads to consideration of the potential for recycling or reusing scrapped products. What it can on the other hand completely fail to focus attention on is the question of whether the cycle should exist in the first place, or how it interacts with other cycles (eg in the case of complementary products). These are not part of the 'map'. An important concursor must therefore be diligent attention to the difference between maps and territories.

Identifying Critical Strategic Parameters

Despite the need to be action-oriented, aware of paradoxes, open to learning and to think about new mental models, and given the great uncertainty of this context, one cannot avoid the necessity of prioritizing action, if action is not to be random and incoherent. Companies developing sustainability-oriented strategic management will therefore routinely identify and prioritize critical strategic parameters or factors which are associated with sustainable development. These must vary greatly depending on the industry and company in question, but in general terms might include the future prices of raw materials and other natural resources, the preferences of customers, trends in environmental regulation, changes in technologies, and, in particular, the firm's own innovativeness and other capacities. Looking beyond future scenarios in which gradual environmentally related changes occur in industries (which seems to be the preferred perspective in much of industry), firms need to ask the question of whether there is any room at all for their processes or products in a future determined by the requirements of sustainable development.

Measuring What Should be Measured

Many things could be measured – especially aspects of a business for which numerical data exists and is regularly generated – but that is no guarantee that they lead to greater insight or better decisions. In their pursuit of developing performance indicators for better environmental reporting, many companies have provided data about their trends in environmental investment. A money figure is usually provided for each quarter or year. While this may look comforting when displayed in a colourful bar chart, it may be close to meaningless, since it is often very difficult to distinguish between environmental and other investments, and also because the magnitude of the investment may have nothing to do with its ecological effectiveness or sustainability. On the other hand, some measures may be quite useful for assessing the direction and rate of change of a company's performance in relation to suspected sustainability criteria, so the overall use of indicators must not be rejected. The key concursor lies in how the company draws the line between 'should' and 'could'.

Reflecting on What Should Not be Measured

Along with the previous concursor, companies attempting to manage their own sustainable industrial development must not forget about items which have been left outside of their systems of indicators. This gets back to the issue of mistaking the map for the territory. Items to which no indicators are attached can experience this fate for two reasons: because they simply do not mean much, or because they may mean a great deal but cannot be usefully quantified. There may be a tendency to lump these two categories together once an environmental management system, for instance, has begun to track performance indicators.

An appropriate concursor might thus be a periodic, systematic procedure for examining and reflecting upon the items left outside the indicator system, and an assessment of the important ones in qualitative terms. Failing to systematically examine and re-examine items which have been left outside of the set of quantitative indicators can lead to difficulties:

> *The first step is to measure whatever can be easily measured. This is OK as far as it goes. The second step is to disregard that which can't be easily measured or give it an arbitrary quantitative value. This is artificial and misleading. The third step is to presume that what can't be measured easily really isn't important. This is blindness. The fourth step is to say that what can't be easily measured really doesn't exist. This is suicide.*

Source: Yankelovich, 1972

Following Relevant Trends

Continuing change in the firm's task and general environments seems to be a dependable aspect of sustainable industrial development. Another concursor must therefore be an adequate strategic consideration of this change. This can be done through the tracking of trends in indicators, but must also be done in relation to more qualitative trends for which no clear numbers are available. Various market research, expert-based, and 'lateral-thinking' methods exist which can serve to produce understandings of the types of trends for which statistics do not exist.

Feeling One's Own Pulse

Organizational research within the area of environmental management is yielding interesting insights. One is that investments in environmental performance tend to lead to overall performance improvements. Another is that environmental performance can be correlated with success in recruiting, with employee loyalty and turnover, and with community relations. On the other hand, uneven greening of organizations can lead to internal conflicts and tensions.

What sustainability-oriented strategic management must always take into consideration is the fact that employees are also members of the greater society, and that they are currently being exposed to considerable opinion, scientific revelation, and political rhetoric about environmental issues when they are off the job. While there may not exist much slack between the internal world of the firm and employees' outside lives on such matters as the profit motive, sexual morality, gender issues, and other more established issues, the rapid change in public understandings of sustainable development may lead to quite a large gap at times. In view of the performance problems or opportunities which may arise from this, a concursor of sustainability-oriented strategic management may therefore be a regular programme for evaluating employee awareness, knowledge, and attitudes, and for discovering how company activities might respond to or benefit from them.

Staying Flexible

In many of the concursors above, the need is mentioned for continually reconsidering and re-evaluating various ideas, goals, strategies and practices with the understanding that – in the uncertain and vague world of sustainable development – fixed reference points are rare and most benchmarks or standards can be expected to evolve or suddenly shift. Overall flexibility must therefore be preserved, no matter how routine and stable something may temporarily appear to become. The appropriate concursor here might therefore be a management approach which incorporates job rotation, continuing training and education, and the strategic use of new ventures, new market entries, reorganizations, and so on as a kind of controlled, managed 'frame-breaking' technique to keep employees and teams flexible.

THE MANAGEMENT OF CONCURSORS

The above list of concursors constitutes a framework for a kind of qualitative accounting and performance management methodology that can be pursued without a need for clear goals, targets, or feedback. It should be possible to systematically compile an account of the firm's development of sustainability-oriented strategic capabilities using these and other appropriate concursors. Nearly all the concursors contain some element of organizational learning or development of the competencies of individual employees. This is why the framework is closely allied to the human resource management function. The central idea here is that sustainability-oriented strategic management must be primarily concerned with equipping firms with the knowledge, skills, experience, practices, and other strategic assets which sustainable industrial development will likely require, even as it attends to the more modest requirements of present day compliance and market demands. The latter must not be allowed to overshadow the former. If we know anything yet about the global environmental crisis and sustainable development, it is that the state of scientific knowledge, the concerns of the public, and ecological conditions can change quite suddenly. This demands foresight, competence, and flexibility of corporations quite apart from prior ability to incrementally comply with regulations and other demands. Systematically tracking and accounting for concursors of sustainable industrial development might serve that purpose.

CONCLUSIONS

HRM practitioners have a potential influence on certain decisions, via the particular functions and processes they are responsible for, and through their influence on the overall strategy and culture of the organization. But, people can only develop to become skilled performers, whatever their roles, if they feel valued and they gain the confidence that comes from feeling valued. People who feel the security of being valued will feel better able to live and work according to the values elaborated in this book. They will place less emphasis on material rewards, and be more prepared to make a creative contribution wherever the opportunity arises.

Much has been written about how sustainable development, or earlier expressions like 'the steady-state economy' and 'the age of ecology', requires some kind of paradigm shift or fundamental change in human values, attitudes, beliefs, and practices. The new paradigm has often been characterized as less exploitive of nature and other humans, less materialistic, more holistic, more farsighted, less violent, more democratic, etc. Whether such a shift is indeed a possibility or even a necessity for sustainable development is impossible to logically prove, but it seems safe to say that human production, consumption, and other aspects of existence will likely undergo much rethinking and re-evaluation as this process unfolds. Staying with traditional corporate environmental management tools and their associated quantitative accounting style methods for defining goals and performance indicators may be necessary to move towards sustainable development but they surely will not be sufficient. Moreover, they also run the risk of slowing progress towards sustainability. Firstly, the standardization of certain tools can lead to inertia as businesses think that they have achieved their goal and need do no more. Secondly, the more incremental of environmental management tools, such as eco-efficiency approaches, can actually stand in the way of important changes which are necessary. And, thirdly, too many corporate environmental management tools quite simply ignore the human dimension, the organization itself and the culture of that organization. We hope that this book has gone some way in redressing that balance.

References

REFERENCES TO CHAPTER 2

Argyris, C and Schon, D (1978) *Organizational Learning: A Theory of Action Perspective* Addison-Wesley, London

Ballard, D (1994) 'Agreeing Environmental Targets' in Taylor, B, Hutchinson, C, Pollack, S and Tapper, R (eds) *Introduction to Environmental Management Handbook* Pitman Publishing, London

Bate, P (1990) 'Using the Culture Concept in an Organization Development Setting' *Journal of Applied Behavioural Sciences*, Vol 26 No 1, pp24–47

Beckhard, R and Harris, R (1987) *Organizational Transitions: Managing Complex Change* Addison-Wesley, London

Bolman, L G and Deal, T E (1991) *Reframing Organization* Jossey Bass, San Francisco

Capra, F (1983) *The Turning Point: Science, Society and the Rising Culture* Wildwood House, San Francisco

Critchley, B (1994) 'Change – Evolution or Revolution?' *Proceedings of South Bank University Consultancy Conference* South Bank University, London

Department of the Environment (1996) *Indicators for Sustainable Development for the UK* HMSO, London

ECOTEC Consultancy (1993) *Reducing Transport Emissions Through Planning* Department of the Environment/HMSO, London

Fineman, S (1997) 'Constructing the Green Manager' *Brit Journal of Management* (forthcoming)

Fischer, K and Schot, J (1994) 'Greening of Industry Network News' *Business Strategy and Environment*, Vol 3, Part 2

Fowler, A (1993) 'Manage Culture Change' *Personnel Management Plus*, Nov 1993, pp37–42

Galbraith, J K (1969) *The Affluent Society* Pelican Books, London

Gore, A (1992) *Earth in the Balance* Earthscan, London

Gummesson, E (1991) *Qualitative Methods in Management Research* Sage, London

Harrison, M (1987) *Diagnosing Organisations: Methods, Models & Processes* Sage, London

Hawkins, P (1995) *Creating A Learning Organisation Through Culture Change* – unpublished Master Class delivered at South Bank University, London

Hawkins, P and Miller, E (1993) 'Psychotherapy in and within the Organisation' in *The Handbook of Psychotherapy* Routledge and Keegan Paul, London

Joseph, S (1996) Editorial in *Transport Report* Vol 19 No 1, pp1–2

Klinkers, L and Nelissen, N (1995) 'Environmental Campaigning: How to Promote Employee Participation' *Greener Management International* 10, pp96–109

Leggett, J (1994) 'Climate Change and the Financial Sector' *Annual Lecture to the Society of Fellows* Chartered Insurance Institute, London

Lewin, K (1951) *Field Theory in Social Science* Harper Row, New York

Margerison, C J (1988) *Practical Consulting Skills* Gower, London

Marsh, P and Collett, P (1986) *Driving Passion – The Psychology of the Car* Jonathon Cape, London

McLaren, D (1995) *Environmental Space – Measuring the Dimensions of Sustainability* Environment Council (UK) Business & Environment Ecofacts Series, London

McKeown, T (1979) *The Role of Medicine: Dream, Mirage or Nemesis?* Blackwell, Oxford

Pettigrew, A, Fairlie, E and McKee, L (1992) *Shaping Strategic Change* Sage, London

Pietroni, P (1986) *Holistic Living* JM Dent, London

Rees, P K (1994), 'Environmental Management in a Construction Business' in Taylor, B, Hutchinson, C, Pollack, S and Tapper, R (eds), *Introduction to Environmental Management Handbook* Pitman Publishing, London

Schein, E (1987) *Process Consultation* Vol 2 Addison-Wesley, London

Stacey, R (1993), *Strategic Management and Organisational Dynamics* Pitman Publishing, London

Welford, R (1994), 'What Environmental Reporting Reveals About Sustainable Development' *Business Strategy and the Environment* Vol 3 Part 1

Whitelegg, J (1993) *Transport for a Sustainable Future* Belhaven, London

Whitelegg, J (1995) 'Up, Up and Away' *New Ground* (Journal of the UK Socialist Environment and Resources Association), Winter 1995, pp8–15

REFERENCES TO CHAPTER 3

Aldrich, P T and Lorentzen, B (1994) 'The Role of the Employees in Companies' Environmental Protection Activities' *Paper presented at the 3rd International Research Conference of the Greening of Industry Network*, Copenhagen, Denmark

Arthur D Little (1995a) 'Hitting the Green Wall' *Perspectives* brochure

Arthur D Little (1995b) *Results of Arthur D. Little's 1995 Survey on 'Hitting the Green Wall'* EHS Communications Office, Cambridge, Massachusetts

Bunge, J, Cohen-Rosenthal, E and Ruiz-Quintanilla, A (1995) 'Employee Participation in Pollution Reduction: Preliminary Analysis of the Toxics Release Inventory' *Paper presented at the 4th International Research Conference of the Greening of Industry Network*, Toronto

Daley, H E and Cobb, J B Jr (1989) *For the Common Good* Beacon Press, Boston, Massachusetts

Denton, D K (1994) *Enviro-Management* Prentice Hall, Englewood Cliffs, New Jersey

Donaldson, L (1995) *American Anti-Management Theories of Organization* Cambridge University Press, Cambridge, UK

Dorfman, M H, Muir, W R and Miller, C G (1992) *Environmental Dividends: Cutting More Chemical Wastes* Inform, New York

Ehrlich, P R and Ehrlich, A H (1991) *Healing the Planet* Addison-Wesley, Reading, Massachusetts

Gabel, H L and Sinclair-Desgagne, B (1993) 'From Market Failure to Organisational Failure', *Paper presented at the 2nd International Research Conference of the Greening of Industry Network*, Cambridge, Massachusetts

Gherardi, S and Turner, B (1987) 'Real Men Don't Collect Soft Data' *Quaderno* 13 Dipartimento di Politica Sociale, Universita di Trento

Gladwin, T N (1993) 'The Meaning of Greening: A Plea for Organizational Theory' in Fischer, K and Schot, J (eds), *Environmental Strategies for Industry – International Perspectives on Research Needs and Policy Implications* Island Press, Covelo, California

Hardin, G (1968) 'The Tragedy of the Commons' *Science*, Vol 162, pp1243–48

Huisingh, D, Martin, L, Hilger, H and Seldman, N (1986) *Proven Profits from Pollution Prevention: Case Studies in Resource Conservation and Waste Reduction* Institute for Local Self-Reliance, Washington, DC

Jones, D R (1996) 'The Sustainable Enterprise: Embracing and Promoting the Paradox' in Ulhøi, J P and Madsen, H (eds), *Industry and the Environment* (published proceedings of the 3rd Conference of the Nordic Business Environmental Management Network, Aarhus, Denmark, March 28–30, 1996), The Aarhus School of Business

March, J G (1994) Lecture on the current state of organization theory, delivered at Copenhagen Business School, May 1994

Martin, J (1992) *Cultures in Organizations – Three Perspectives* Oxford University Press, New York

Mayo, E (1946) *Human Problems in an Industrial Civilization* Macmillan, New York

Meima, R (1996) 'The Alpha Case. A Grounded Theory of Corporate Environmental Management in an IT Company' in Ulhøi, J P and Madsen, H (eds), *Industry and the Environment* (published proceedings of the 3rd Conference of the Nordic Business Environmental Management Network, Aarhus, Denmark, March 28–30, 1996), The Aarhus School of Business

Morgan, G (1986) *Images of Organization* Sage, London

Nielsen, L and Remmen, A (1994) 'Environmental Management – Employee Participation and Continuous Improvements' *Paper presented at the 3rd International Research Conference of the Greening of Industry Network*, Copenhagen, Denmark

Peters, T J and Waterman, R H Jr (1982) *In Search of Excellence* Harper and Row, New York

Piasecki, B W (1995) *Corporate Environmental Strategy – The Avalanche of Change Since Bhopal* John Wiley and Sons, New York

Pinchot, G 3rd (1985) *Intrapreneuring* Harper and Row, New York

Räsänen, K (1994) 'Pioneering Descriptions of Corporate Greening: Notes and Doubts on the Emerging Discussion' *Business Strategy and the Environment*, Vol 3 (4), pp9–16

Robèrt, K-H (1994) *Den Naturliga Utmaningen (The Natural Challenge)* Ekerlids Förlag, Stockholm

Roethlisberger, F J and Dickson, W J (1947) *Management and the Worker* Harvard University Press, Cambridge, Massachusetts

Romm, J J (1994) *Lean and Clean Management* Kodansha International Ltd, New York

Smart, B (1992) *Beyond Compliance – A New Industry View of the Environment* World Resources Institute, Washington, DC

Stacey, R D (1995) 'The Science of Complexity: An Alternative Perspective for Strategic Change Processes' *Strategic Management Journal*, Vol 16 (6), pp477–495

von Krogh, J and Roos, J (1995) *Organizational Epistemology* St. Martin's Press, New York

Weick, K E (1969) *The Social Psychology of Organizing* Addison-Wesley, Reading, Massachusetts

Weick, K E (1989) 'Theory Construction as Disciplined Imagination' *Academy of Management Review*, Vol 14 (4), pp516–531

Weick, K E (1995) *Sensemaking in Organizations* Sage, Thousand Oaks, California

Weick, K E and Roberts, K H (1993) 'Collective Mind in Organizations: Heedful Interrelating on Flight Decks' *Administrative Science Quarterly* Vol 38, pp357–81

REFERENCES TO CHAPTER 4

Abraham, K and Houseman, S (1994) 'Does Employment Protection Inhibit Labour Market Flexibility?' *US National Bureau of Economic Research (NBER) Working Paper* 4390

Argyris, C (1982) 'Research as Action: Usable Knowledge for Understanding and Changing the Status Quo' in Nicholson, N and Wall, T (eds) *The Theory and Practice of Organizational Psychology* Academic Press, London

Argyris, C and Schon, D (1978) *Organizational Learning: A Theory of Action Perspective* Addison-Wesley, London

Commoner, B (1974) *The Closing Circle* Cape, London

Co-operative Advisory Group (CAG Consultancy) (1986) *Greater London Council's Co-operative Development Plans 1981–6: an Evaluation* CAG/Greater London Enterprise Board, London

De Board, R (1978) *The Psychoanalysis of Organizations* Tavistock Publications, London

Freeman, J (1972) 'The Tyranny of Structurelessness' *Berkeley Journal of Sociology*, 72, pp151–164

Gore, A (1992) *Earth in the Balance* Earthscan, London

Gorz, A (1989) 'A Land of Cockayne' *New Statesman and Society*, 12 May

Galbraith, J K (1969) *The Affluent Society* Pelican Books, London

Handy, C (1985) *Understanding Organizations* Penguin, Harmondsworth

Handy, C (1994) *The Empty Raincoat* Hutchinson, London

Harrison, R (1987) 'Organization Culture and Quality of Service' *UK Association for Management Education and Development Focus Paper*, London

Hirschhorn, L (1990) *The Work Place Within* MIT Press, Massachusetts

Hofstede, G (1983) *Culture and Management Development* International Labour Office, Geneva

Hutton, W (1994) 'Happiness that Money Truly Cannot Buy' *The Guardian* 27 Dec p13

Landry, C et al (1985) *What a Way to Run a Railroad* Comedia, London

March, J G (1984) 'Theories of Choice and Making Decisions' in Paton, R et al (ed) *Organizations – Cases, Issues, Concepts* Harper/Open University, Milton Keynes

Marsh, P and Collett, P (1986) *Driving Passion – The Psychology of the Car* Jonathon Cape, London

Menzies, I E P (1970) *The Functioning of Social Systems as a Defence against Anxiety* Tavistock Institute of Human Relations, London

Moore, T and Hanton A (1995) *Company Cars (a briefing document)* Environmental Transport Association/Transport 2000, London

Paton, R (1978) *Some Problems of Co-operative Organisation* Co-operatives Research Unit (Open University), Milton Keynes

Pedlar, M, Boydell, T and Burgoyne, J (1988) *Learning Company Project Report* (UK Govt) Employment Department Training Group, London

Prowse, P (1990) 'Assessing the Flexible Firm' *Personnel Review*, Vol 19, No 6, pp27–31

Pugh, D and Hickson, D (1989) *Writers on Organisations* Penguin, London

Seabrook, J (1988) *The Race for Riches* Green Print/Marshall Pickering, Sheffield

Skynner, R (1992) 'A Kind of Unloving' *Guardian Weekend*, 30 May p8

Skynner, R (1995) *Family Matters* Methuen, London

Steiner, C M (1979) *Scripts People Live* Bantam Books, New York

Walker, M (1993) 'Clinton Inherits a Windfall Economic Miracle' *The Guardian* 23 Dec, p11

REFERENCES TO CHAPTER 5

Aerschot, A and Heikura, P (1995) 'Tampere Hall: An Environmentally Conscious Congress Venue in Finland' *UNEP Industry and Environment*, April–Sept, pp105–107

Aldrich, P T and Lorentzen, B (1994) 'The Role of the Employees in the Companies' Environmental Protection Activities' *Paper presented at the Greening of the Industry Conference*, Copenhagen, Denmark, Nov pp13–15

Barrett, S and Murphy, D (1995) 'The Implications of the Corporate Environmental Policy Process for Human Resources Management' *Greener Management International*, Vol 10, pp49–68

Bartunek, J (1984) 'Changing Interpretative Schemes and Organizational Restructuring: The Example of a Religious Order' *Administrative Science Quarterly*, Vol 29, pp355–372

Bettis, R and Pralahad, C (1995) 'The Dominant Logic: Retrospective and Extension' *Strategic Management Journal*, Vol 16, pp5–14

Brauchlin, E (1988) 'Ökogerechte Unternehmungs-Strategien' *Thexis* 3

Callenbach, E, Capra, F, Goldman, L, Lutz, R and Marburg, S (1993) *EcoManagement* Berrett-Koehler Publishers, San Francisco

Cialdini, R. (1988) *Influence* HarperCollins Publishers, New York

Dutton, J and Duncan, R (1987) 'The Creation of Momentum for Change Through the Process of Strategic Issue Diagnosis' *Strategic Management Journal*, Vol 8, pp279–295

Ekholm, R (1996) 'Hoechst Stumbles in Environmental Issues' *Tekniikka ja Talous* 22.2, 8 (in Finnish)

Gersick, C (1991) 'Revolutionary Change Theories: A Multilevel Exploration of the Punctuated Equilibrium Paradigm' *Academy of Management Review*, Vol 16, No 1, pp10–36

Goodpaster, K (1989) 'Can Corporations Have Environmental Conscience?' in Hoffman, M, Frederick, R and Petry, E (eds) *The Corporation, Ethics and the Environment* Quorum Books, Connecticut

Halme, M (1996) 'Shifting Environmental Management Paradigms in Two Finnish Paper Facilities: A Broader View of Institutional Theory' *Business Strategy and the Environment*, Vol 5, p2

Halme, M (1995) *Environmental Management Experiences in SMEs* University of Tampere A2:62 (in Finnish)

Halme, M (1994a) *Environmental Issues in Product Development Process: Paradigm Shift in a Packaging Company* University of Tampere A1:39

Halme, M (1994b) 'Managerial Processes Behind Organizations' Environmental Transformation Efforts' *Paper presented at the Greening of the Industry Conference*, Copenhagen, Denmark, Nov 13–15

Hedberg, B (1981) 'How Organizations Learn and Unlearn?' in Nyström, P C and Starbuck, W (eds) *Handbook of Organizational Design* Oxford University Press, London

Hendry, J and Hope, V (1994) 'Cultural Change and Competitive Performance' *European Management Journal*, Vol 12, No 4, pp401–406

Jennings, P D and Zandbergen, P (1995) 'Ecologically Sustainable Organizations: An Institutional Approach' *Academy of Management Review*, Vol 20, No 4, pp1015–1052

Jones, D R (1995) 'The Sustainable Enterprise: Embracing and Promoting the Paradox' *Paper presented at the Greening of the Industry Conference*, Toronto, Canada, Nov pp12–14

Jose, P D (1995) 'Greening through Strategic Adaption: A Process Study of Selected Firms in the Indian Industry' *Paper presented at the Greening of the Industry Conference*, Toronto, Canada, Nov pp12–14

Karlsson, M (1995) *Green Concurrent Development – En Konceptidé för Miljöanpassad Utveckling* University of Lund, the International Institute for Industrial Environmental Economics. Unpublished

Kerr, J and Slocum, J (1987) 'Managing Corporate Culture through Reward Systems' *Academy of Management Executive*, Vol 1, No 2, pp99–108

Klinkers, L and Nelissen, N (1995) 'Environmental Campaigning: How to Promote Employee Participation in Environmental Policies' *Greener Management International*, Vol 10, pp96–109

Linnanen, L, Boström, T and Miettinen, P (1994) *Life Cycle Management* Weilin and Göös, Espoo, Finland

Linnanen, L (1995) Market Dynamics and Sustainable Organizations: HRM Implications in the Pulp and Paper Industry's Management of Environmental Issues *Greener Management International*, Vol 10, pp85–124

McCann, J and Galbraith, J (1981) 'Interdepartmental Relations' in Nystrom, P and Starbuck, W (eds) *Handbook of Organizational Design: Remodeling Organizations and Their Environments* Oxford University Press, Oxford

Meima, R (1995) '"The Vanguard" A Story of Corporate Environmental Management in an IT Company' *Paper presented at the Greening of the Industry Conference*, Toronto, Canada, Nov pp2–14

Milliman, J and Clair, J (1995) 'Environmental HRM Best Practices in the USA: A Review of the Literature' *Greener Management International*, Vol 10, pp34–48

Netherwood, A (1996) 'Environmental Management Systems' in Welford, R (ed) *Corporate Environmental Management: Systems and Strategies* Earthscan Publications, London

Nielsen, L and Remmen, A (1994) 'Environmental Management – Employee Participation and Continuous Improvements' *Paper presented at the Greening of the Industry Conference*, Copenhagen, Denmark, Nov pp13–15

Nonaka, I (1994) 'A Dynamic Theory of Organizational Knowledge Creation' *Organization Science*, Vol 5, No 1, pp14–37

Post, J and Altman, B (1992) 'Models of Corporate Greening: How Corporate Social Policy and Organizational Learning Inform Leading-Edge Environmental Management' *Research in Corporate Social Performance and Policy*, Vol 13, pp3–29

Schmidheiny, S (1992) *Changing Course* MIT Press, Cambridge, MA

Shrivastava, P. (1995) 'Ecocentric Management for a Risk Society' *Academy of Management Review*, Vol 20, No 1, pp118–137

Servatius, H-G (1992) 'Umsetzung Umweltbewusster Führung als Prozess eines Kulturellen Wandels' in *Umweltmanagement als Chance – Ökologische Wege in die Zukunft* Studentinitiative Wirtschaft und Umwelt, Druckwerstatt, Münster

Smart, B (1992) *Beyond Compliance: A New Industry View of the Environment* World Resources Institute, Washington DC

Tushman, M and Romanelli, E (1985) 'Organizational Evolution: A Metamorphosis Model of Convergence and Reorientation' in Cummings, L and Staw, B (eds) *Research in Organizational Behavior*, Vol 7, pp171–22 JAI Press, Greenwich, CT

Weick, K (1995) *Sensemaking in Organizations* Sage, Thousand Oaks, New York

Welford, R (1996) *Corporate Environmental Management: Systems and Strategies* Earthscan Publications, London

Wolters, T, Bouman, M and Peeters, M (1995) 'Environmental Management and Employment' *Greener Management International*, Vol 11, issue July, pp64–71

Wuori, M (1995) *Dream of Faust* Weilinn and Göös, Helsinki (in Finnish)

REFERENCES TO CHAPTER 6

Ansoff, H I and McDonnell, E J (1987) *The New Corporate Strategy* John Wiley and Sons, New York

Bass, B M (1985) *Leadership and Performance Beyond Expectations* Free Press, New York

Blake, R A and Mouton, J S (1985) *The Managerial Grid III* Gulf Publishing, Houston, Texas

Buzzell, R D and Gale, B T (1987) *The PIMS Principles: Linking Strategy to Performance* Free Press, New York

Chandler, A D (1962) *Strategy and Structure* MIT Press, Boston, MA

Chatman, J A (1991) 'Matching People and Organizations: Selection and Socialization in Public Accounting Firms' *Administrative Science Quarterly*, Vol 36, pp459–484

Dodge, J L (1995) *Organizational Perspectives on Strategic Environmental Management and Performance* PhD Thesis, University of Bradford, UK

Fiedler, F E (1967) *A Theory of Leadership Effectiveness* McGraw-Hill, New York

Fiedler, F E (1986) 'The Contribution of Cognitive Resources to Leadership Performance' *Journal of Applied Social Psychology*, Vol 16, pp532–548

Fiedler, F E and Garcia, J E (1987) *New Approaches to Effective Leadership: Cognitive Resources and Organizational Performance* John Wiley and Sons, New York

Grant, R M (1991) 'The Resource-Based Theory of Competitive Advantage: Implications for Strategy Formulation' *California Management Review*, Vol 33 (3), pp114–135

Greiner, L E (1972) 'Evolution and Revolution as Organizations Grow' *Harvard Business Review*, July–August pp119–140

Hersey, P and Blanchard, K H (1988) *Management of Organizational Behavior: Utilizing Human Resources* (5th ed) Prentice-Hall, Englewood Cliffs, NJ

Hill, C and Jones, G (1992) *Strategic Management: An Integrated Approach* Houghton Mifflin Company, Boston, MA

Hofner, C W and Schendel, D (1978) *Strategy Formulation: Analytic Concepts* West Publications, St Paul MN

Killmann, R H, Saxton, M J and Serpa, R (1986) 'Issues in Understanding and Changing Culture' *California Management Review*, Vol 28, pp87–94

Lawrence, P R and Lorsch, J W (1967) *Organization and Environment* Irwin, Homewood, Illinois

Liedtka, J (1989) 'Managerial Values and Corporate Decision Making: An Empirical Analysis of Value Congruence in Two Organizations' *Research in Corporate Social Performance and Policy*, Vol 11, pp55–91

Lublin, J S (1991) 'Green Executives Find Their Mission Isn't a Natural Part of Corporate Culture' *The Wall Street Journal*, B1/B4, March 5

Meglino, B M, Ravine, E C and Adkins, C L (1989) 'A Work Values Approach to Corporate Culture: A Field Test of the Value Congruence Process and Its Relationship to Individual Outcomes' *Journal of Applied Psychology*, Vol 74 (3), pp424–432

Mintzberg, H (1983) *Power in and Around Organizations* Prentice-Hall, Englewood Cliffs, NJ

Mintzberg, H (1985) 'Of Strategies, Deliberate and Emergent' *Strategic Management Journal*, Vol 6, pp257–272

Mintzberg, H and Quinn, J B (1992) *The Strategy Process: Concepts, Context, Cases* (2nd ed) Prentice-Hall, Englewood Cliffs, NJ

O'Reilly, C (1989) 'Corporations, Culture and Commitment: Motivation and Social Control in Organizations' *California Management Review*, Vol 31 (4), pp9–25

Ouchi, W G (1979) 'A Conceptual Framework for the Design of Organizational Control Systems' *Management Science*, Vol 25, pp833–849

Pearce II, J A and Robinson, R B (1991) *Strategic Management: Formulation, Implementation and Control* (4th ed) Irwin, Homeword, Illinois

Pettigrew, A and Whipp, A (1991) 'Managing the Twin Processes of Competition and Change: The Role of Intangible Assets', proceedings of the 'Strategic Processes Research Conference', Oslo: Centre For Corporate Strategy and Change, University of Warwick

Pettigrew, A M (1977) 'Strategy Formulation as a Political Process' *International Studies of Management and Organization*, Vol 7, pp78–87

Pfeffer, J (1981) *Power in Organizations* Pitman Publishing, Boston

Rokeach, M (1979) *The Nature of Human Values* Free Press, New York

Roome, N (1992) 'Developing Environmental Management Strategies' *Business Strategy and the Environment*, Vol 1 (1) pp10–18

Tannenbaum, R and Schmidt, W H (1973) 'How to Choose a Leadership Pattern' *Harvard Business Review*, Vol 51, May–June, p164

Welford, R (1992) 'Linking Quality and the Environment: A Strategy for the Implementation of Environmental Management Systems' *Business Strategy and the Environment*, Vol 1 (1), pp9–18

Welford, R (1995) *Environmental Strategy and Sustainable Development: The Corporate Challenge for the 21st Century* Routledge, London

REFERENCES TO CHAPTER 7

Ansoff, H I (1979) 'The changing shape of the strategic problem' in Schendel, D and Hofer, C (eds) *Strategic Management: A New View of Business Policy and Planning* pp30–44 Little, Brown, Boston

Bartunek, J M and Moch, M K (1987) 'First-Order, Second-Order, and Third-Order Change and Organization Development Interventions: A Cognitive Approach' *Journal of Applied Behavioural Science*, Vol 23, pp483–500

Bate, P (1994) *Strategies for Cultural Change* Butterworth–Heinemann, Oxford

Beaumont, J R, Pedersen, L M and Whitaker, B D (1993) *Managing the Environment* Butterworth–Heinemann, Oxford

Burrows, B, Mayne, A and Newbury, P (1991) *Into the 21st Century. A Handbook for a Sustainable Future* Adamantine, Twickenham

References

Callenbach, E, Capra, F, Goldman, L, Lutz, R and Marburg, S (1993) *EcoManagement: The Elmwood Guide to Ecological Auditing and Sustainable Business* Berrett–Koehler Publishers, San Francisco

Cavanagh, G, Moberg, D and Valasquez, M (1981) 'The Ethics of Organizational Politics' *Academy of Management Review*, Vol 6 (3), pp363–374

Daly, H E and Cobb, J B Jr (1989) *For the Common Good* Beacon, Boston

Deal, T E and Kennedy, A A (1982) *Corporate Cultures* Addison–Wesley, New York

Deci, E L and Ryan, R M (1985) *Intrinsic Motivation and Self-Determination in Human Behaviour* Plenum, New York

Drambo, L (1988) 'The Futures Circle' *Social Inventions*, No 11, pp3–9

Ernst, K R, and Baginski, R M (1989) 'Visioning: The Key to Effective Strategic Planning' in Glass H E (ed) *Handbook of Business Strategy* (Chap. 22), Warren, Gorham and Lamont, Boston

Etzioni, A (1991) 'What Community, What Responsiveness?' *The Responsive Community*, Vol 2 (1), pp5–8

Freeman, R E and Gilbert, D R Jr (1988) *Corporate Strategy and the Search for Ethics* Prentice-Hall, Englewood Cliffs, NJ

Gray, R H (1994) 'Corporate Reporting for Sustainable Development: Accounting for Sustainability in 2000 AD' *Environmental Values*, Vol 3 (1), pp17–45

Halal, W E (1986) *The New Capitalism* John Wiley and Sons, New York

Heisenberg, W (1985) 'Scientific and Religious Truths' in Wilber K (ed) *Quantum Questions* (pp39–44), New Science Library, Boston

Hoe, S (1978) *The Man Who Gave His Companies' Power Away* William Heinemann, London

Jungk, R and Mullert, N (1987) *Future Workshops – How to Create Desirable Futures* Institute for Social Interventions, London

Koestler, A (1964) *The Act of Creation* Hutchinson, London

Martin, J and Siehl, A (1983) 'Organizational Culture and Counter Culture: An Uneasy Symbiosis' *Organizational Dynamics*, Vol 12 (2), pp52–64

Mayne, A J (1965) 'Creativity, Psi and Human Personality' *Research Journal of Philosophy and Social Sciences*, Vol 2, No 1, pp232–252

Milbrath, L W (1989) *Envisioning a Sustainable Society* State University of New York Press, Albany

Montaigne, M de (1958a) 'On the Education of Children', in Cohen, J M (trans) *Michel de Montaigne Essays* (pp60–65), Penguin, Middlesex, UK (Original work published in 1580)

Montaigne, M de (1958b) 'That One Man's Profit is Another's Loss', in Cohen, J M (trans), *Michel de Montaigne Essays* (pp48–53), Penguin, Middlesex, UK (Original work published in 1580)

Morgan, G (1986) *Images of Organizations* Sage, Newbury Park, CA

Ochse, R (1990) *Before the Gates of Excellence – the Determinants of Creative Genius* Cambridge University Press, Cambridge and New York

Ornstein, R and Ehrlich, P (1990) *New World, New Mind* Touchstone, New York

Peters, T J and Waterman, R H Jr (1982) *In Search of Excellence* Harper and Row, New York

Peters, T (1990) 'Prometheus Barely Unbound' *Academy of Management Executive*, Vol 4 (4), pp70–84

Post, J E and Altman, B (1991) 'Corporate Environmentalism: The Challenge of Organizational Learning' *National Academy of Management Meeting*, Miami, Florida, August 12th

Plant, J (1987) *Managing Change and Making it Stick* Fontana, London

Rickards, T (1974) *Problem Solving Through Creative Analysis* Gower Press, Epping, Essex

Rose, F (1990) 'A New Age for Business?' *Fortune*, Oct 8, pp156–164

Schein, E H (1985) *Organizational Culture and Leadership* Jossey–Bass, San Francisco

Schumacher, E F (1973) *Small is Beautiful: Economics as if People Mattered* Harper and Row, New York

Schumacher, E F (1979) *Good Work* Harper and Row, New York

Senge, P M (1990) *The Fifth Discipline: The Art and Practice of the Learning Organization* Doubleday/Currency, New York

Silk, L and Vogel, D (1976) *Ethics and Profits: The Crisis of Confidence in America* Simon and Schuster, New York

Sinclair, A (1993) 'Approaches to Organizational Culture and Ethics' *Journal of Business Ethics*, Vol 12, pp63–73

Speth, G (1990) 'The Crucial Decade: Environmental Imperatives for the 1990s' in *Proceedings of the Business Week Symposium on the Environment: Corporate Stewardship and Business Opportunity in the Decade of Global Awakening* (pp1–4), Journal Graphics, New York

Stead, W E and Stead, J E (1992) *Management for a Small Planet* Sage Publications, Newbury Park

Welford, R and Jones, D R (1996) 'Beyond Environmentalism and Towards the Sustainable Organization' in Welford, R J (ed) *Corporate Environmental Management: Systems and Strategies* Earthscan, London

Welford, R J and Prescott, C E (1994) *European Business: An Issue Based Approach* Pitman Publishing, London

Welford, R J (1995) *Environmental Strategy and Sustainable Development* Routledge, London

Welford, R J (1997) *Hijacking Environmentalism: Corporate Responses to Sustainable Development* Earthscan, London

Zenisek, T J (1979) 'Corporate Social Responsibility: A Conceptualisation Based on Organizational Literature' *Academy of Management Review*, Vol 4 (2), pp359–368

REFERENCES TO CHAPTER 8

ADL (1991) *Seizing Strategic Environmental Advantage* Arthur D. Little, Centre for Environmental Assurance, London

References

ADL (1996) *Sustainable Industrial Development – Sharing Responsibilities in a Competitive World* Conference paper prepared for the Dutch Ministries of Housing, Spatial Planning and the Environment, and Economic Affairs, Arthur D. Little, Environmental Management Europe, Brussels

Argyris, C and Schön, D A (1978) *Organizational Learning: A Theory of Action Perspective* Addison-Wesley, Reading, MA

Blyton, P and Turnbull, P (1992) *Reassessing Human Resource Management* Sage, London

Burgoyne, J (1995) 'Feeding Minds to Grow the Business' *People Management,* 21st Sept 1995, pp9–12

Callenbach, E, Capra, F, Goldman, L, Lutz, R and Marburg, S (1993) *EcoManagement – The Elmwood Guide to Ecological Auditing and Sustainable Business* Berrett-Koehler Publishers, San Francisco

Clark, I (1993) 'HRM: Prescription, Description and Content' *Personnel Review,* Vol 22 No 4, pp3–15

Elkington, J et al (1995) *Who Needs It?* Sustainability Consultancy, London

Fineman, S (1997) 'Constructing the Green Manager' *British Journal of Management* (forthcoming)

Gray, R (1993) *Accounting for the Environment* Paul Chapman Publishing Limited, London

Hutchinson, C (1992) 'Corporate Strategy and the Environment' *Long Range Planning,* Vol 25, No 4, pp140–161

International Chamber Of Commerce (1991) *Business Charter for Sustainable Development* ICC, Paris

March, J G and Olsen, J P (eds) (1976) *Ambiguity and Choice in Organizations* Universitetsforlaget, Bergen

McLaren, D (1995) *Environmental Space – Measuring the Dimensions of Sustainability* Environment Council (UK) Business and Environment Ecofacts Series, London

Michaelson, G A (1987) *Winning the Marketing War* Abt Books, London

Milliman, J and Clair, J (1995) 'Environmental HRM Best Practices in the USA' *Greener Management International,* Vol 10, pp34–48

Payne, R (1991) 'Taking Stock of Corporate Culture' *Personnel Management,* July 1995, pp49–52

Pedlar, M, Burgoyne, J and Boydell, T (1991) *The Learning Company: A Strategy for Sustainable Development* McGraw-Hill, London

Senge, P M (1990) *The Fifth Discipline – The Art and Practice of the Learning Organization* Doubleday, New York

Stacey, R (1993) *Strategic Management and Organizational Dynamics* Pitman, London

Steger, U (1993) *Umweltmanagement: Erfahrungen und Instrumente einer umweltorientierten Unternehmensstrategie* Frankfurter Allgemeine Zeitung/Wiesbaden, Gabler, Frankfurt

Wallace, D (1995) *Environmental Policy and Industrial Innovation: Strategies in Europe, the US and Japan* Earthscan Publications Ltd, London

Wehrmeyer, W (1996) *Greening People: Human Resources and Environmental Management* Greenleaf, Sheffield

Welford, R J (1995) *Environmental Strategy and Sustainable Development* Routledge, London

Welford, R (1996) *Corporate Environmental Management – Systems and Strategies* Earthscan, London

Yankelovich, D (1972) *Corporate Priorities: A Continuing Study of the New Demands on Business*, Daniel Yankelovich Inc, Stamford, CT

Index

Other Relevant Publications Available from Earthscan

Corporate Environmental Management
Systems and Strategies
Edited by Richard Welford

A clear, comprehensive guide for companies looking to build an effective environmental profile, including examinations of: environmental management systems and standards; environmental auditing; environmental policies; environmental reporting; and measuring environmental performance. It introduces the theme of systems-based environmental management and considers how it might be integrated within local authorities and small and medium-sized companies, and then extended to cover continuous environmental improvement.

£15.95 paperback   ISBN 1 85383 308 8
£35 hardback   ISBN 1 85383 303 7

A–Z of Corporate Environmental Management
Kit Sadgrove

With over 800 entries, the *A–Z of Corporate Environmental Management* provides a clear and authoritative summary of the subject. Its encyclopedic coverage includes:
- Management strategies such as ISO 14001
- UK, EU and international legislation
- General issues, eg timber
- Toxic substances, eg organochlorines
- Waste management, eg landfill
- Disasters, eg contamination at the Union Carbide plant, Bhopal
- Water pollutants, eg chlorine
- Air pollutants, eg carbon monoxide

The *A–Z* will help you to:
• Reduce your organization's impacts
• Understand major issues
• Decide which chemicals to use
• Assess whether you are complying with legislation
• Communicate with staff and customers
• Implement an environmental management system

With hundreds of best practice points, the *A–Z* shows how to reduce pollution, cut costs, improve staff motivation, increase sales and avoid litigation. Its checklists, charts and tables makes it a highly practical tool for anyone needing to understand and implement environmental management.

£18.95 paperback   ISBN 1 85383 330 4

ISO 14001
The Missed Opportunities
Riva Krut and Harris Gleckman

ISO 14001 is the new International Standard for environmental management systems. But what difference will it make to the environmental performance of companies that receive it? More crucially, will it do anything to further *sustainable* industrial development? The authors argue that it won't, and – further – that it does not have a legitimate place in discussions of sustainable industrial development.

In this compelling and alarming volume, the authors point to a massive democratic deficit in the process of establishing the standard, in which small and medium-sized enterprises, developing country companies, public opinion and environmental groups were unable to participate. This has, in turn, put up barriers to the full participation of these parties. The authors also describe how the standard reverses the trend for firms to innovate to meet the challenge of sustainability. Furthermore, under new international trade rules this new private sector standard will have an unassailable status which may result in it being used to undermine the substance of decades of debate and agreement on international environmental standards. It does not just fail to contribute to sustainable industrial development; it actually has the potential to subvert that goal. All those concerned with corporate environmental management, whether from a legal, business or environmental standpoint, should read this book.

Published in association with UNCTAD
£14.95 paperback   ISBN 1 85383 507 2
£35 hardback   ISBN 1 85383 506 4

Clean and Competitive?

Motivating Environmental Performance in Industry

Rupert Howes, Jim Skea and Bob Whelan

Reconciling wealth creation with environmental sustainability is one of the key challenges to sustainable development. Motivating business to take its environmental responsibilities seriously is also central. This book draws on the research and experience of Sussex University's Science Policy Research Unit (SPRU) and the Centre for the Exploitation of Science and Technology (CEST) to explore vexed questions of industrial motivation.

The first theme it addresses is the compatibility of environmental and economic performance – can companies become more competitive while reducing the environmental impact of their activities? A second theme is the apparent paradox of business and the environment – why do some companies' management systems and policy statements appear so virtuous when the same companies respond obstructively and negatively to environmental problems? The third is the appropriate roles of business and public policy makers – how much policy and regulation is needed? To what extent will industry put its own house in order? What role can public–private partnerships play?

The book explores in detail responses to three sets of environmental issues at the global, national and regional–local levels. The issues addressed include climate change, air quality and contaminated land. It also addresses various approaches to dealing with environmental problems, including traditional regulation, partnership approaches, voluntary agreements and market-based instruments. It concludes by offering practical ways forward for addressing an ever more complex environmental agenda. This thoughtful and articulate text will appeal to students on environmental management courses, policy makers and environmental officers within industry.

£14.95 paperback   ISBN 1 85383 490 4
£35 hardback   ISBN 1 85383 491 2

Building Corporate Accountability

Emerging Practices in Social and Ethical Accounting, Auditing and Reporting

Edited by Simon Zadek, Peter Pruzan and Richard Evans

The practice of social and ethical accounting is emerging as a key tool for companies in the 1990s in response to calls for greater transparency and accountability to different stakeholders, and as a means for managing companies in increasingly complex situations where social and environmental issues are significant in securing business success. This is the first book to address the practice of social and ethical accounting, auditing and reporting, and its implications for the development of corporate social, ethical and environmental responsibility. It includes ten case studies, as well as an historical overview of the development of social and ethical accounting and reporting. The editors introduce a methodological framework that allows emerging practice worldwide to be analysed, understood and improved; and the case studies are written by the practitioners, giving insight into the experiences described.

This innovative book, written by internationally acknowledged leaders in the field, will be of enormous value to business managers, particularly those with responsibility for corporate affairs, human resources, environmental management, financial management, or planning. It will also be a useful text for business students.

£13.95 paperback   ISBN 1 85383 413 0
£35 hardback   ISBN 1 85383 418 1

Building to Last
The Challenge for Business Leaders

Colin Hutchinson

The major challenge for companies is to create a business that will last. This means they will have to take seriously the issue of sustainable development, rather than simply having an environmental policy, conducting social or environmental audits or consulting the stakeholder. It requires more radical change; a thorough review of core values and purposes, with attention to the 'triple bottom line' of money, people and nature.

Building to Last shows the way. Part One lays out the factors, including market trends and changing mindsets, which businesses will in future have to take into account. Part Two looks at some of the most enlightened steps so far taken by companies to preserve or enhance profitability while positioning themselves for the next century. The final part examines the different ways in which businesses can adopt principles of sustainability: independently, through industry associations, with those in their local community and through initiatives such as industrial ecology. It shows how businesses can manage the new challenges, monitor their performance and measure progress – towards solutions that will last.

This is a useful guide for environmental managers, senior and middle managers and managers of SMEs; and an essential text for academics and students of business schools or courses.

£15.95 paperback   ISBN 1 85383 478 5
£40 hardback   ISBN 1 85383 431 9

For further details, please contact:
Earthscan Publications Ltd
120 Pentonville Road
London N1 9JN
Telephone: 0171 278 0433
Fax: 0171 278 1142
Email: earthinfo@earthscan.co.uk *or* earthsales@earthscan.co.uk
World Wide Web: http://www.earthscan.co.uk